Garfield FEEDS HIS FACE

BY JIM DAVIS

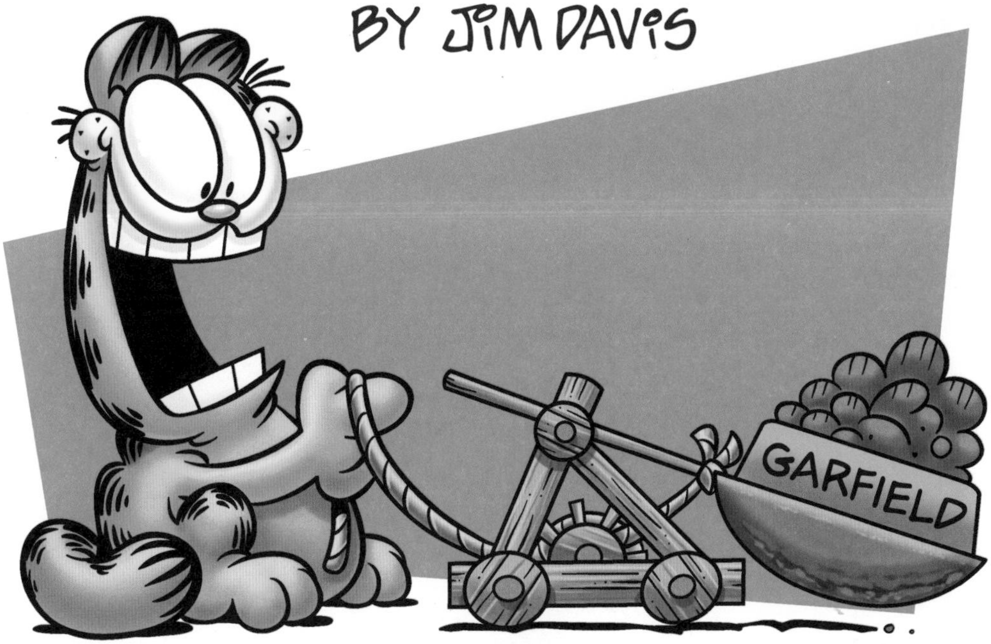
GARFIELD

Ballantine Books • New York

A Ballantine Books Trade Paperback Original

Copyright © 2017 by PAWS, Inc. All Rights Reserved.
"GARFIELD" and the GARFIELD characters are trademarks of PAWS, Inc.

Published in the United States by Ballantine Books, an imprint of Random House,
a division of Penguin Random House LLC, New York.

BALLANTINE and the HOUSE colophon are registered trademarks of Penguin Random House LLC.

ISBN 978-0-425-28567-1
Ebook ISBN 978-0-425-28568-8

Printed in China on acid-free paper

randomhousebooks.com

9 8 7 6 5 4 3

GARFIELD'S PET FORCE

ORDINARY PETS GARFIELD, ODIE, ARLENE, AND NERMAL HAVE THEIR LIVES CHANGED FOREVER WHEN THEY'RE SUCKED INTO A PARALLEL UNIVERSE AND TRANSFORMED INTO FOUR FURRY SUPERPOWERED DEFENDERS OF JUSTICE: GARZOOKA, ODIOUS, STARLENA, AND ABNERMAL.

TOGETHER, THIS TITANIC TEAM PROTECTS THE COSMOS FROM EVIL VETERINARIAN VETVIX AND HER MANIACAL MUTANT MINIONS.

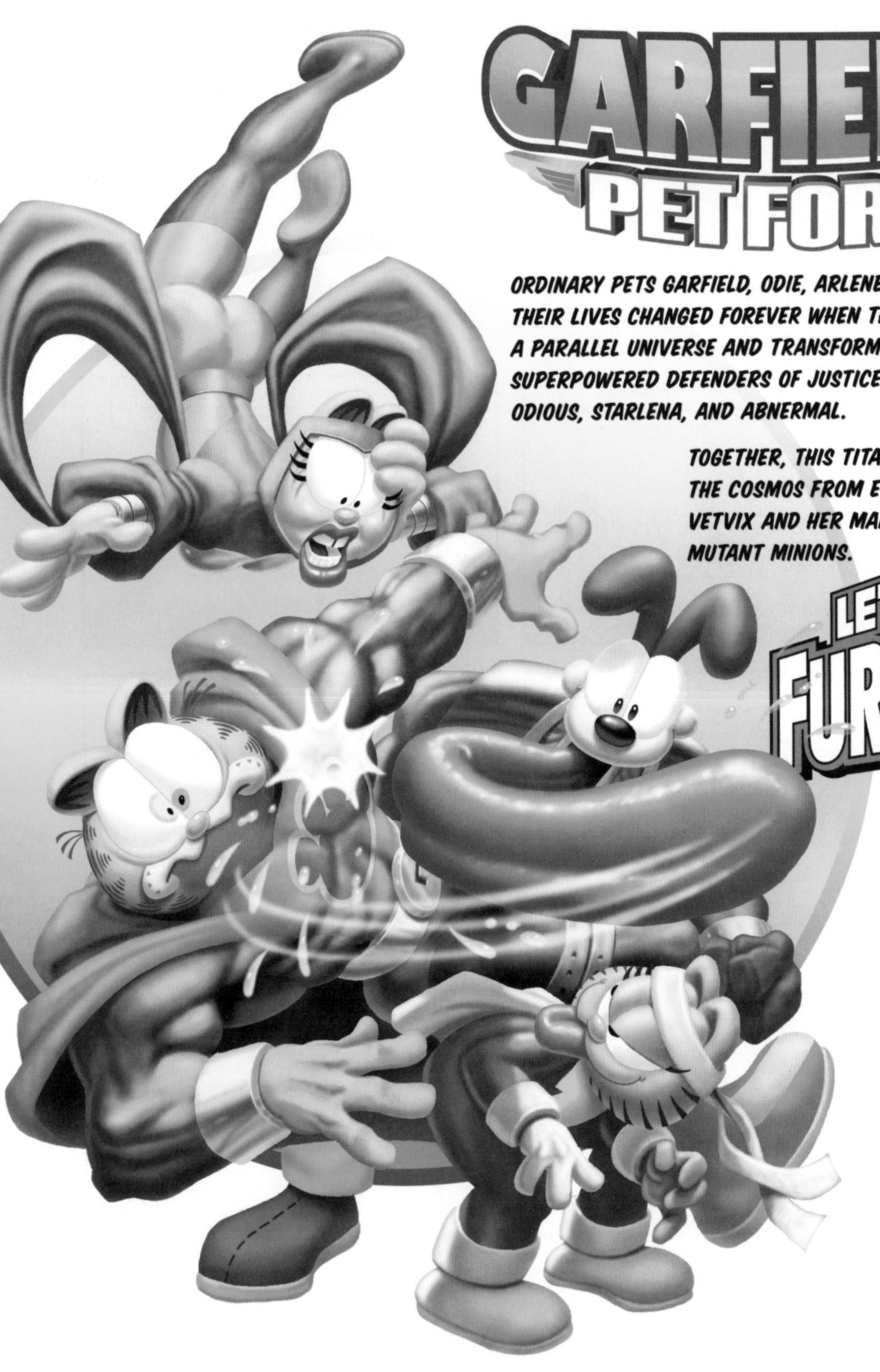

LET THE FUR FLY!

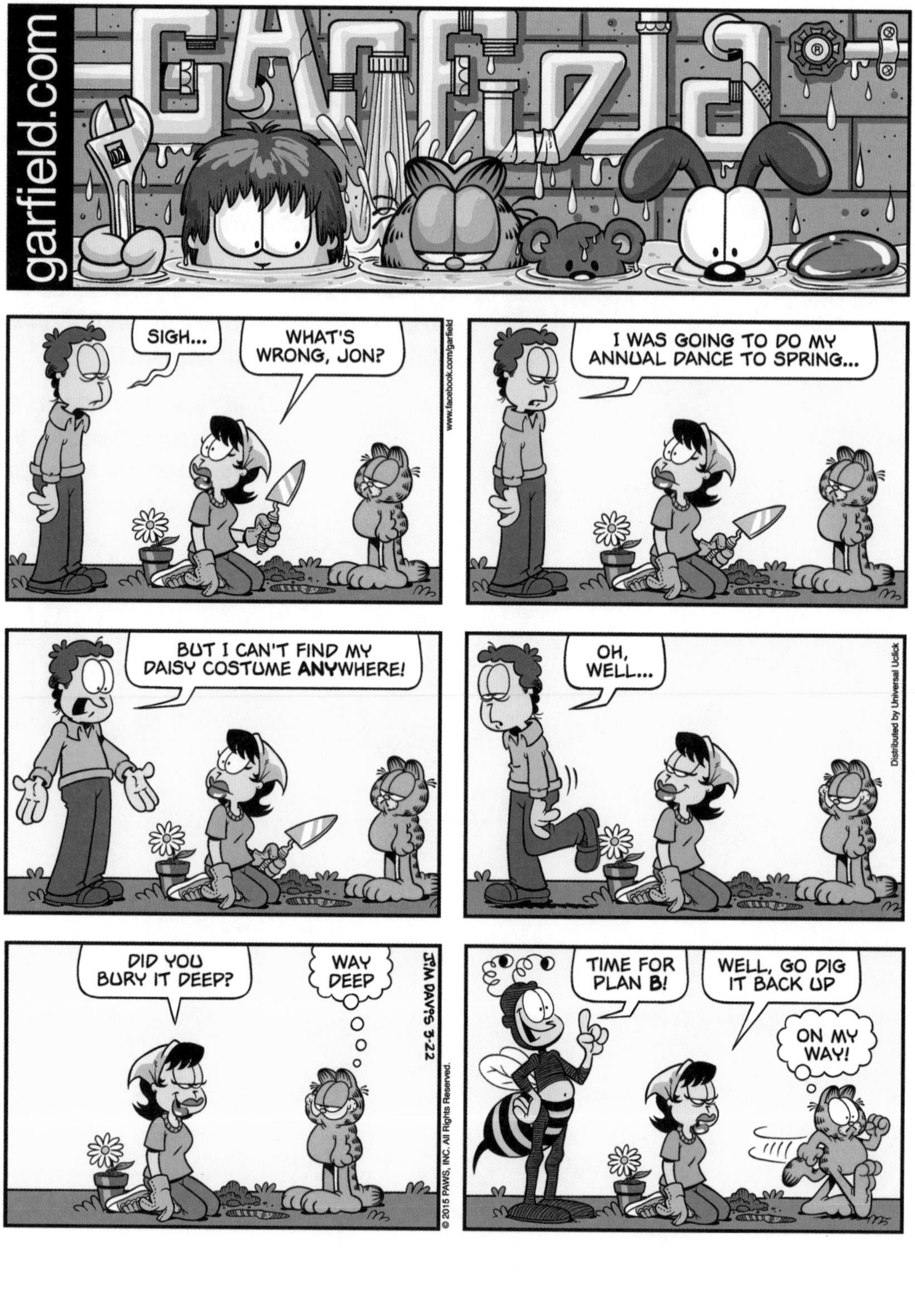
garfield.com
GARFIELD
SIGH...
WHAT'S WRONG, JON?
www.facebook.com/garfield
I WAS GOING TO DO MY ANNUAL DANCE TO SPRING...
BUT I CAN'T FIND MY DAISY COSTUME **ANY**WHERE!
OH, WELL...
Distributed by Universal Uclick
DID YOU BURY IT DEEP?
WAY DEEP
JIM DAVIS 3-22
© 2015 PAWS, INC. All Rights Reserved.
TIME FOR PLAN **B**!
WELL, GO DIG IT BACK UP
ON MY WAY!

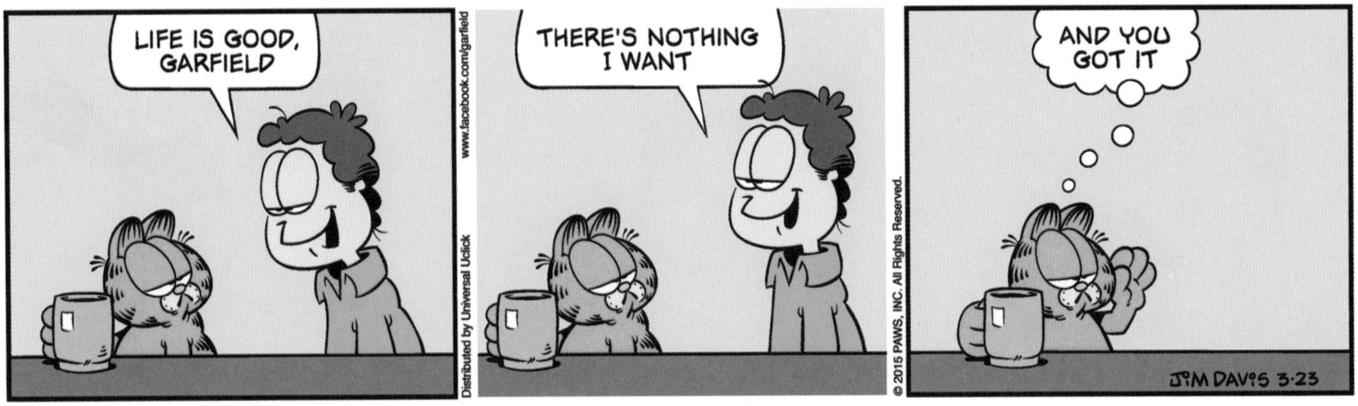
LIFE IS GOOD, GARFIELD
THERE'S NOTHING I WANT
AND YOU GOT IT
Distributed by Universal Uclick
www.facebook.com/garfield
© 2015 PAWS, INC. All Rights Reserved.
JIM DAVIS 3-23

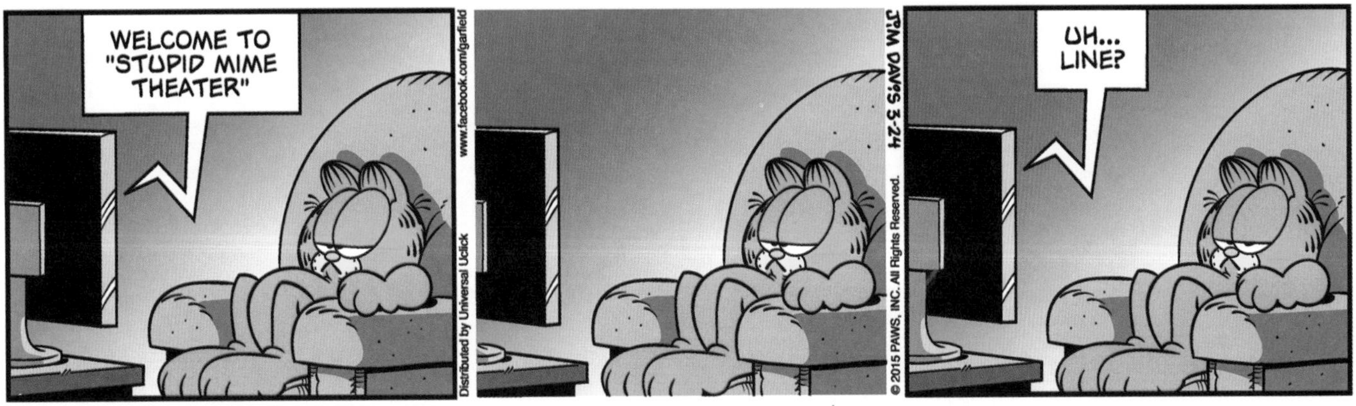
WELCOME TO "STUPID MIME THEATER"
UH... LINE?
Distributed by Universal Uclick
www.facebook.com/garfield
© 2015 PAWS, INC. All Rights Reserved.
JIM DAVIS 3-24

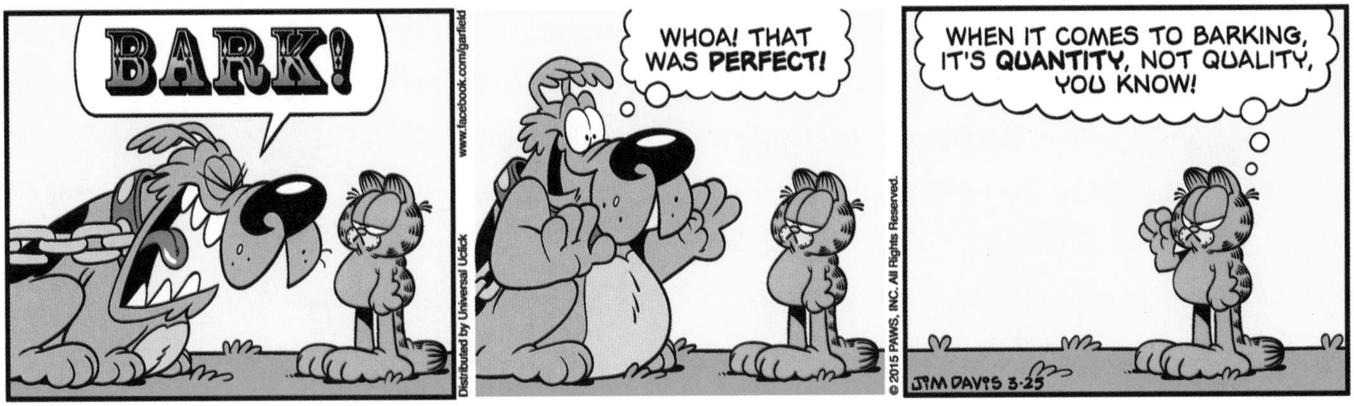
BARK!
WHOA! THAT WAS PERFECT!
WHEN IT COMES TO BARKING, IT'S QUANTITY, NOT QUALITY, YOU KNOW!
Distributed by Universal Uclick
www.facebook.com/garfield
© 2015 PAWS, INC. All Rights Reserved.
JIM DAVIS 3-25

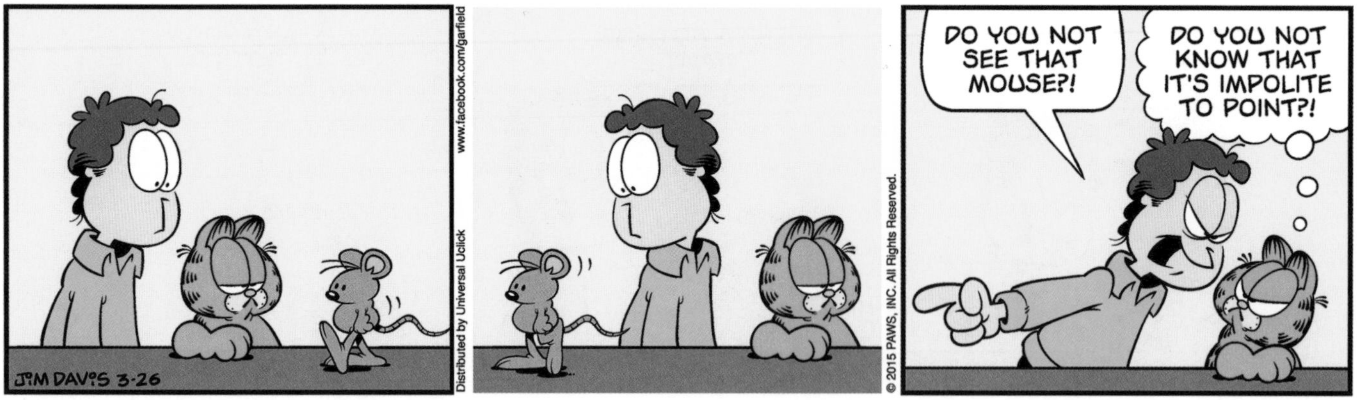
JIM DAVIS 3-26
www.facebook.com/garfield
Distributed by Universal Uclick
© 2015 PAWS, INC. All Rights Reserved.
DO YOU NOT SEE THAT MOUSE?!
DO YOU NOT KNOW THAT IT'S IMPOLITE TO POINT?!

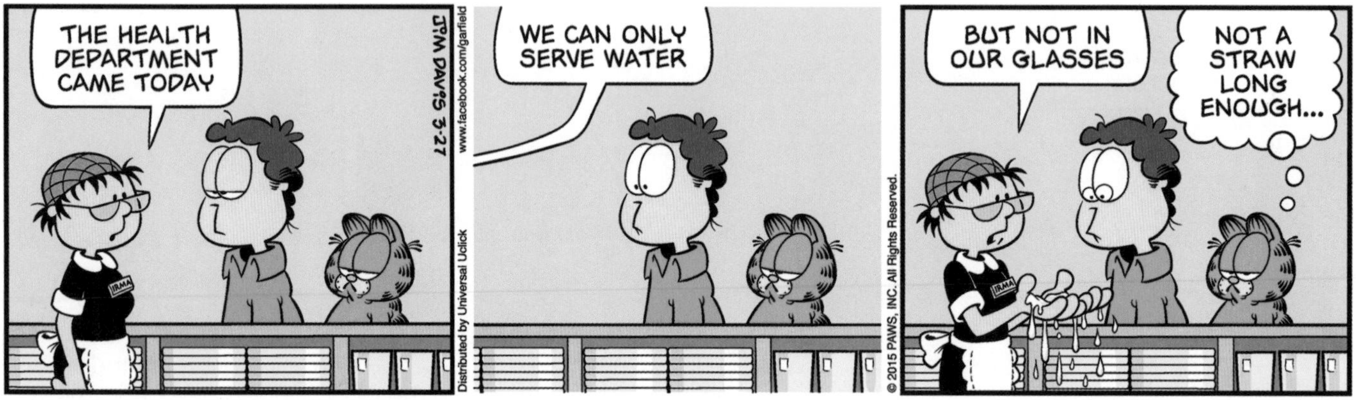
THE HEALTH DEPARTMENT CAME TODAY
JIM DAVIS 3-27
www.facebook.com/garfield
Distributed by Universal Uclick
WE CAN ONLY SERVE WATER
© 2015 PAWS, INC. All Rights Reserved.
BUT NOT IN OUR GLASSES
NOT A STRAW LONG ENOUGH...

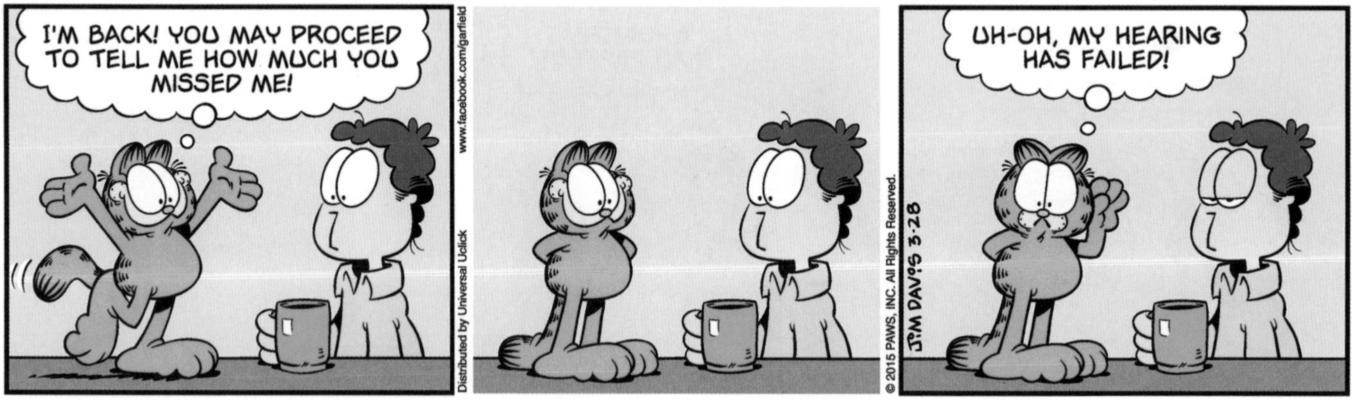
I'M BACK! YOU MAY PROCEED TO TELL ME HOW MUCH YOU MISSED ME!
www.facebook.com/garfield
Distributed by Universal Uclick
© 2015 PAWS, INC. All Rights Reserved.
JIM DAVIS 3-28
UH-OH, MY HEARING HAS FAILED!

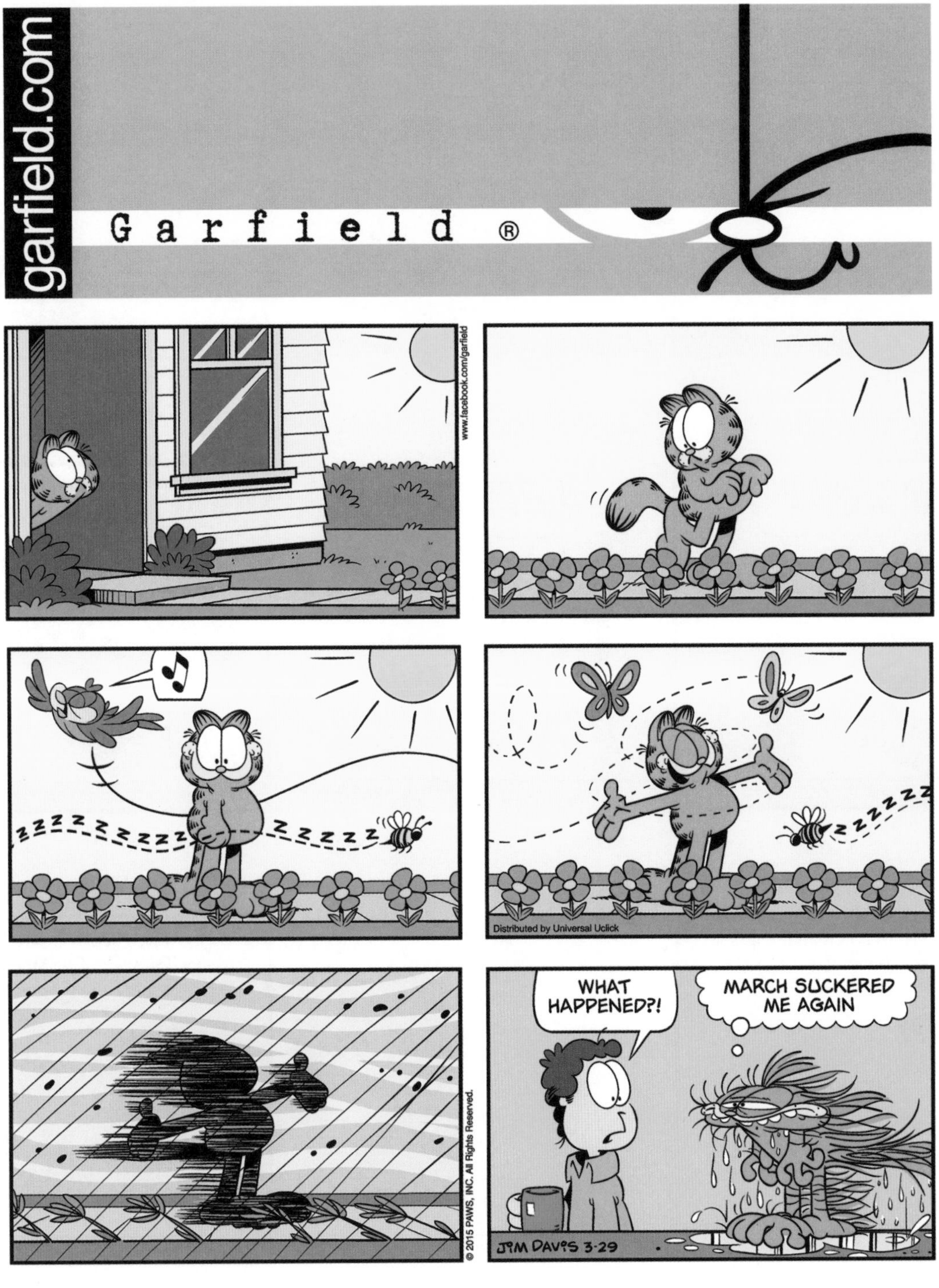
garfield.com
Garfield ®
www.facebook.com/garfield
Distributed by Universal Uclick
© 2015 PAWS, INC. All Rights Reserved.
WHAT HAPPENED?!
MARCH SUCKERED ME AGAIN
JIM DAVIS 3-29

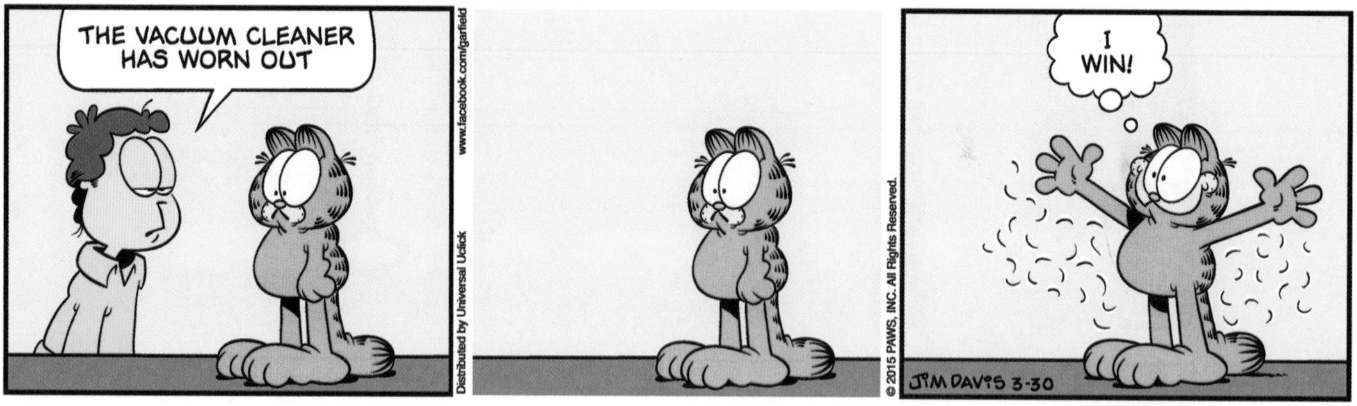
THE VACUUM CLEANER HAS WORN OUT
I WIN!
Distributed by Universal Uclick
www.facebook.com/garfield
© 2015 PAWS, INC. All Rights Reserved.
JIM DAVIS 3-30

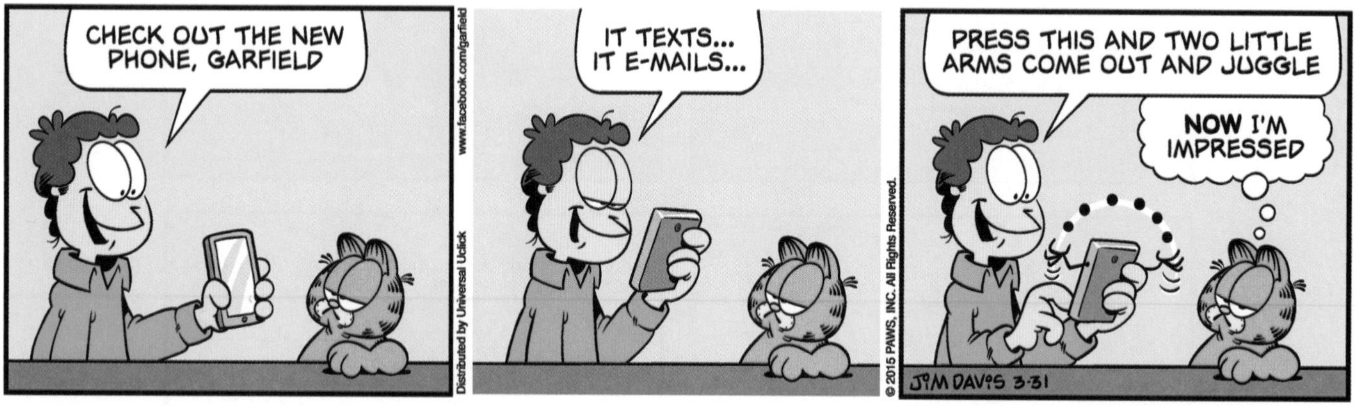
CHECK OUT THE NEW PHONE, GARFIELD
IT TEXTS... IT E-MAILS...
PRESS THIS AND TWO LITTLE ARMS COME OUT AND JUGGLE
NOW I'M IMPRESSED
Distributed by Universal Uclick
www.facebook.com/garfield
© 2015 PAWS, INC. All Rights Reserved.
JIM DAVIS 3-31

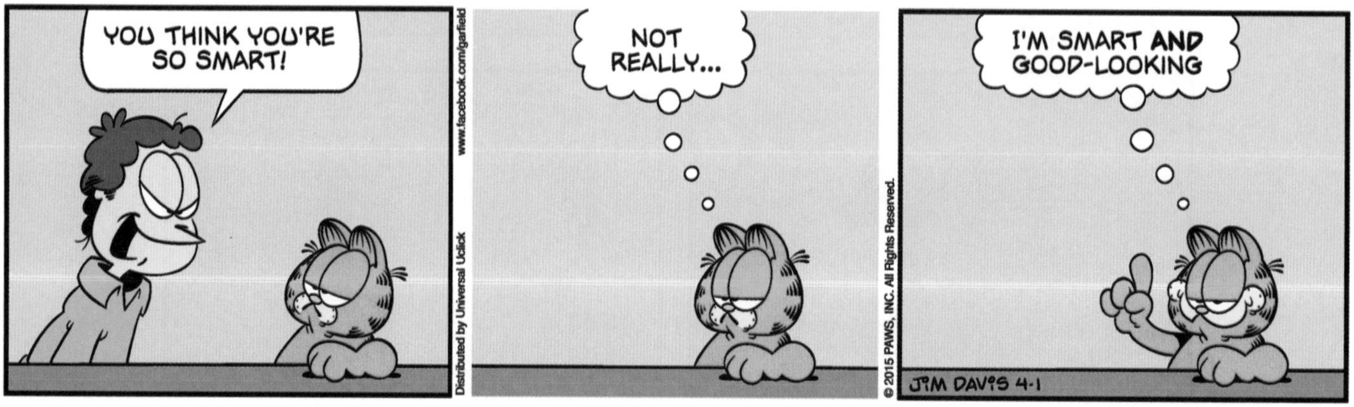
YOU THINK YOU'RE SO SMART!
NOT REALLY...
I'M SMART AND GOOD-LOOKING
Distributed by Universal Uclick
www.facebook.com/garfield
© 2015 PAWS, INC. All Rights Reserved.
JIM DAVIS 4-1

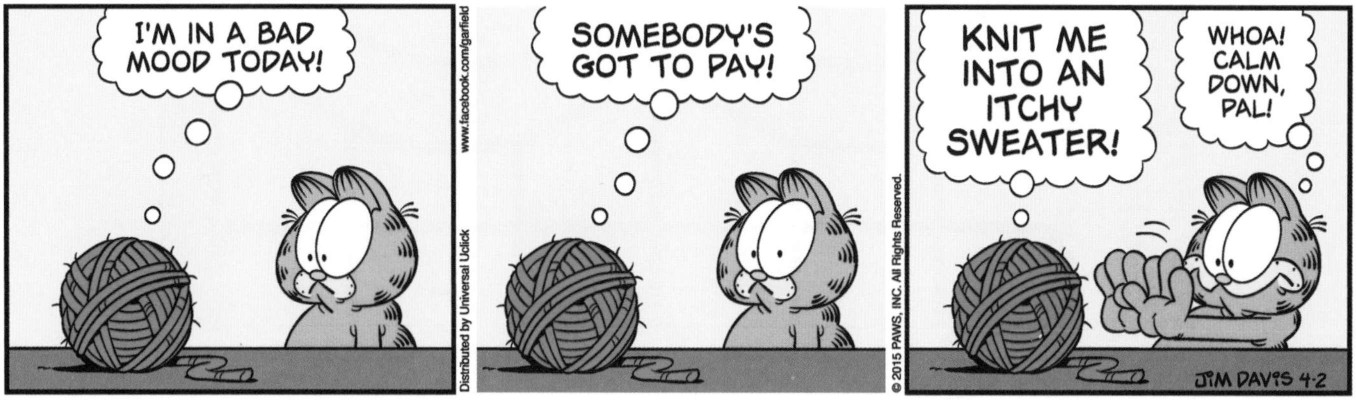
I'M IN A BAD MOOD TODAY!
SOMEBODY'S GOT TO PAY!
KNIT ME INTO AN ITCHY SWEATER!
WHOA! CALM DOWN, PAL!
JIM DAVIS 4-2
Distributed by Universal Uclick www.facebook.com/garfield
© 2015 PAWS, INC. All Rights Reserved.

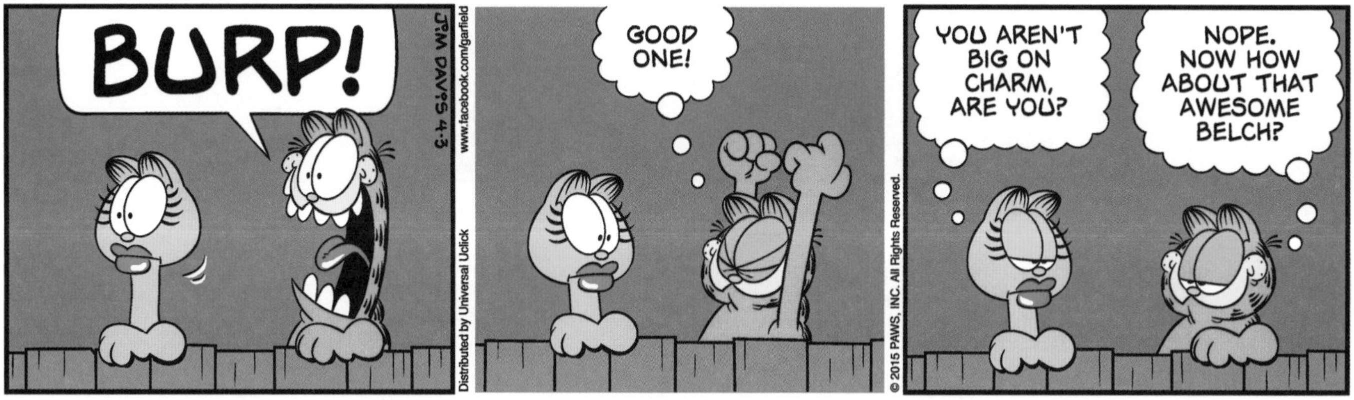
BURP!
JIM DAVIS 4-3
GOOD ONE!
YOU AREN'T BIG ON CHARM, ARE YOU?
NOPE. NOW HOW ABOUT THAT AWESOME BELCH?
Distributed by Universal Uclick www.facebook.com/garfield
© 2015 PAWS, INC. All Rights Reserved.

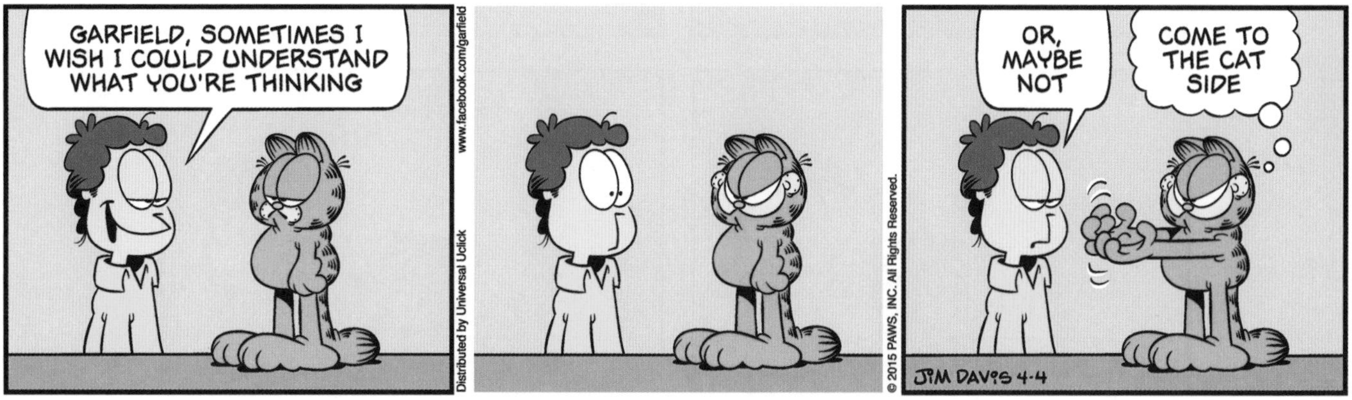
GARFIELD, SOMETIMES I WISH I COULD UNDERSTAND WHAT YOU'RE THINKING
OR, MAYBE NOT
COME TO THE CAT SIDE
JIM DAVIS 4-4
Distributed by Universal Uclick www.facebook.com/garfield
© 2015 PAWS, INC. All Rights Reserved.

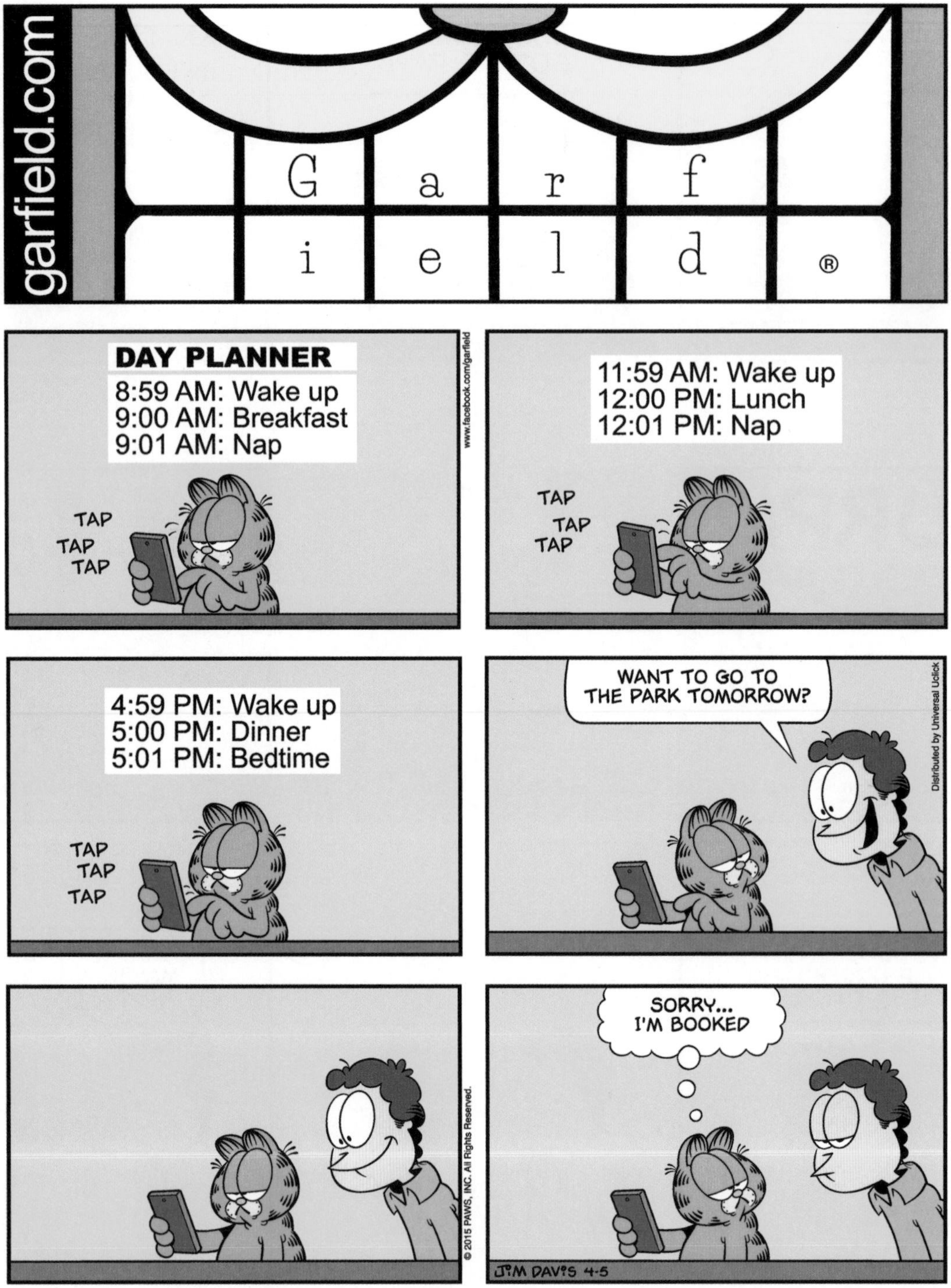

garfield.com
Garfield®
DAY PLANNER
8:59 AM: Wake up
9:00 AM: Breakfast
9:01 AM: Nap
TAP TAP TAP
11:59 AM: Wake up
12:00 PM: Lunch
12:01 PM: Nap
TAP TAP TAP
4:59 PM: Wake up
5:00 PM: Dinner
5:01 PM: Bedtime
TAP TAP TAP
WANT TO GO TO THE PARK TOMORROW?
SORRY... I'M BOOKED
JIM DAVIS 4-5
www.facebook.com/garfield
Distributed by Universal Uclick
© 2015 PAWS, INC. All Rights Reserved.

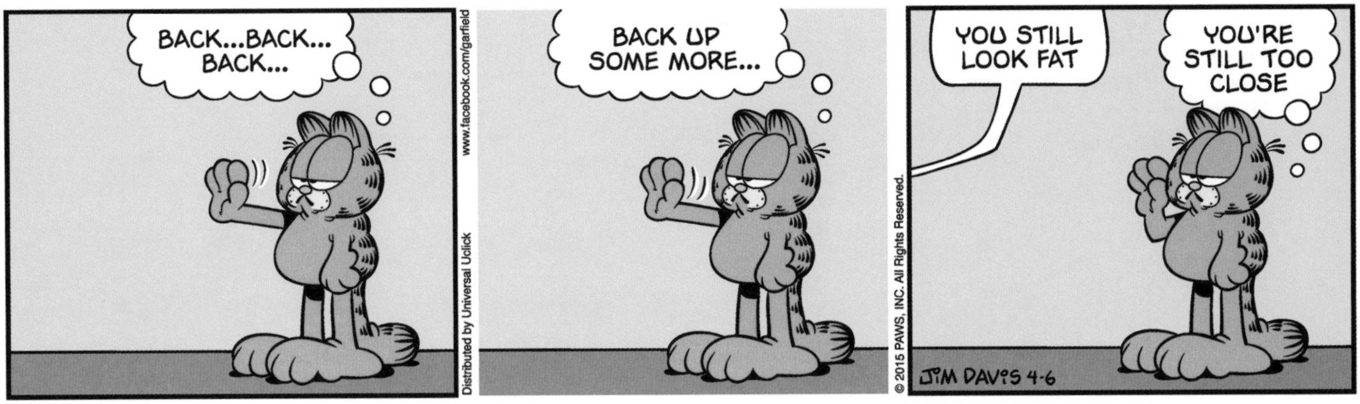
BACK...BACK...
BACK...
www.facebook.com/garfield
Distributed by Universal Uclick
BACK UP
SOME MORE...
© 2015 PAWS, INC. All Rights Reserved.
YOU STILL
LOOK FAT
YOU'RE
STILL TOO
CLOSE
JIM DAVIS 4-6

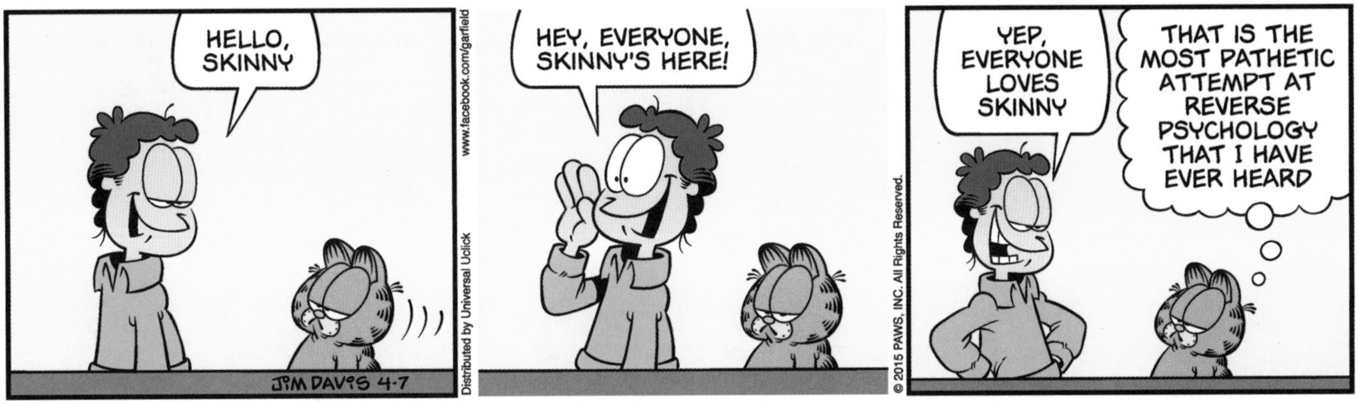
HELLO,
SKINNY
JIM DAVIS 4-7
www.facebook.com/garfield
Distributed by Universal Uclick
HEY, EVERYONE,
SKINNY'S HERE!
© 2015 PAWS, INC. All Rights Reserved.
YEP,
EVERYONE
LOVES
SKINNY
THAT IS THE
MOST PATHETIC
ATTEMPT AT
REVERSE
PSYCHOLOGY
THAT I HAVE
EVER HEARD

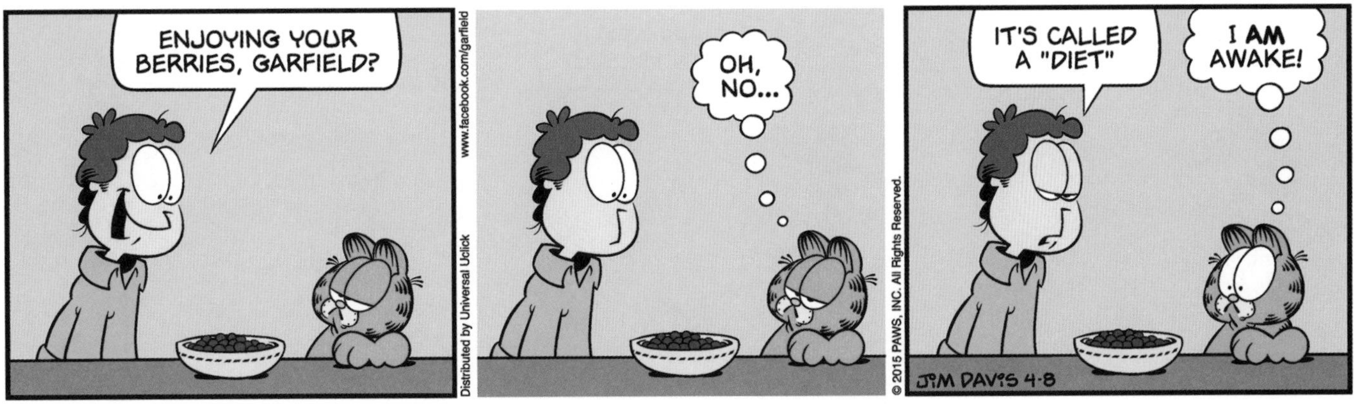
ENJOYING YOUR
BERRIES, GARFIELD?
www.facebook.com/garfield
Distributed by Universal Uclick
OH,
NO...
© 2015 PAWS, INC. All Rights Reserved.
IT'S CALLED
A "DIET"
I **AM**
AWAKE!
JIM DAVIS 4-8

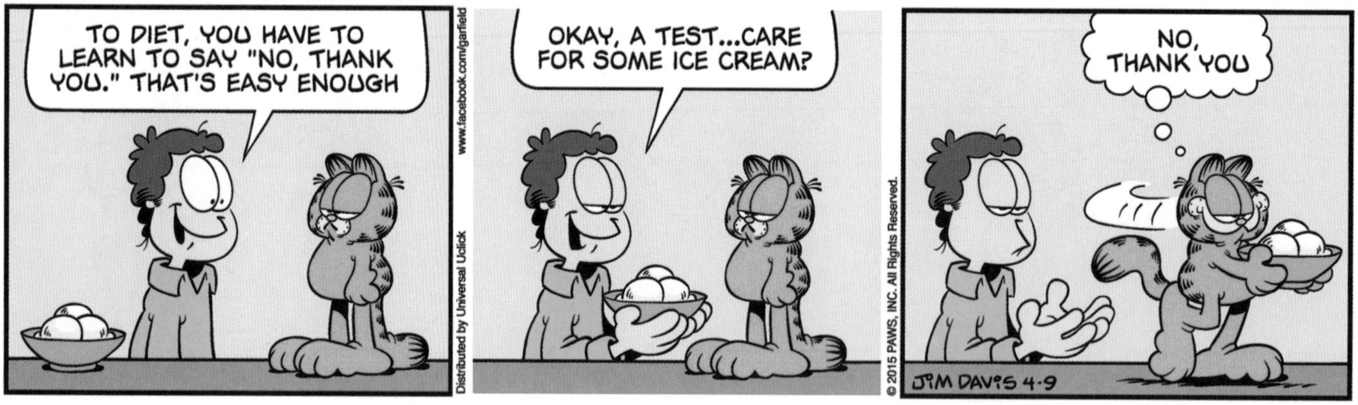
TO DIET, YOU HAVE TO LEARN TO SAY "NO, THANK YOU." THAT'S EASY ENOUGH
Distributed by Universal Uclick www.facebook.com/garfield
OKAY, A TEST...CARE FOR SOME ICE CREAM?
© 2015 PAWS, INC. All Rights Reserved.
NO, THANK YOU
JIM DAVIS 4-9

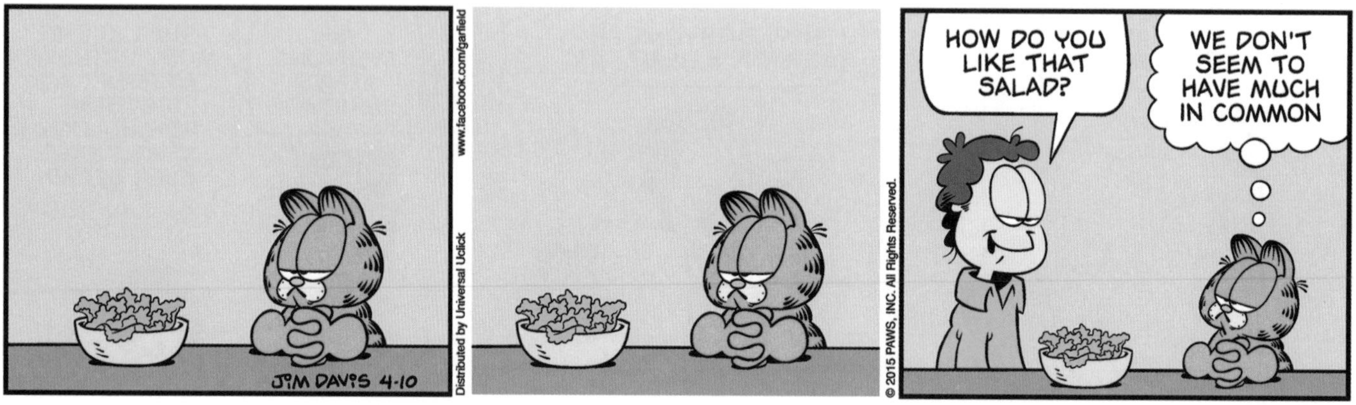
JIM DAVIS 4-10
Distributed by Universal Uclick www.facebook.com/garfield
© 2015 PAWS, INC. All Rights Reserved.
HOW DO YOU LIKE THAT SALAD?
WE DON'T SEEM TO HAVE MUCH IN COMMON

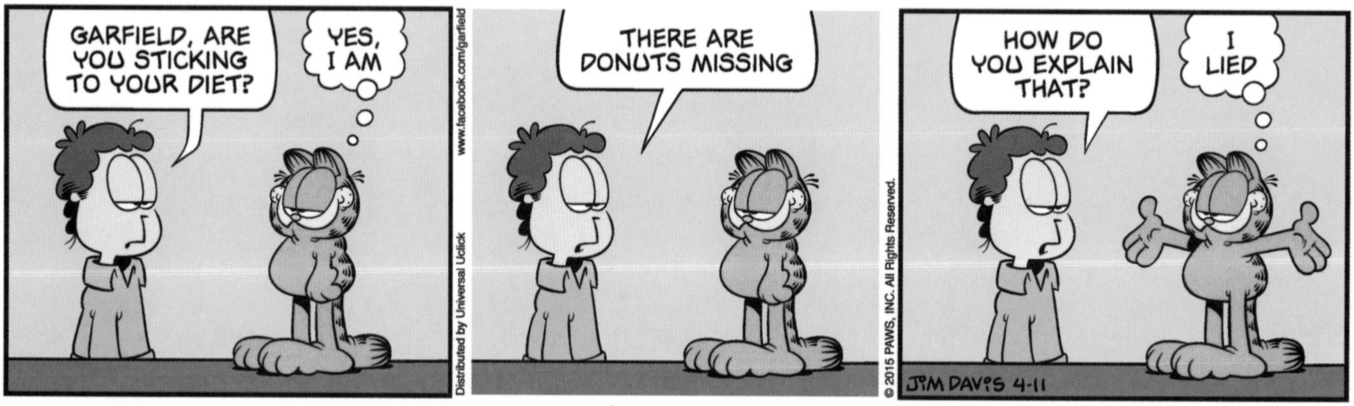
GARFIELD, ARE YOU STICKING TO YOUR DIET?
YES, I AM
Distributed by Universal Uclick www.facebook.com/garfield
THERE ARE DONUTS MISSING
© 2015 PAWS, INC. All Rights Reserved.
HOW DO YOU EXPLAIN THAT?
I LIED
JIM DAVIS 4-11

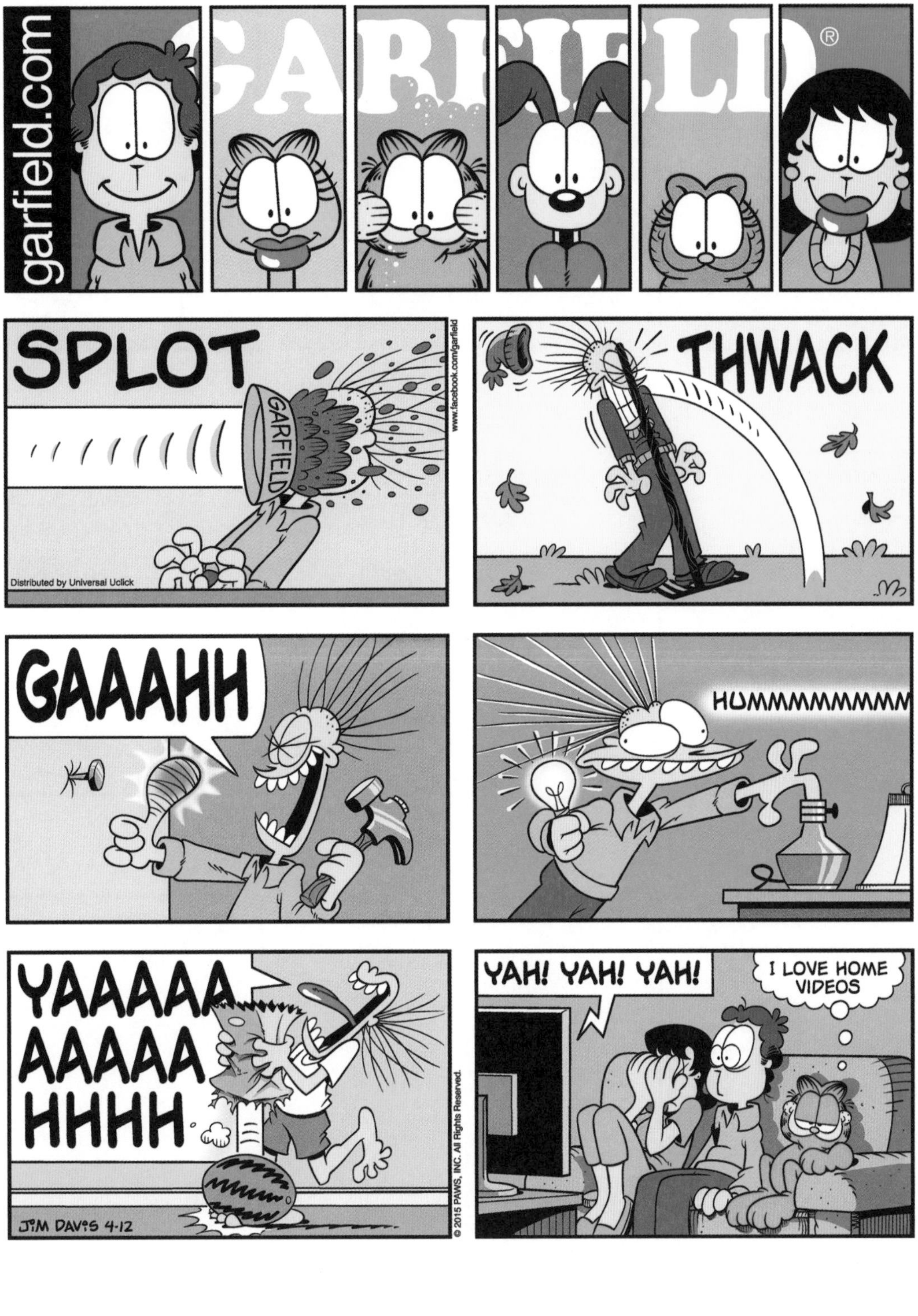
garfield.com
GARFIELD®
SPLOT
GARFIELD
www.facebook.com/garfield
Distributed by Universal Uclick
THWACK
GAAAHH
HUMMMMMMMM
YAAAAA
AAAAA
HHHH
JIM DAVIS 4-12
© 2015 PAWS, INC. All Rights Reserved.
YAH! YAH! YAH!
I LOVE HOME VIDEOS

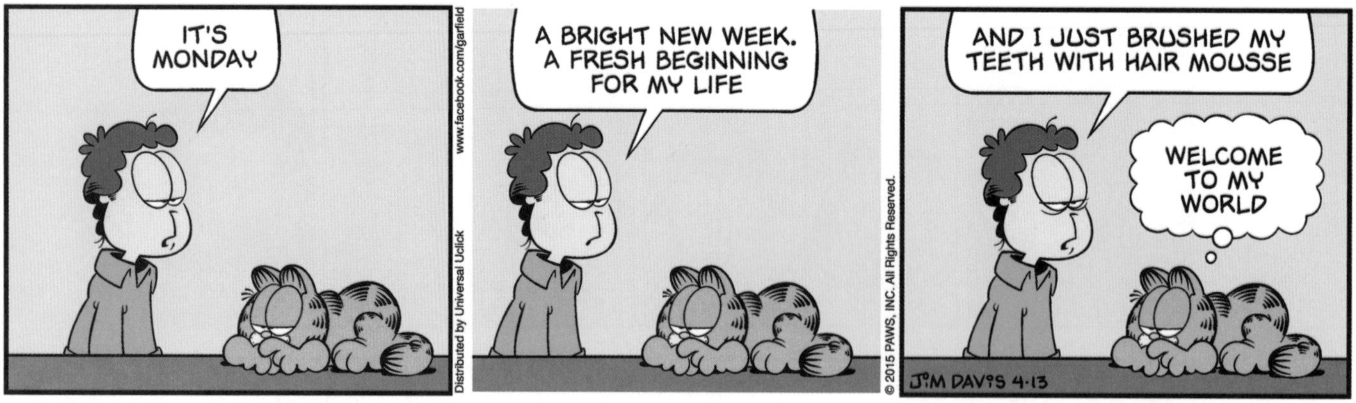
IT'S MONDAY
www.facebook.com/garfield
Distributed by Universal Uclick
A BRIGHT NEW WEEK. A FRESH BEGINNING FOR MY LIFE
© 2015 PAWS, INC. All Rights Reserved.
AND I JUST BRUSHED MY TEETH WITH HAIR MOUSSE
WELCOME TO MY WORLD
JIM DAVIS 4-13

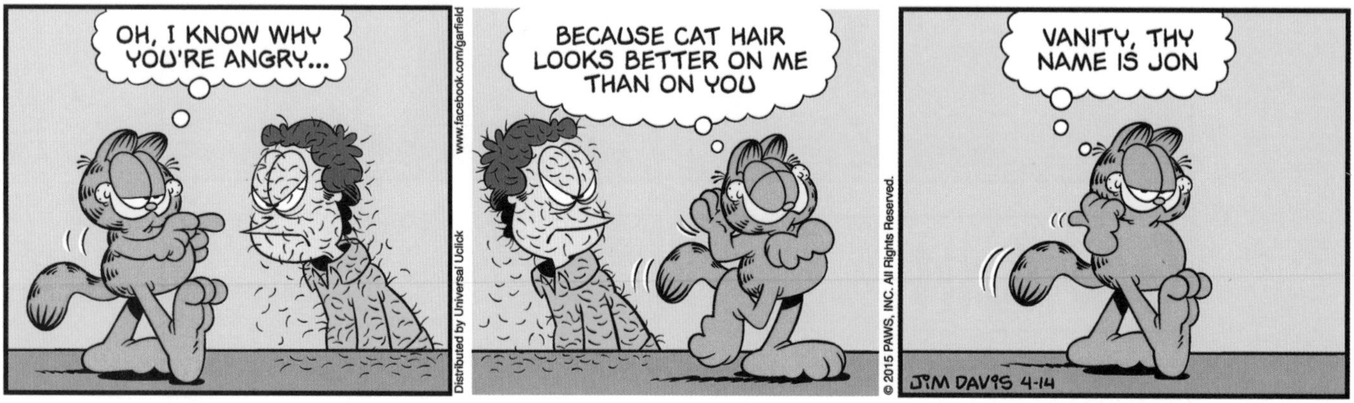
OH, I KNOW WHY YOU'RE ANGRY...
www.facebook.com/garfield
Distributed by Universal Uclick
BECAUSE CAT HAIR LOOKS BETTER ON ME THAN ON YOU
© 2015 PAWS, INC. All Rights Reserved.
VANITY, THY NAME IS JON
JIM DAVIS 4-14

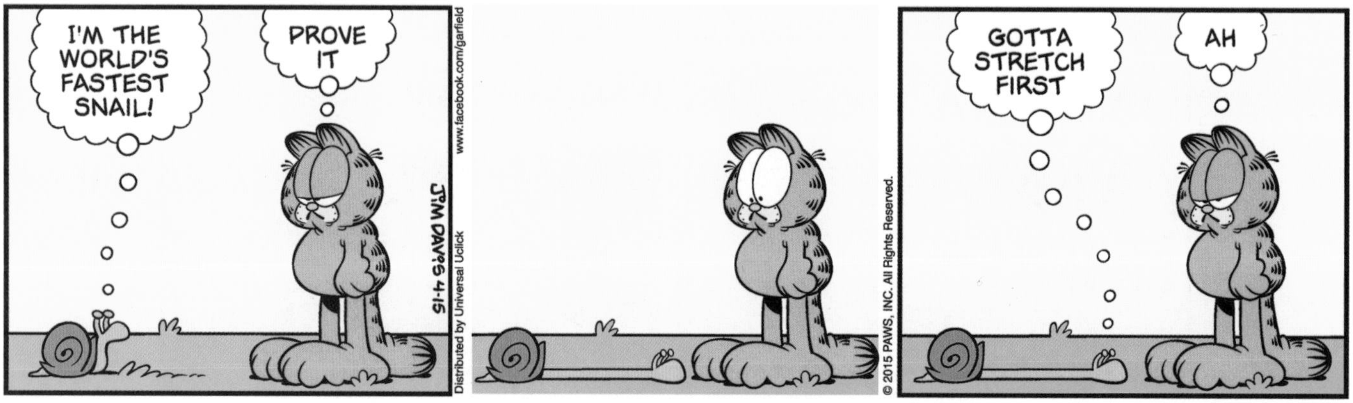
I'M THE WORLD'S FASTEST SNAIL!
PROVE IT
JIM DAVIS 4-15
www.facebook.com/garfield
Distributed by Universal Uclick
© 2015 PAWS, INC. All Rights Reserved.
GOTTA STRETCH FIRST
AH

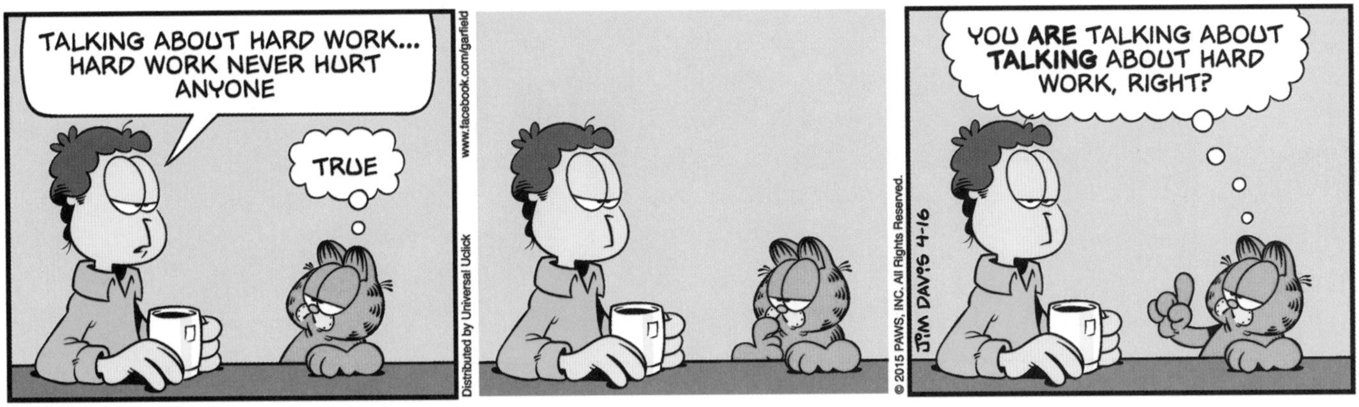
TALKING ABOUT HARD WORK... HARD WORK NEVER HURT ANYONE
TRUE
www.facebook.com/garfield
Distributed by Universal Uclick
YOU **ARE** TALKING ABOUT **TALKING** ABOUT HARD WORK, RIGHT?
JIM DAVIS 4-16
© 2015 PAWS, INC. All Rights Reserved.

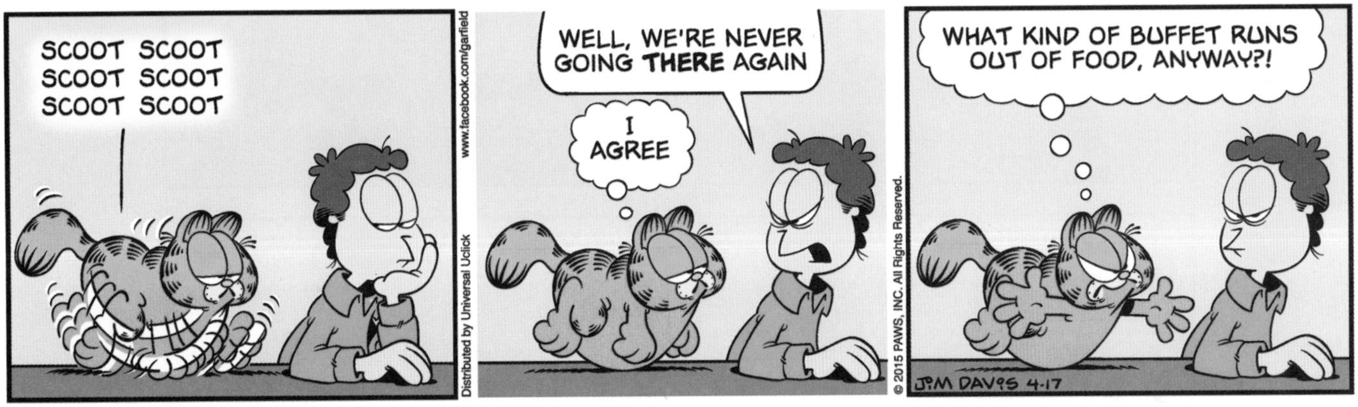
SCOOT SCOOT SCOOT SCOOT SCOOT SCOOT
www.facebook.com/garfield
Distributed by Universal Uclick
WELL, WE'RE NEVER GOING **THERE** AGAIN
I AGREE
WHAT KIND OF BUFFET RUNS OUT OF FOOD, ANYWAY?!
JIM DAVIS 4-17
© 2015 PAWS, INC. All Rights Reserved.

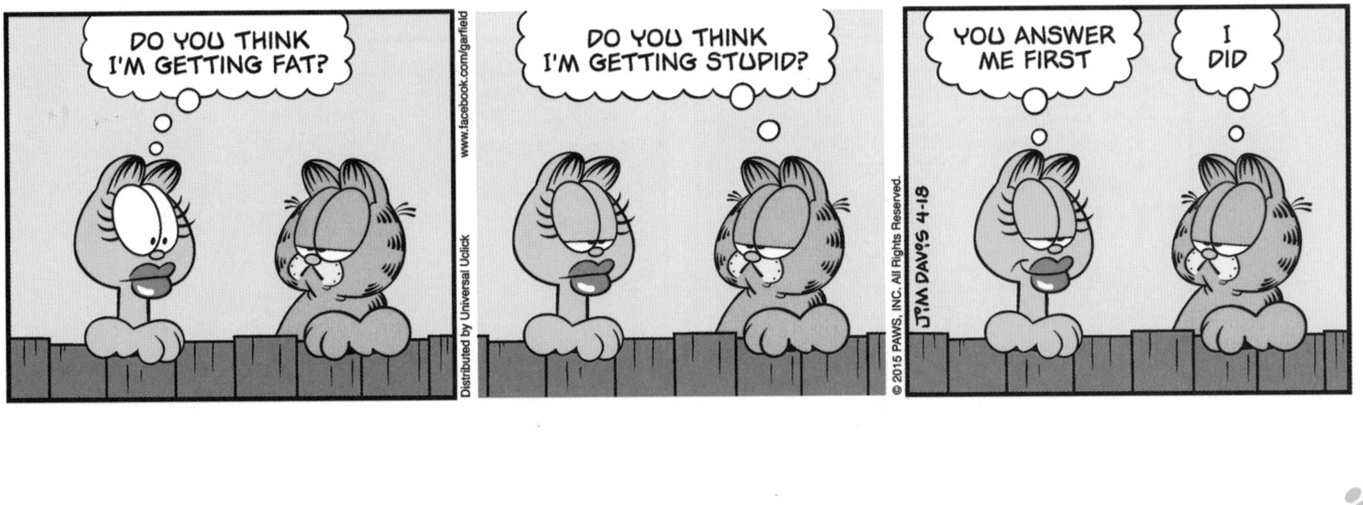
DO YOU THINK I'M GETTING FAT?
www.facebook.com/garfield
Distributed by Universal Uclick
DO YOU THINK I'M GETTING STUPID?
YOU ANSWER ME FIRST
I DID
JIM DAVIS 4-18
© 2015 PAWS, INC. All Rights Reserved.

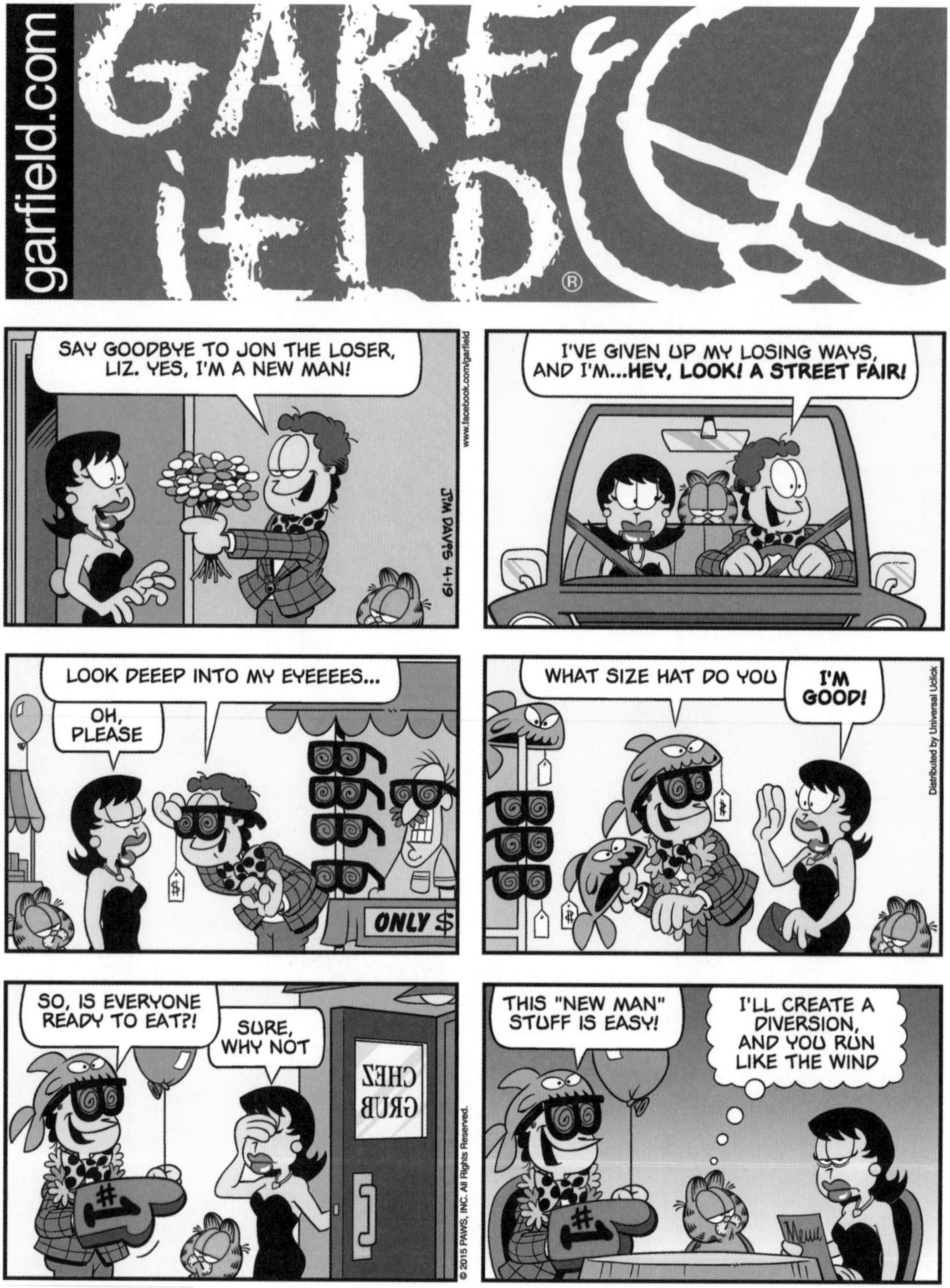
garfield.com
GARFIELD
SAY GOODBYE TO JON THE LOSER, LIZ. YES, I'M A NEW MAN!
JIM DAVIS 4-19
www.facebook.com/garfield
I'VE GIVEN UP MY LOSING WAYS, AND I'M...HEY, LOOK! A STREET FAIR!
LOOK DEEEP INTO MY EYEEEES...
OH, PLEASE
ONLY $
WHAT SIZE HAT DO YOU
I'M GOOD!
Distributed by Universal Uclick
SO, IS EVERYONE READY TO EAT?!
SURE, WHY NOT
CHEZ GRUB
© 2015 PAWS, INC. All Rights Reserved.
THIS "NEW MAN" STUFF IS EASY!
I'LL CREATE A DIVERSION, AND YOU RUN LIKE THE WIND
Menu

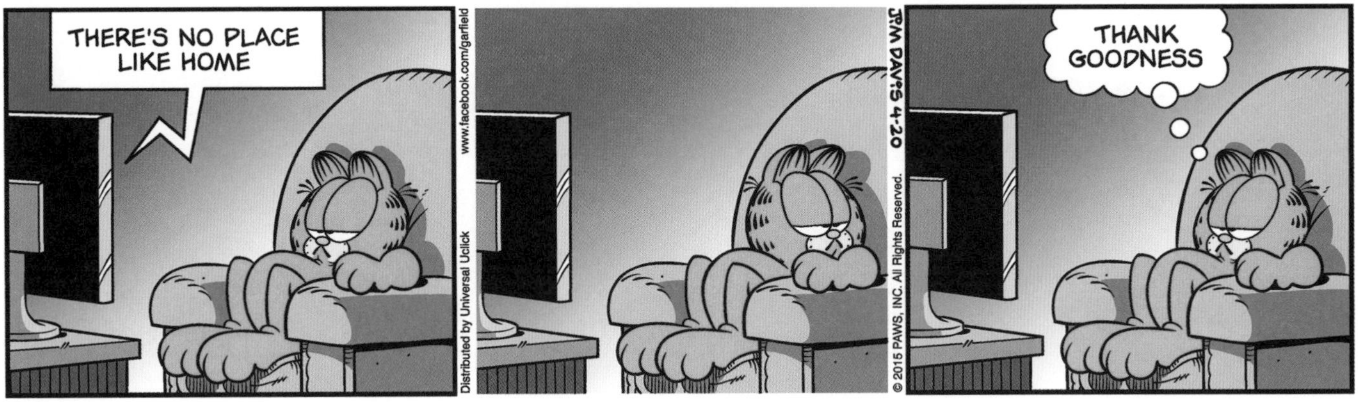
THERE'S NO PLACE LIKE HOME
THANK GOODNESS
JIM DAVIS 4-20
Distributed by Universal Uclick www.facebook.com/garfield
© 2015 PAWS, INC. All Rights Reserved.

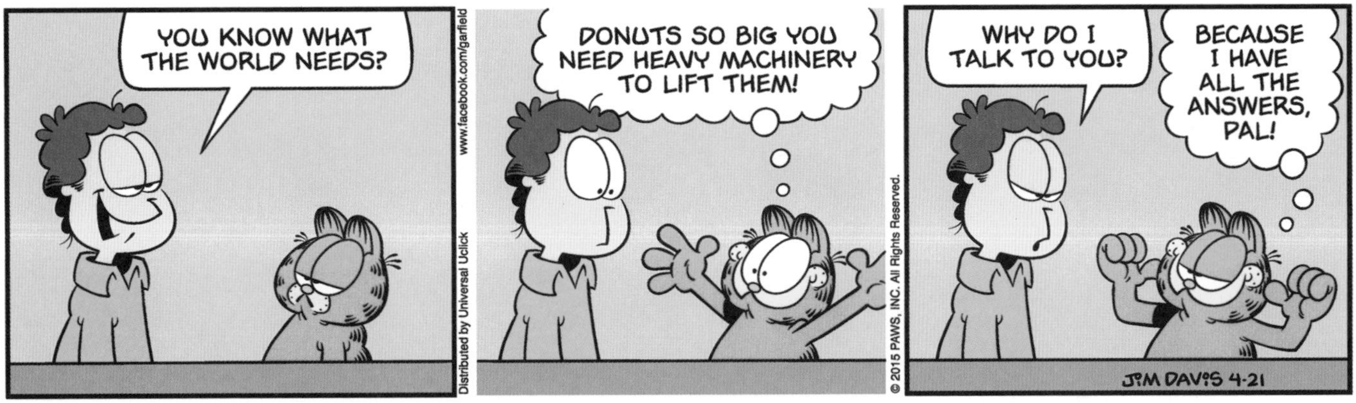
YOU KNOW WHAT THE WORLD NEEDS?
DONUTS SO BIG YOU NEED HEAVY MACHINERY TO LIFT THEM!
WHY DO I TALK TO YOU?
BECAUSE I HAVE ALL THE ANSWERS, PAL!
JIM DAVIS 4-21
Distributed by Universal Uclick www.facebook.com/garfield
© 2015 PAWS, INC. All Rights Reserved.

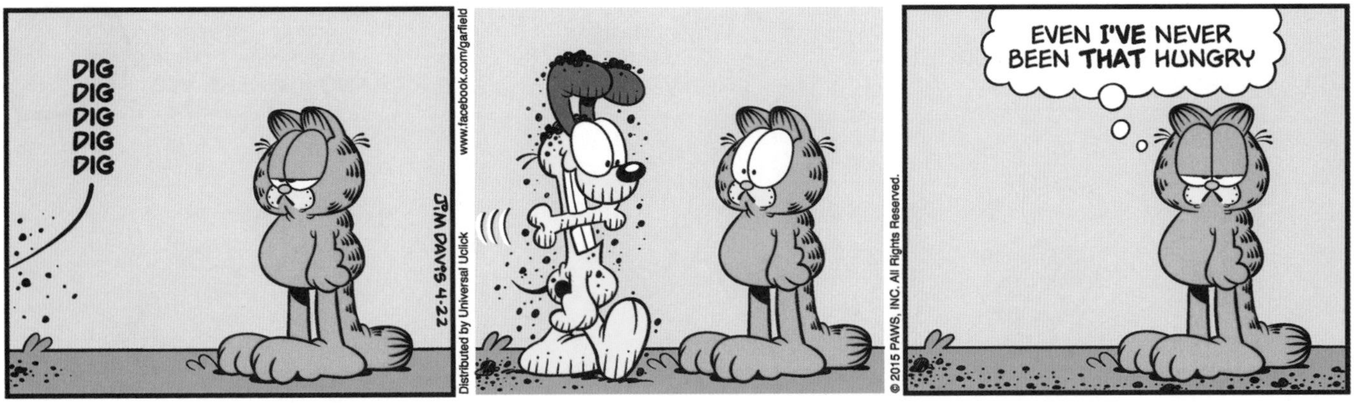
DIG DIG DIG DIG DIG
EVEN I'VE NEVER BEEN THAT HUNGRY
JIM DAVIS 4-22
Distributed by Universal Uclick www.facebook.com/garfield
© 2015 PAWS, INC. All Rights Reserved.

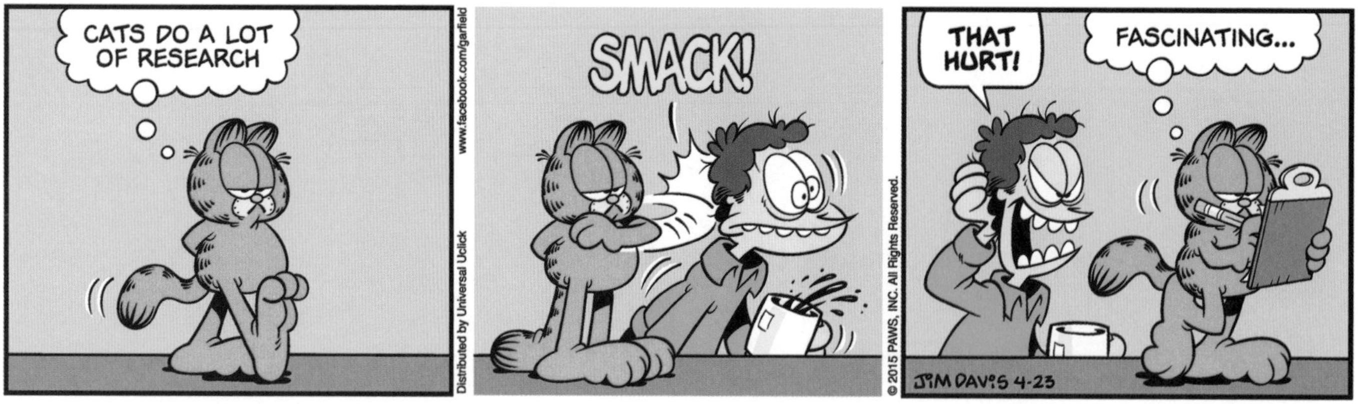
CATS DO A LOT OF RESEARCH
SMACK!
THAT HURT!
FASCINATING...

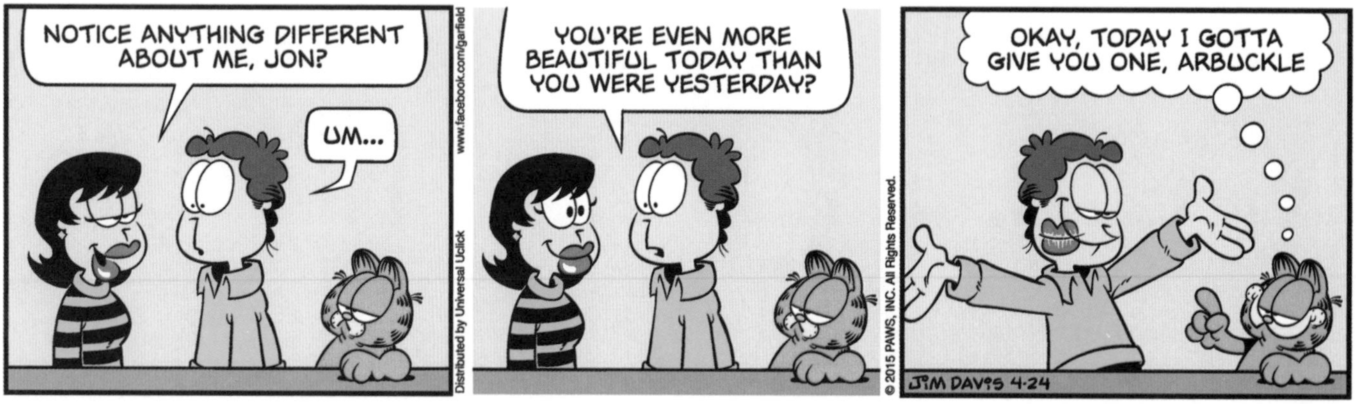
NOTICE ANYTHING DIFFERENT ABOUT ME, JON?
UM...
YOU'RE EVEN MORE BEAUTIFUL TODAY THAN YOU WERE YESTERDAY?
OKAY, TODAY I GOTTA GIVE YOU ONE, ARBUCKLE

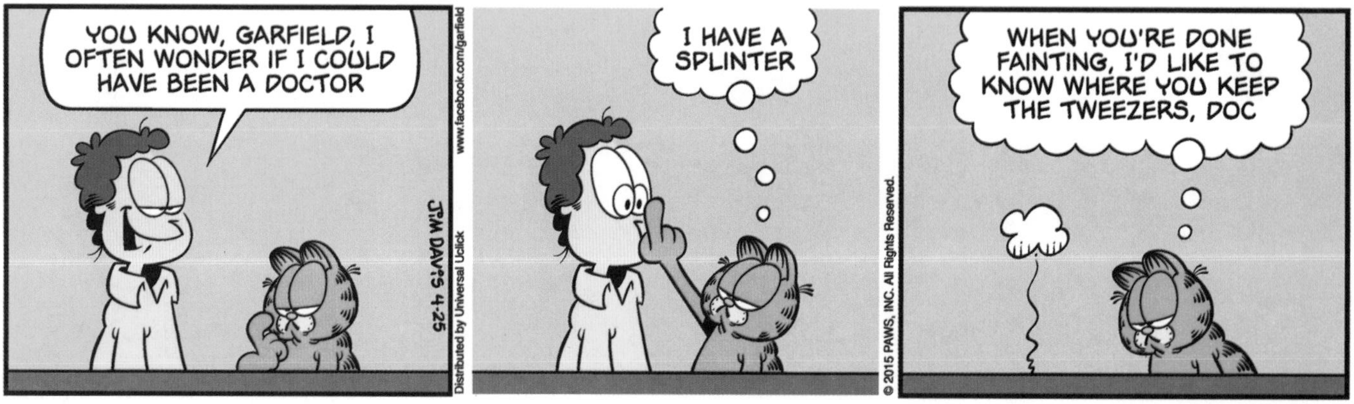
YOU KNOW, GARFIELD, I OFTEN WONDER IF I COULD HAVE BEEN A DOCTOR
I HAVE A SPLINTER
WHEN YOU'RE DONE FAINTING, I'D LIKE TO KNOW WHERE YOU KEEP THE TWEEZERS, DOC

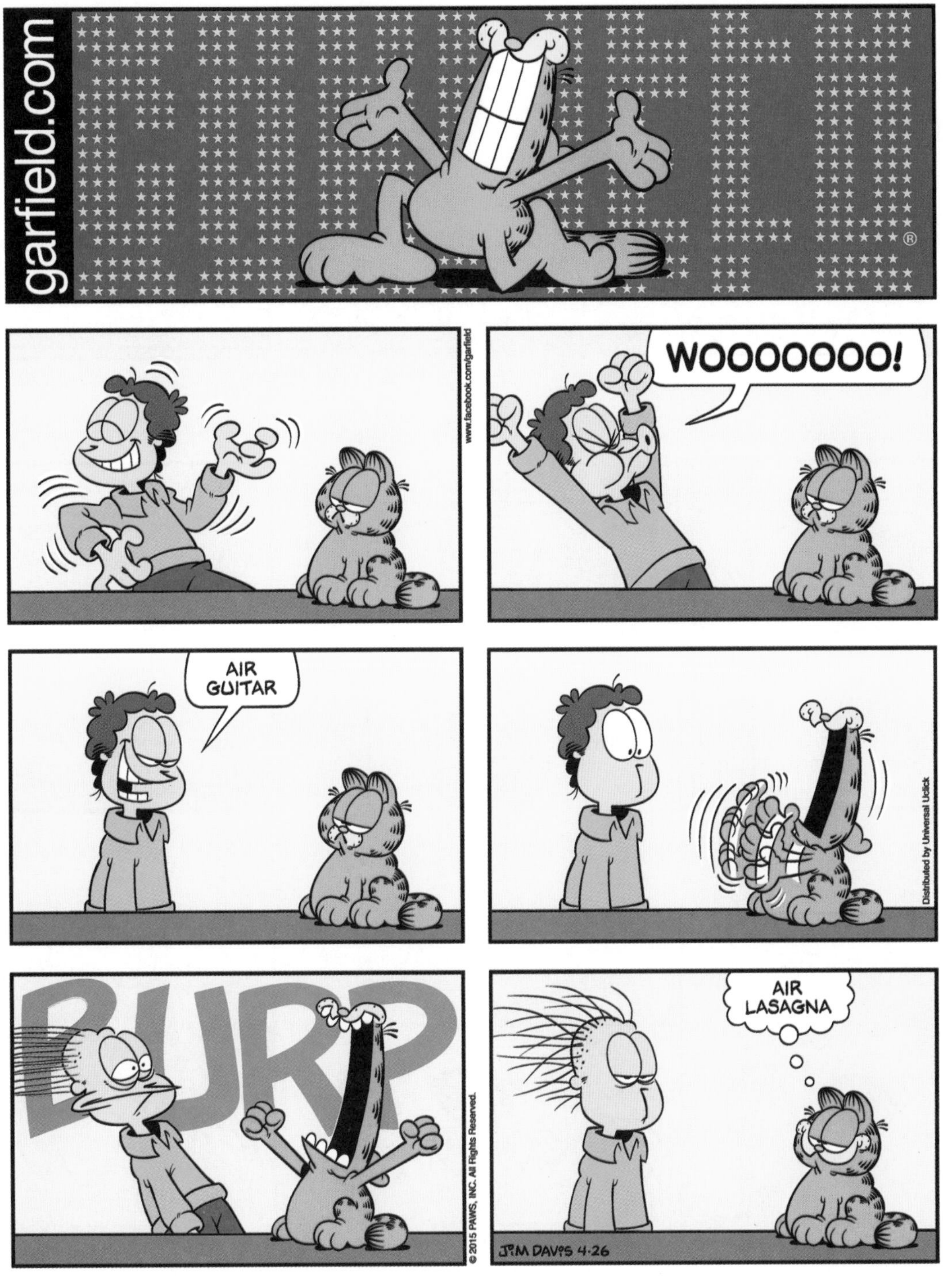
garfield.com
www.facebook.com/garfield
WOOOOOOO!
AIR GUITAR
Distributed by Universal Uclick
BURP
© 2015 PAWS, INC. All Rights Reserved.
AIR LASAGNA
JIM DAVIS 4-26

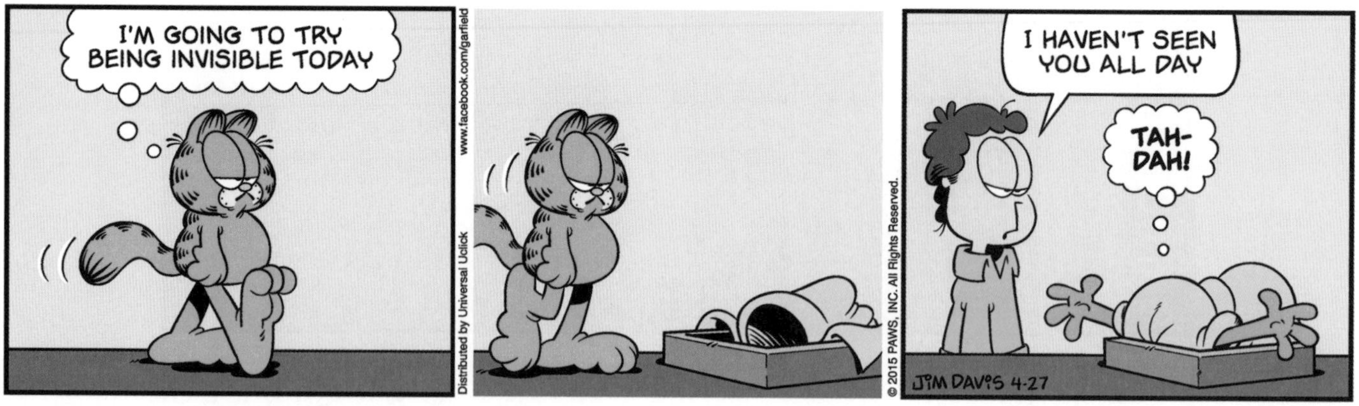
I'M GOING TO TRY BEING INVISIBLE TODAY
Distributed by Universal Uclick www.facebook.com/garfield
I HAVEN'T SEEN YOU ALL DAY
TAH-DAH!
© 2015 PAWS, INC. All Rights Reserved.
JIM DAVIS 4-27

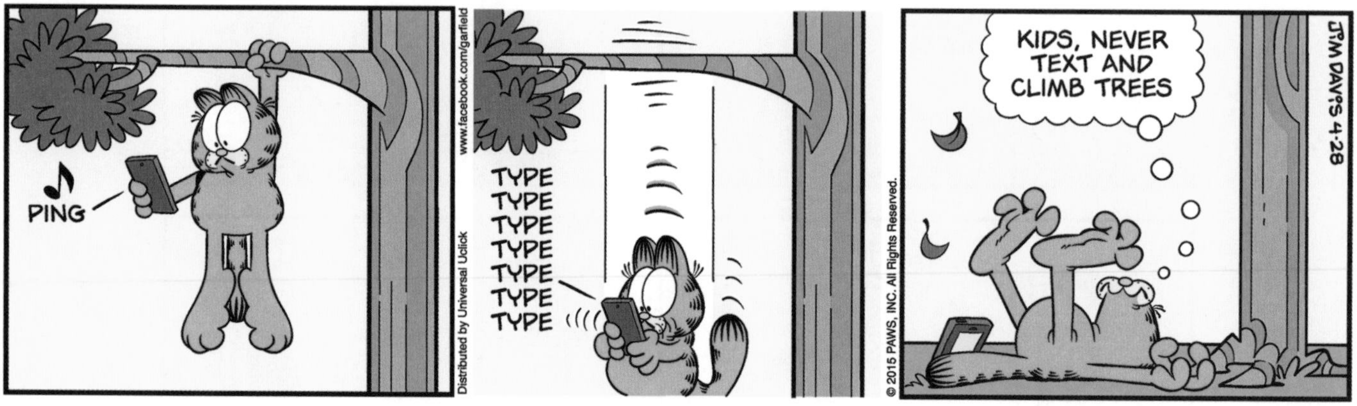
PING
Distributed by Universal Uclick www.facebook.com/garfield
TYPE TYPE TYPE TYPE TYPE TYPE TYPE
KIDS, NEVER TEXT AND CLIMB TREES
© 2015 PAWS, INC. All Rights Reserved.
JIM DAVIS 4-28

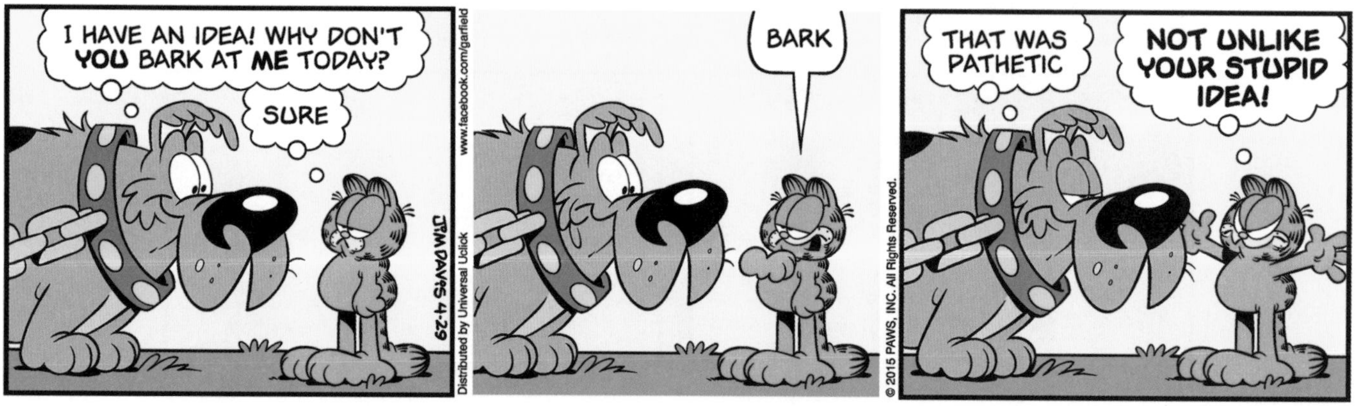
I HAVE AN IDEA! WHY DON'T YOU BARK AT ME TODAY?
SURE
JIM DAVIS 4-29
Distributed by Universal Uclick www.facebook.com/garfield
BARK
© 2015 PAWS, INC. All Rights Reserved.
THAT WAS PATHETIC
NOT UNLIKE YOUR STUPID IDEA!

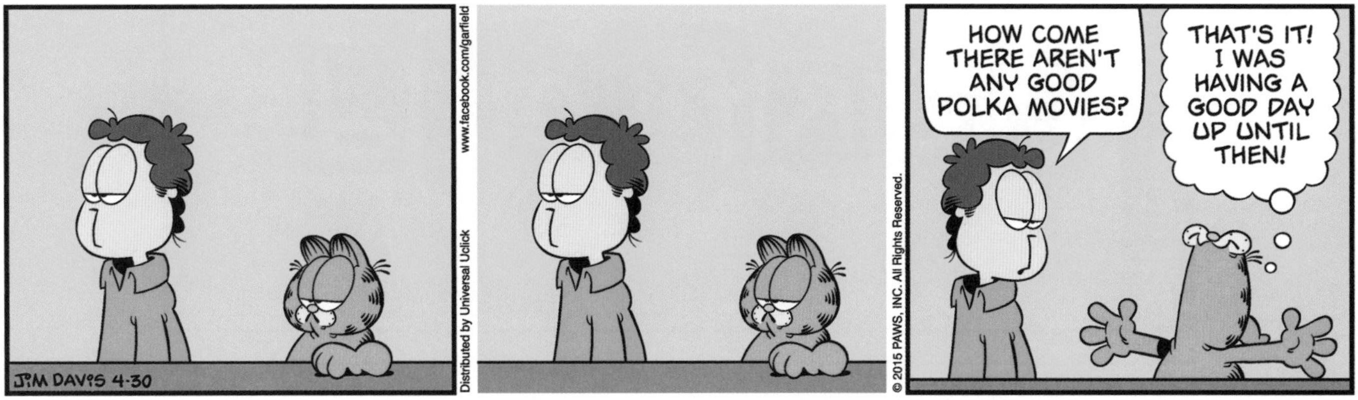
JIM DAVIS 4-30
Distributed by Universal Uclick www.facebook.com/garfield
© 2015 PAWS, INC. All Rights Reserved.
HOW COME THERE AREN'T ANY GOOD POLKA MOVIES?
THAT'S IT! I WAS HAVING A GOOD DAY UP UNTIL THEN!

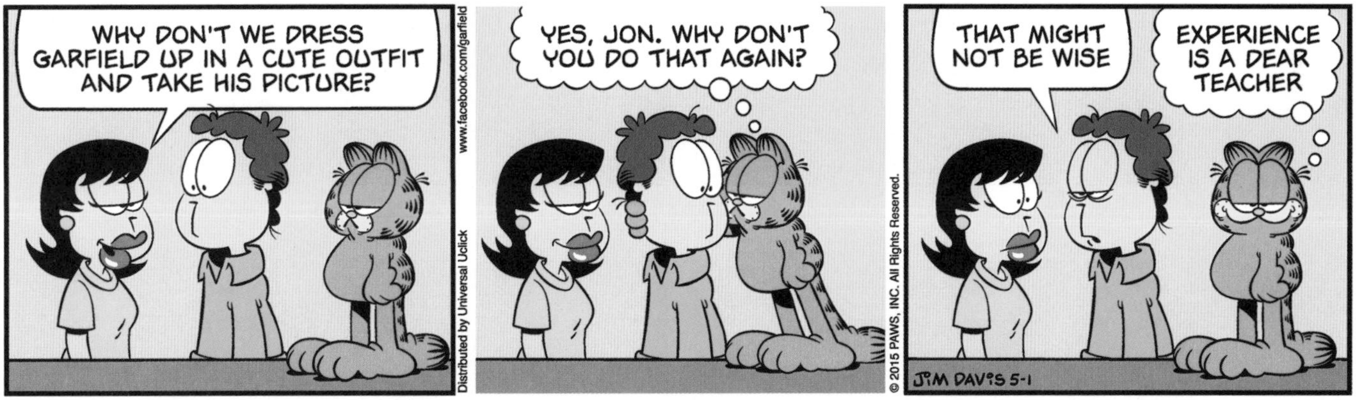
WHY DON'T WE DRESS GARFIELD UP IN A CUTE OUTFIT AND TAKE HIS PICTURE?
Distributed by Universal Uclick www.facebook.com/garfield
YES, JON. WHY DON'T YOU DO THAT AGAIN?
© 2015 PAWS, INC. All Rights Reserved.
THAT MIGHT NOT BE WISE
EXPERIENCE IS A DEAR TEACHER
JIM DAVIS 5-1

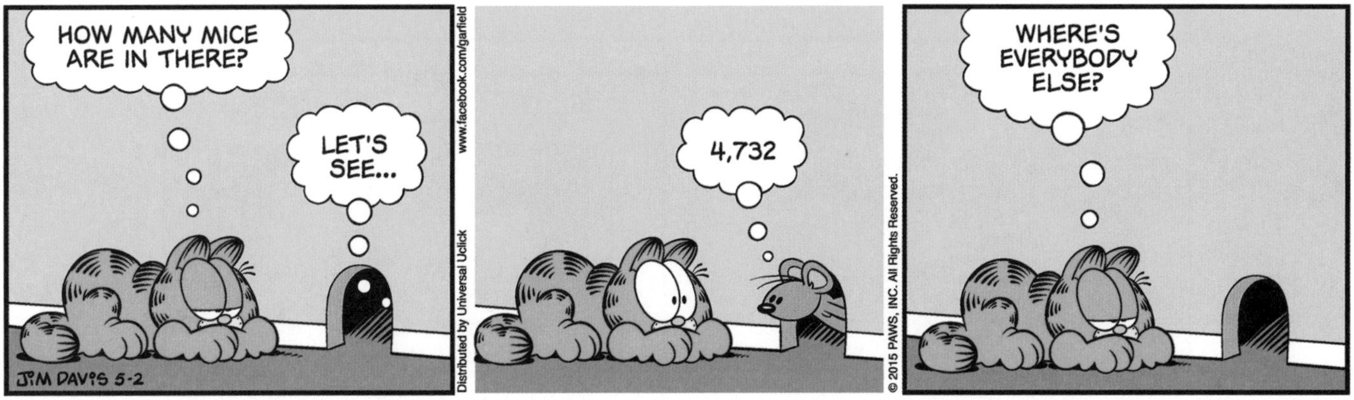
HOW MANY MICE ARE IN THERE?
LET'S SEE...
JIM DAVIS 5-2
Distributed by Universal Uclick www.facebook.com/garfield
4,732
© 2015 PAWS, INC. All Rights Reserved.
WHERE'S EVERYBODY ELSE?

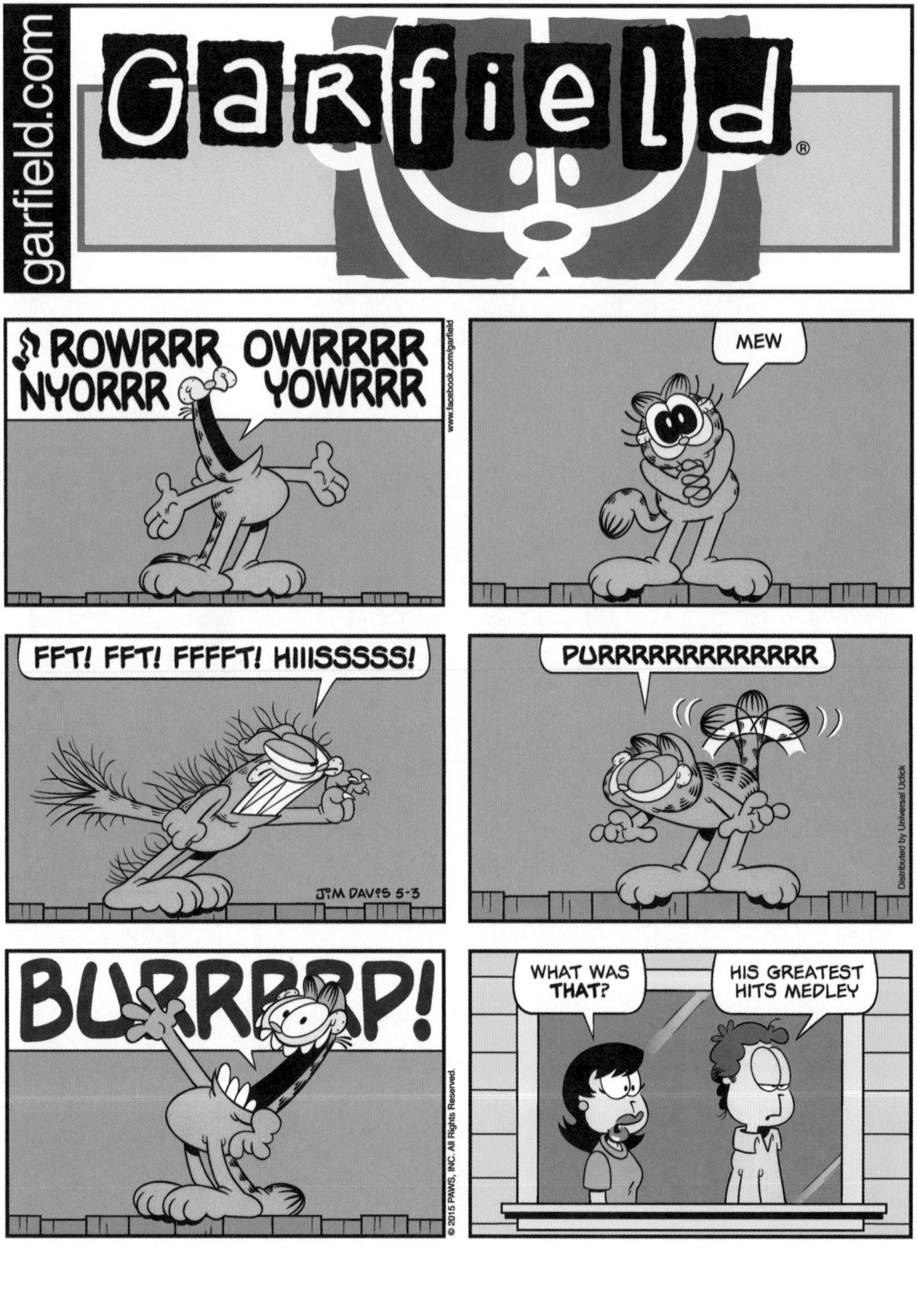
garfield.com
Garfield®
♪ ROWRRR OWRRRR NYORRR YOWRRR
www.facebook.com/garfield
MEW
FFT! FFT! FFFFT! HIIISSSSS!
JIM DAVIS 5-3
PURRRRRRRRRRRRR
Distributed by Universal Uclick
BURRRRP!
© 2015 PAWS, INC. All Rights Reserved.
WHAT WAS THAT?
HIS GREATEST HITS MEDLEY

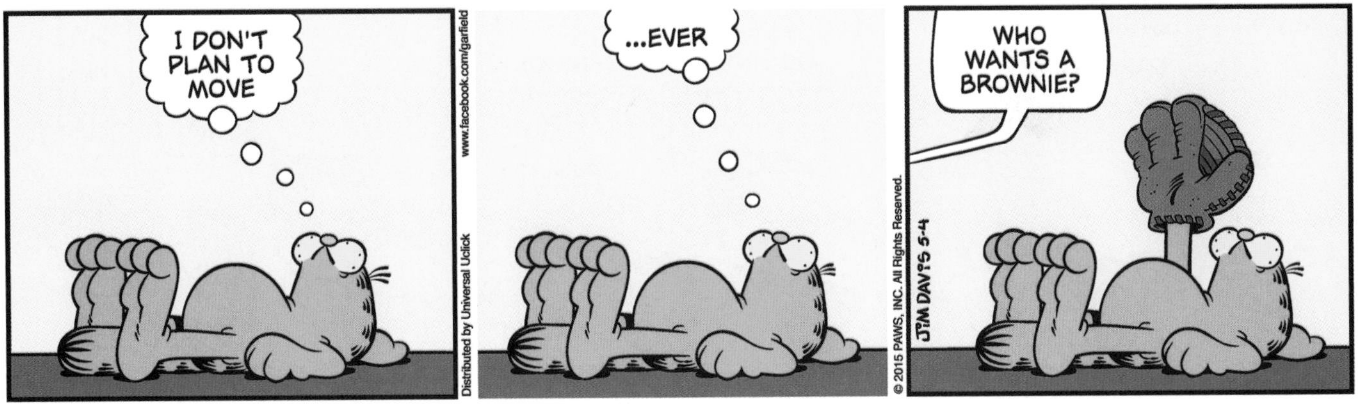
I DON'T PLAN TO MOVE
...EVER
WHO WANTS A BROWNIE?
Distributed by Universal Uclick
www.facebook.com/garfield
© 2015 PAWS, INC. All Rights Reserved.
JIM DAVIS 5-4

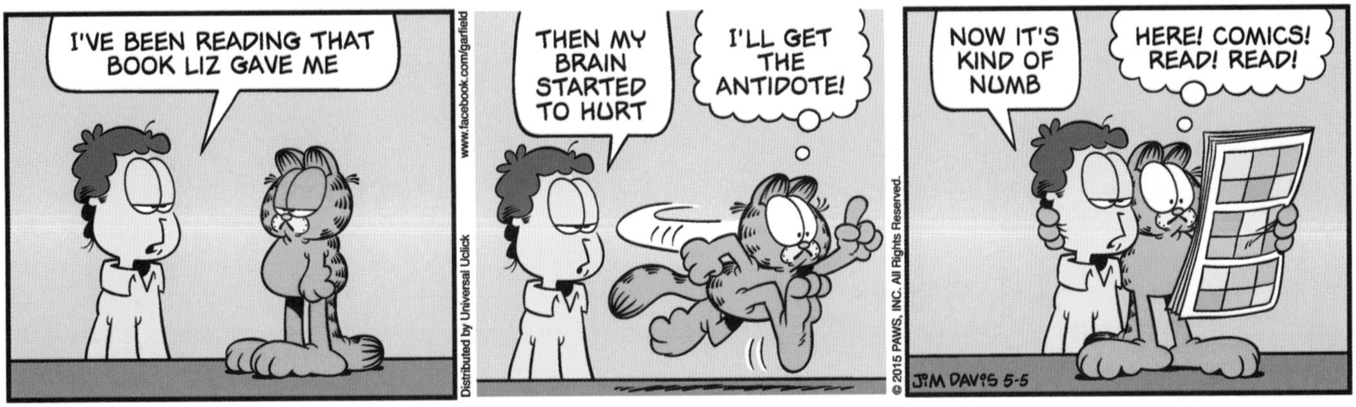
I'VE BEEN READING THAT BOOK LIZ GAVE ME
THEN MY BRAIN STARTED TO HURT
I'LL GET THE ANTIDOTE!
NOW IT'S KIND OF NUMB
HERE! COMICS! READ! READ!
Distributed by Universal Uclick
www.facebook.com/garfield
© 2015 PAWS, INC. All Rights Reserved.
JIM DAVIS 5-5

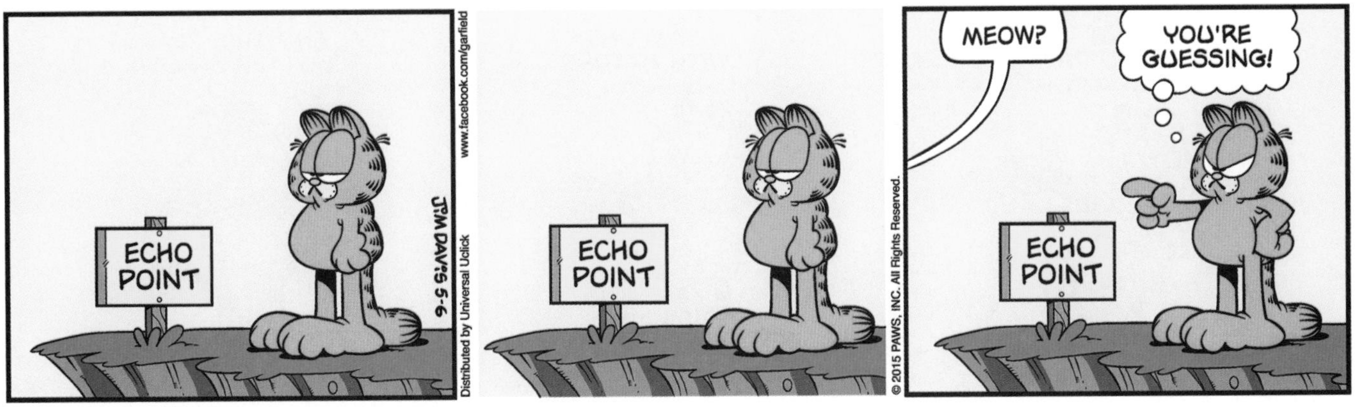
ECHO POINT
JIM DAVIS 5-6
ECHO POINT
MEOW?
YOU'RE GUESSING!
ECHO POINT
Distributed by Universal Uclick
www.facebook.com/garfield
© 2015 PAWS, INC. All Rights Reserved.

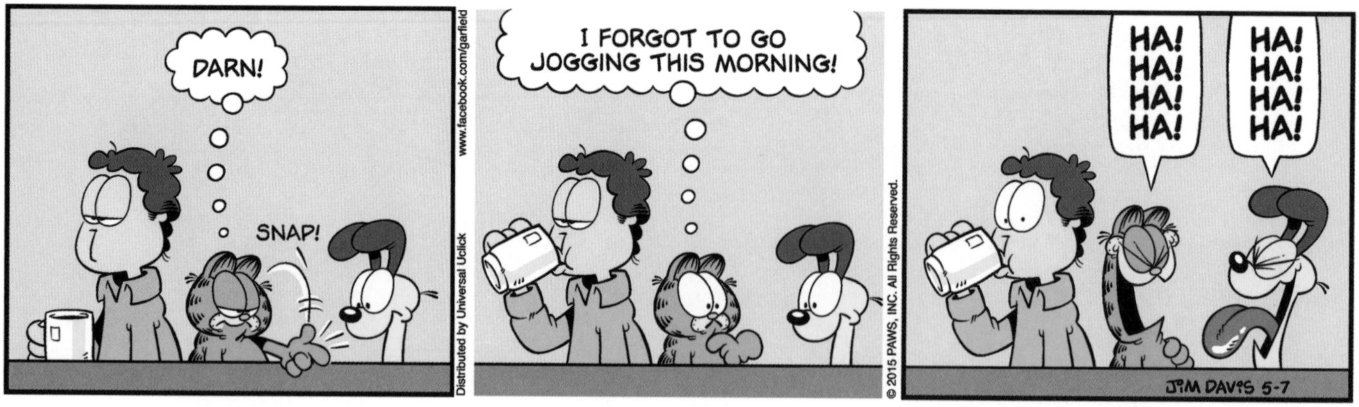
DARN!
SNAP!
I FORGOT TO GO JOGGING THIS MORNING!
HA! HA! HA! HA!
HA! HA! HA! HA!
JIM DAVIS 5-7
Distributed by Universal Uclick www.facebook.com/garfield
© 2015 PAWS, INC. All Rights Reserved.

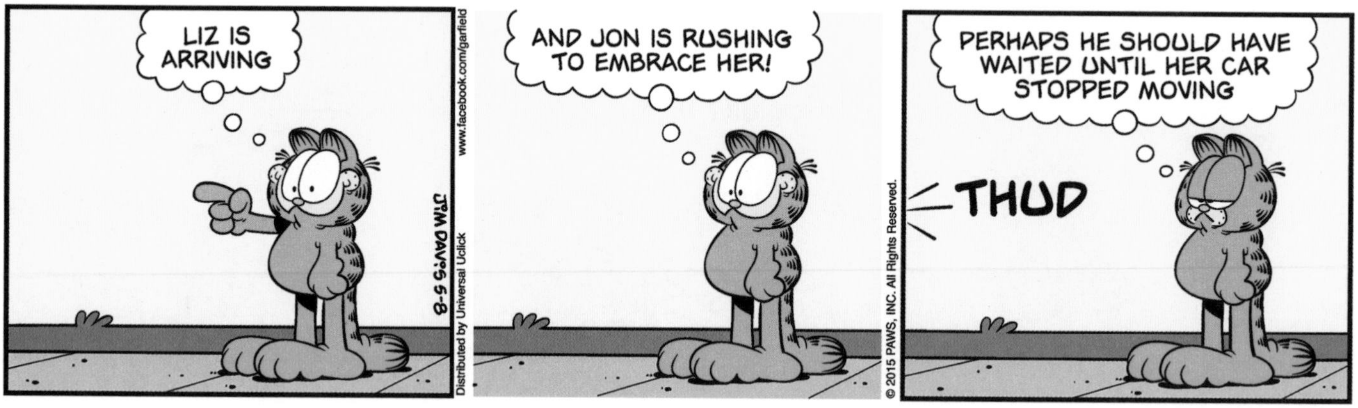
LIZ IS ARRIVING
JIM DAVIS 5-8
AND JON IS RUSHING TO EMBRACE HER!
PERHAPS HE SHOULD HAVE WAITED UNTIL HER CAR STOPPED MOVING
THUD
Distributed by Universal Uclick www.facebook.com/garfield
© 2015 PAWS, INC. All Rights Reserved.

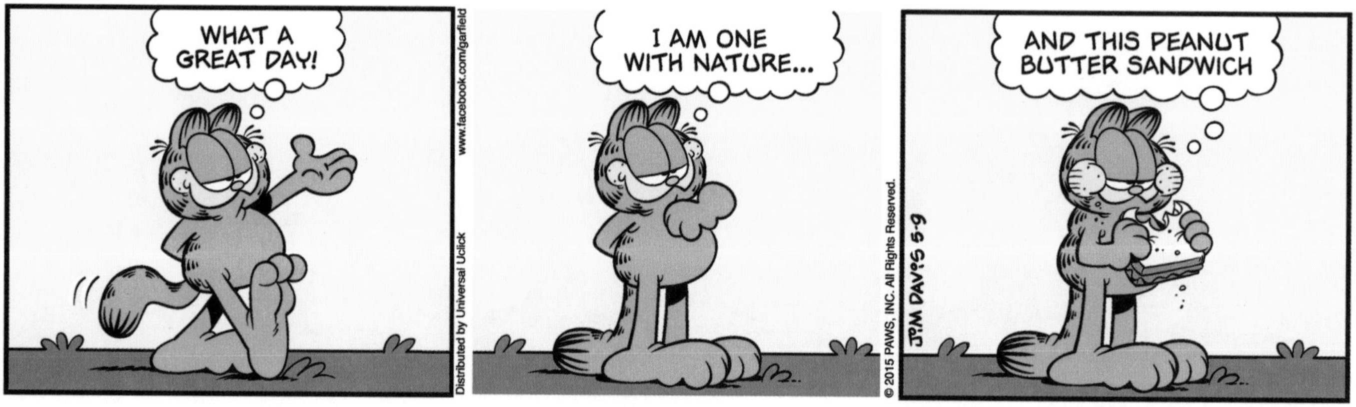
WHAT A GREAT DAY!
I AM ONE WITH NATURE...
AND THIS PEANUT BUTTER SANDWICH
JIM DAVIS 5-9
Distributed by Universal Uclick www.facebook.com/garfield
© 2015 PAWS, INC. All Rights Reserved.

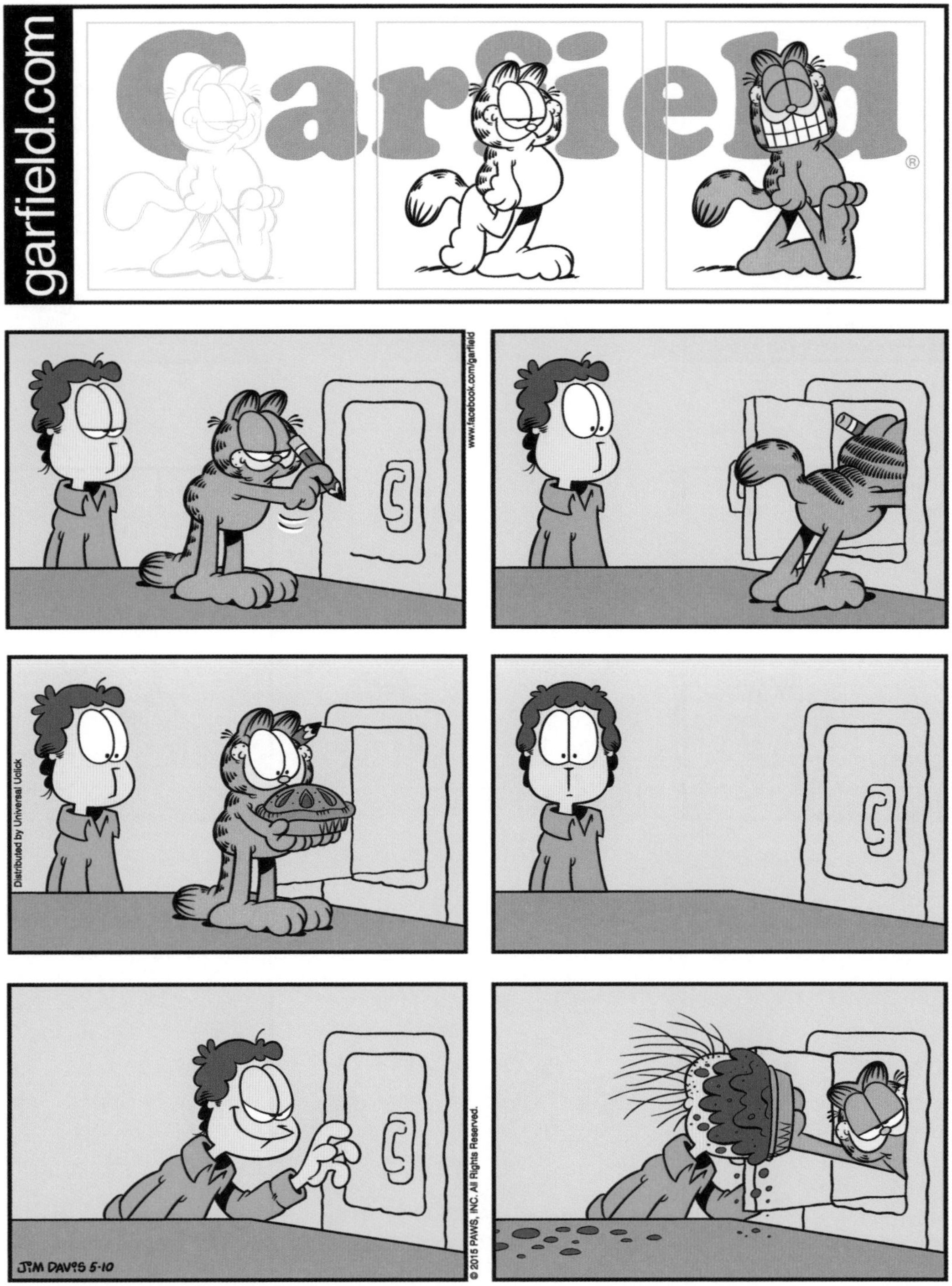
garfield.com
Garfield
www.facebook.com/garfield
Distributed by Universal Uclick
© 2015 PAWS, INC. All Rights Reserved.
JIM DAVIS 5-10

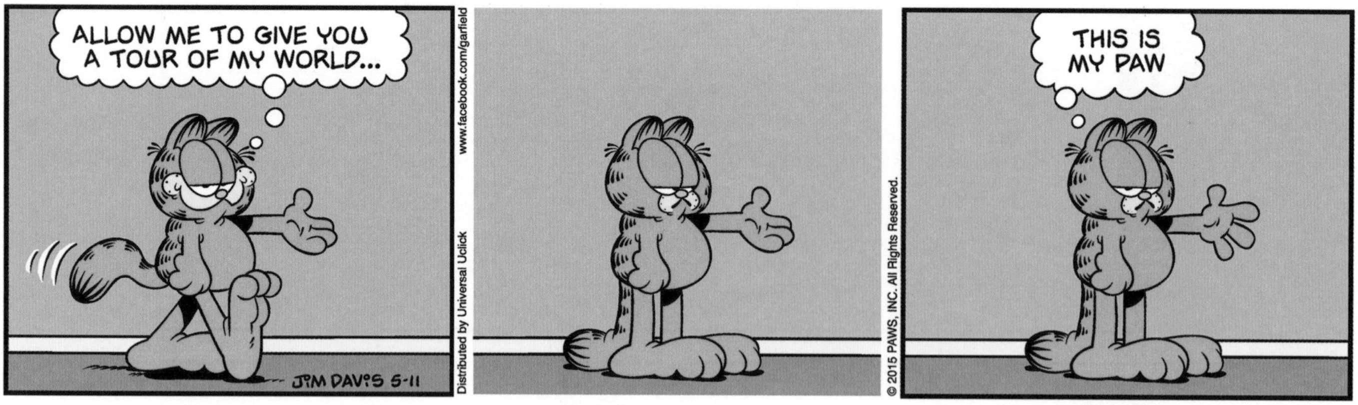
ALLOW ME TO GIVE YOU A TOUR OF MY WORLD...
JIM DAVIS 5-11
Distributed by Universal Uclick www.facebook.com/garfield
THIS IS MY PAW
© 2015 PAWS, INC. All Rights Reserved.

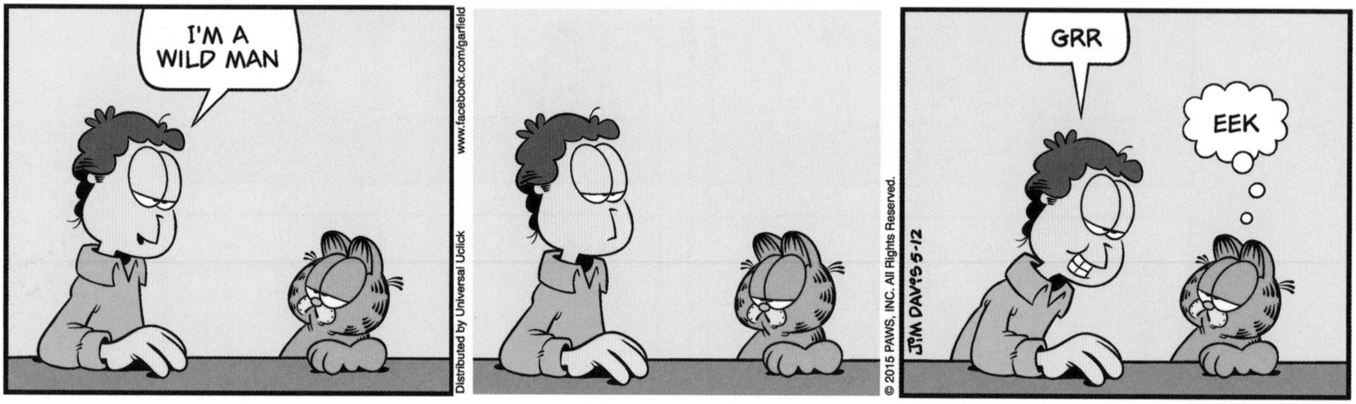
I'M A WILD MAN
Distributed by Universal Uclick www.facebook.com/garfield
GRR
EEK
© 2015 PAWS, INC. All Rights Reserved.
JIM DAVIS 5-12

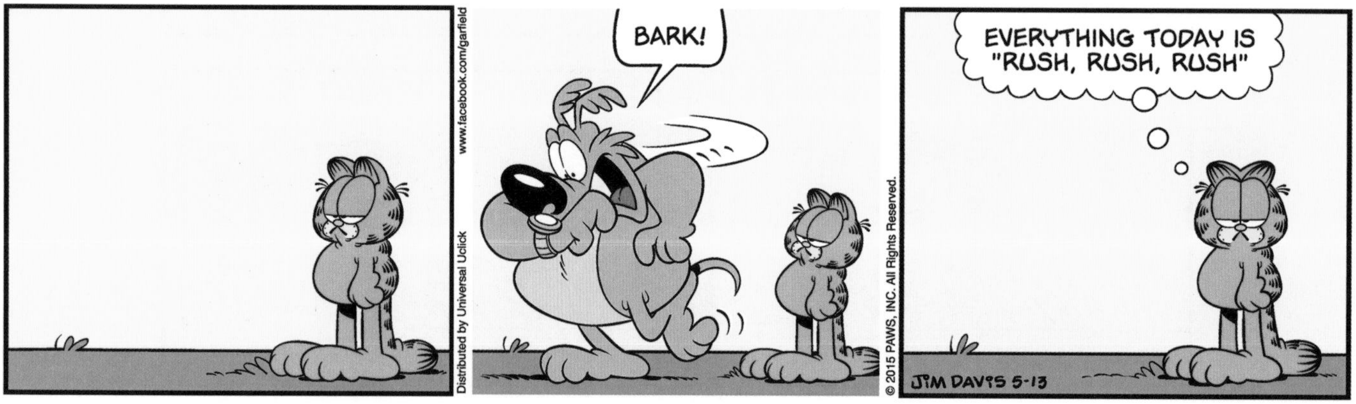
Distributed by Universal Uclick www.facebook.com/garfield
BARK!
EVERYTHING TODAY IS "RUSH, RUSH, RUSH"
© 2015 PAWS, INC. All Rights Reserved.
JIM DAVIS 5-13

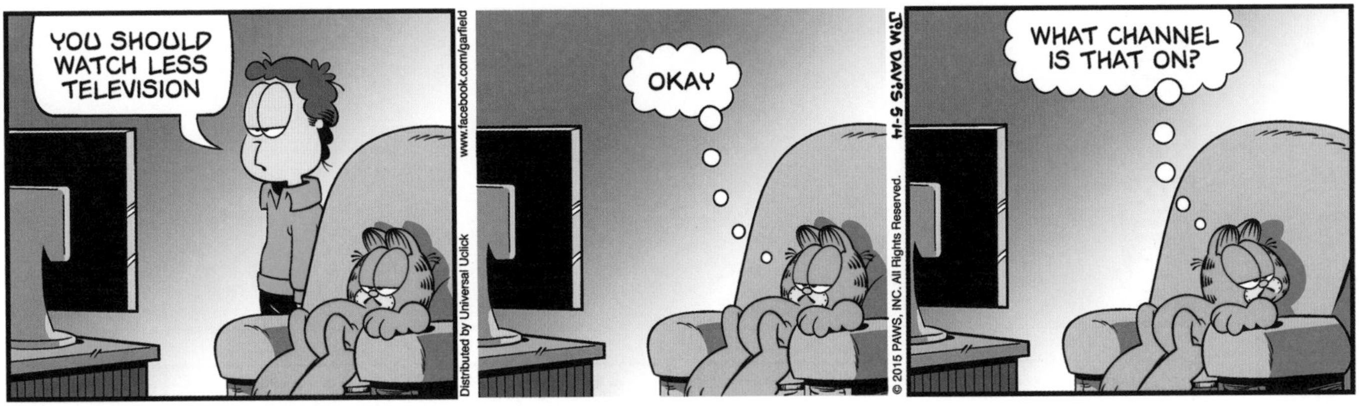
YOU SHOULD WATCH LESS TELEVISION
Distributed by Universal Uclick www.facebook.com/garfield
OKAY
JIM DAVIS 5-14
© 2015 PAWS, INC. All Rights Reserved.
WHAT CHANNEL IS THAT ON?

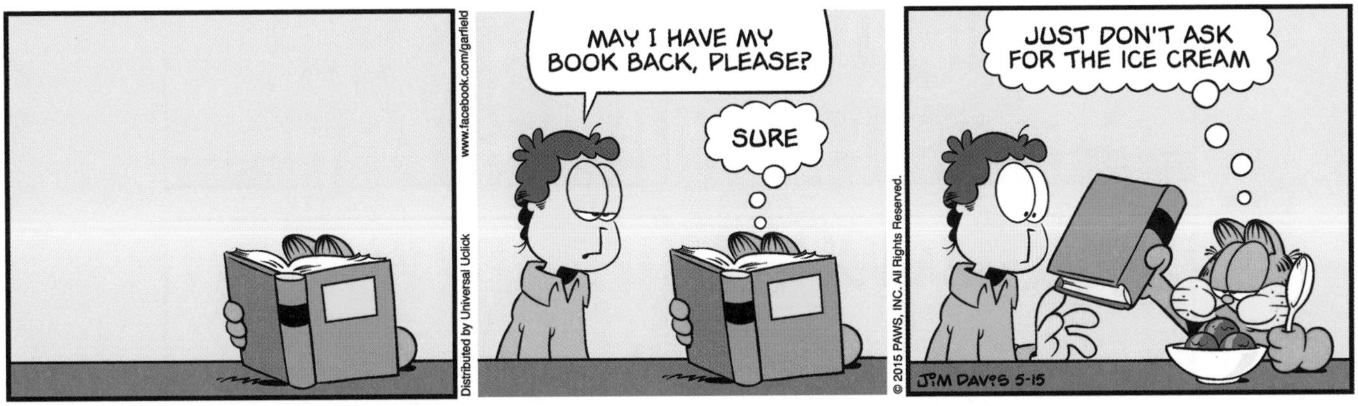
Distributed by Universal Uclick www.facebook.com/garfield
MAY I HAVE MY BOOK BACK, PLEASE?
SURE
© 2015 PAWS, INC. All Rights Reserved.
JUST DON'T ASK FOR THE ICE CREAM
JIM DAVIS 5-15

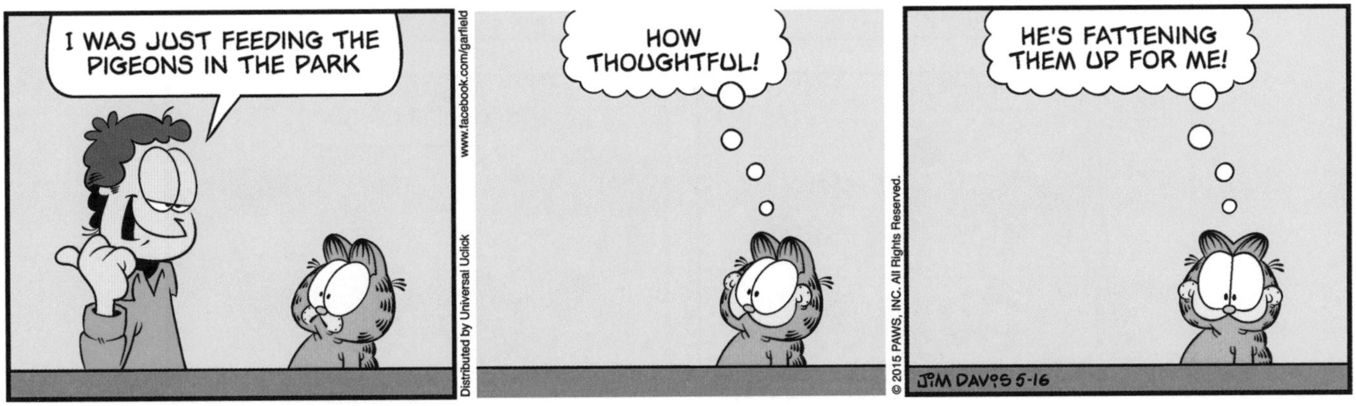
I WAS JUST FEEDING THE PIGEONS IN THE PARK
Distributed by Universal Uclick www.facebook.com/garfield
HOW THOUGHTFUL!
© 2015 PAWS, INC. All Rights Reserved.
HE'S FATTENING THEM UP FOR ME!
JIM DAVIS 5-16

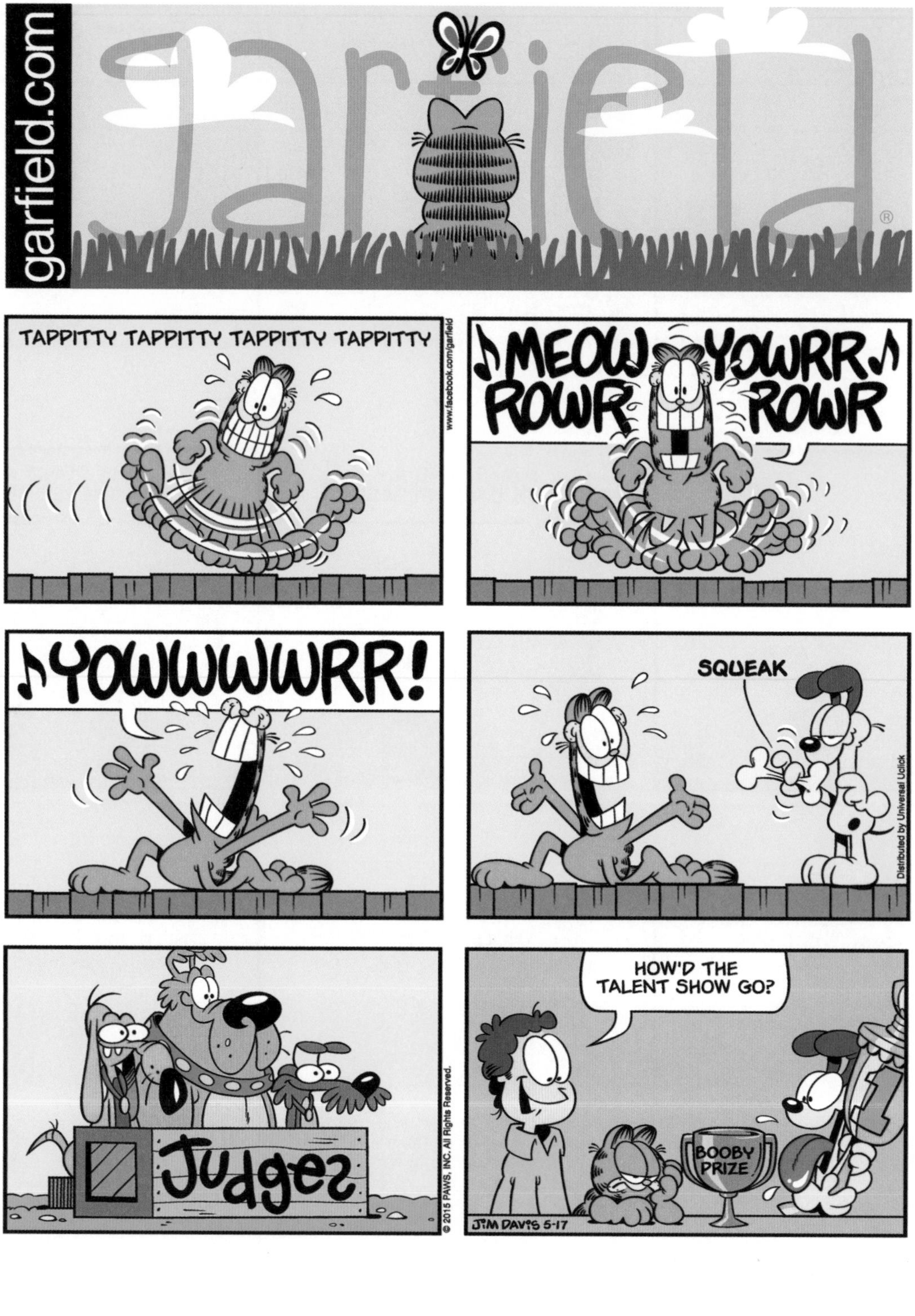
garfield.com
garfield®
www.facebook.com/garfield
TAPPITTY TAPPITTY TAPPITTY TAPPITTY
♪MEOW ROWR
YOWRR ROWR♪
♪YOWWWWRR!
SQUEAK
Distributed by Universal Uclick
Judges
© 2015 PAWS, INC. All Rights Reserved.
HOW'D THE TALENT SHOW GO?
BOOBY PRIZE
JIM DAVIS 5-17

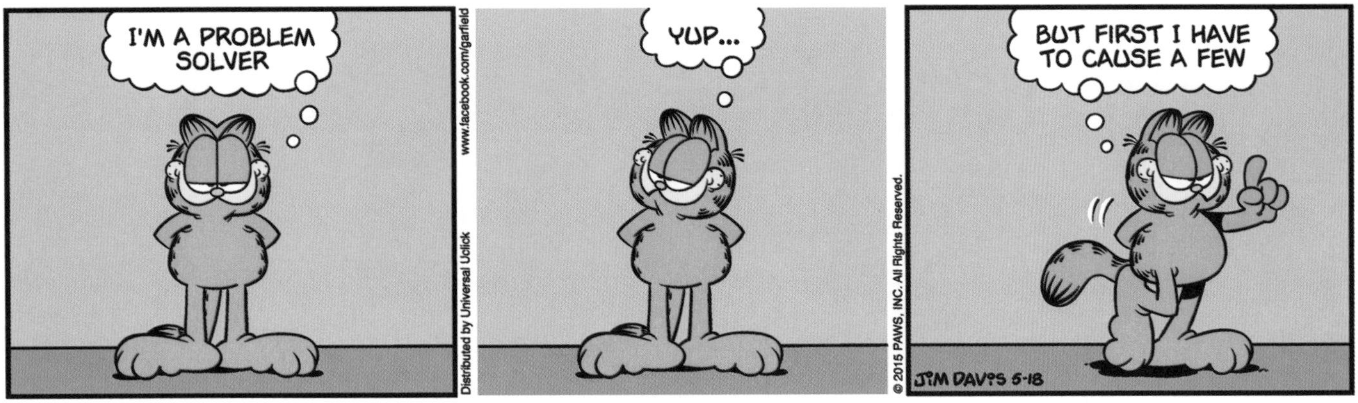
I'M A PROBLEM SOLVER
YUP...
BUT FIRST I HAVE TO CAUSE A FEW
Distributed by Universal Uclick www.facebook.com/garfield
© 2015 PAWS, INC. All Rights Reserved.
JIM DAVIS 5-18

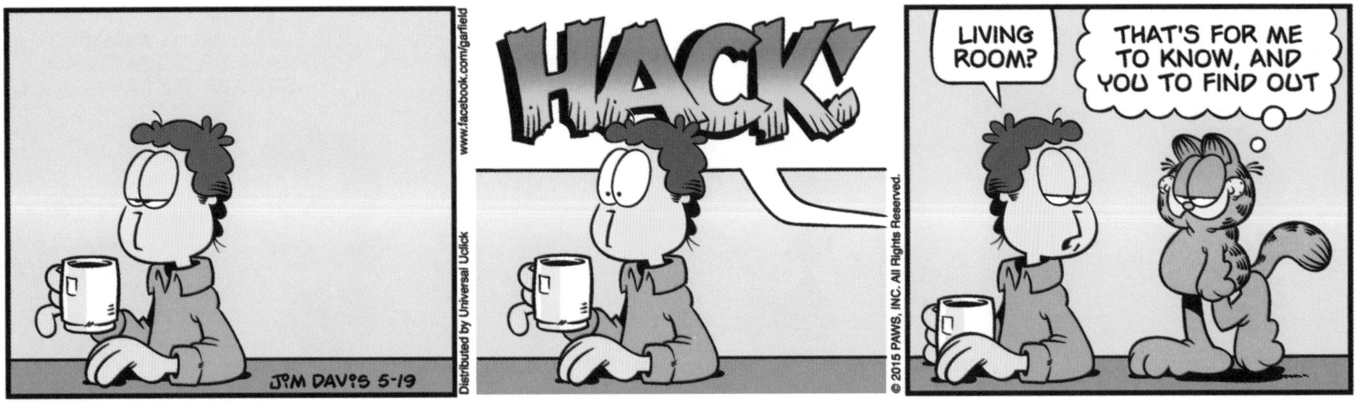
JIM DAVIS 5-19
Distributed by Universal Uclick www.facebook.com/garfield
HACK!
© 2015 PAWS, INC. All Rights Reserved.
LIVING ROOM?
THAT'S FOR ME TO KNOW, AND YOU TO FIND OUT

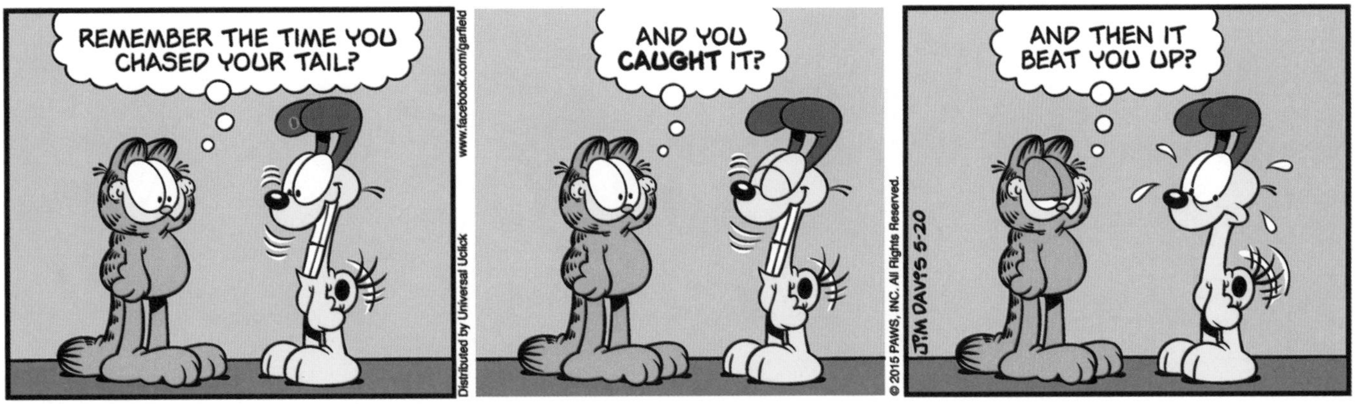
REMEMBER THE TIME YOU CHASED YOUR TAIL?
Distributed by Universal Uclick www.facebook.com/garfield
AND YOU **CAUGHT** IT?
© 2015 PAWS, INC. All Rights Reserved.
JIM DAVIS 5-20
AND THEN IT BEAT YOU UP?

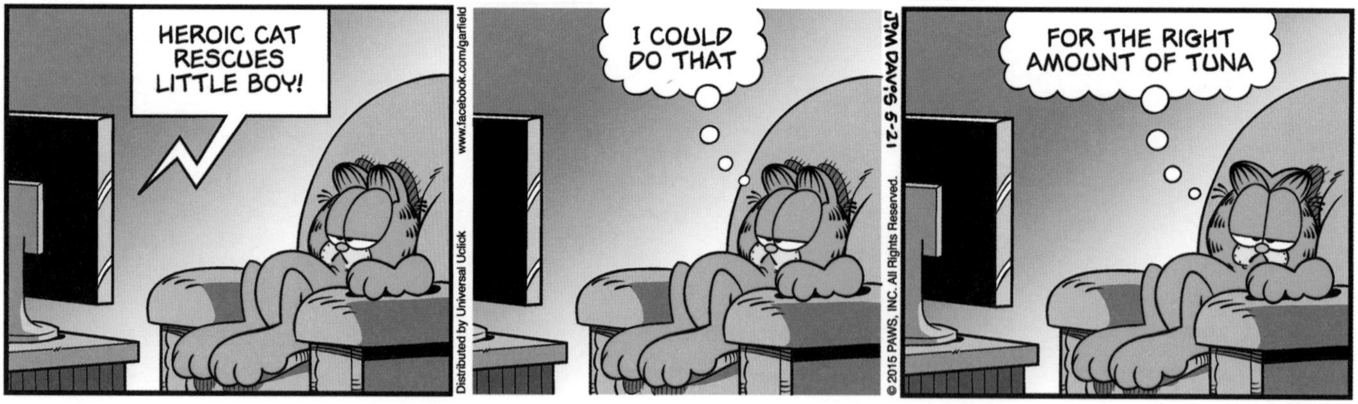
HEROIC CAT RESCUES LITTLE BOY!
I COULD DO THAT
FOR THE RIGHT AMOUNT OF TUNA
JIM DAVIS 5-21
Distributed by Universal Uclick www.facebook.com/garfield
© 2015 PAWS, INC. All Rights Reserved.

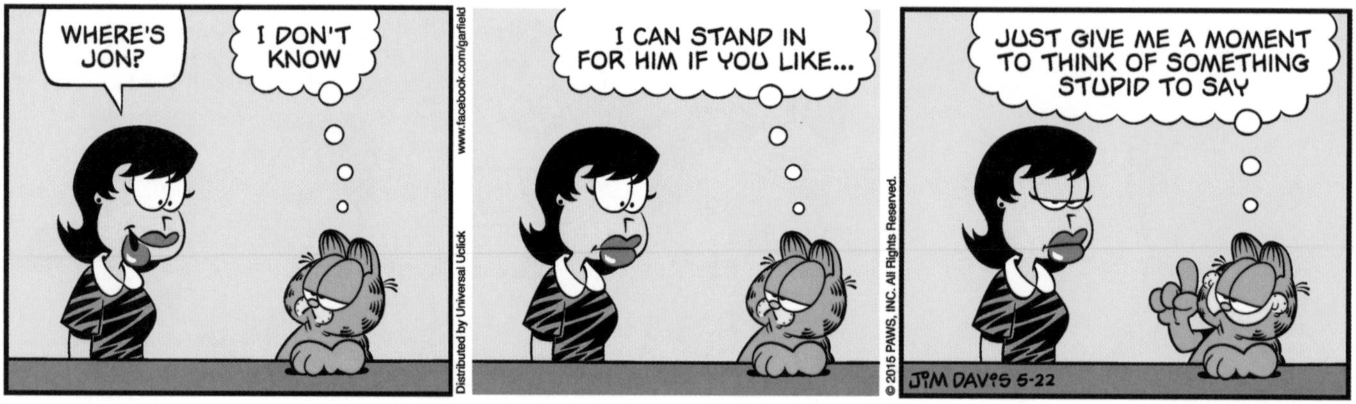
WHERE'S JON?
I DON'T KNOW
I CAN STAND IN FOR HIM IF YOU LIKE...
JUST GIVE ME A MOMENT TO THINK OF SOMETHING STUPID TO SAY
JIM DAVIS 5-22
Distributed by Universal Uclick www.facebook.com/garfield
© 2015 PAWS, INC. All Rights Reserved.

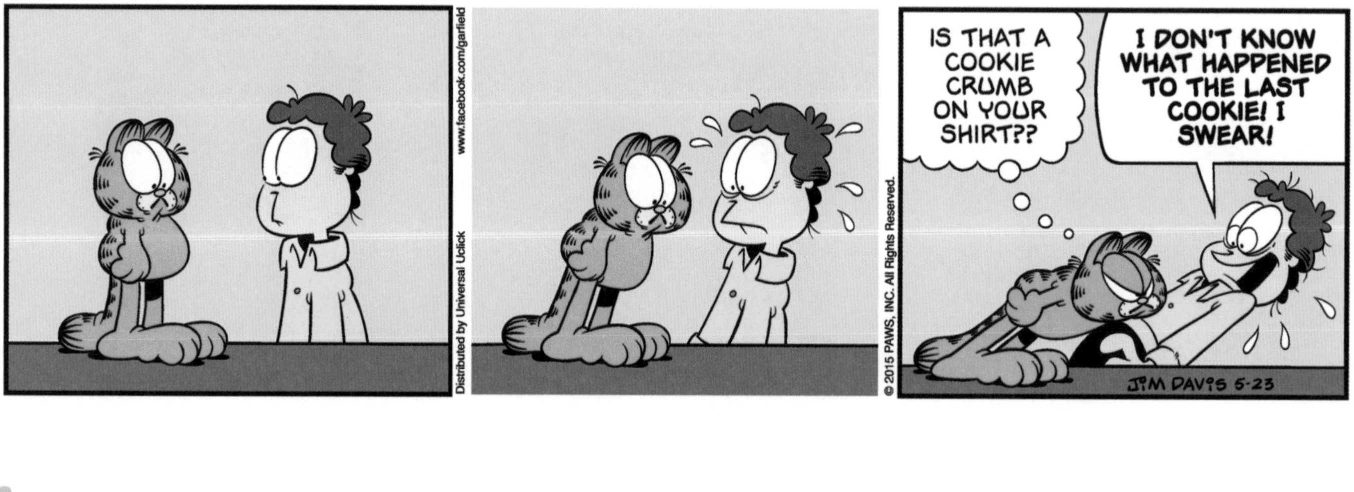
IS THAT A COOKIE CRUMB ON YOUR SHIRT??
I DON'T KNOW WHAT HAPPENED TO THE LAST COOKIE! I SWEAR!
JIM DAVIS 5-23
Distributed by Universal Uclick www.facebook.com/garfield
© 2015 PAWS, INC. All Rights Reserved.

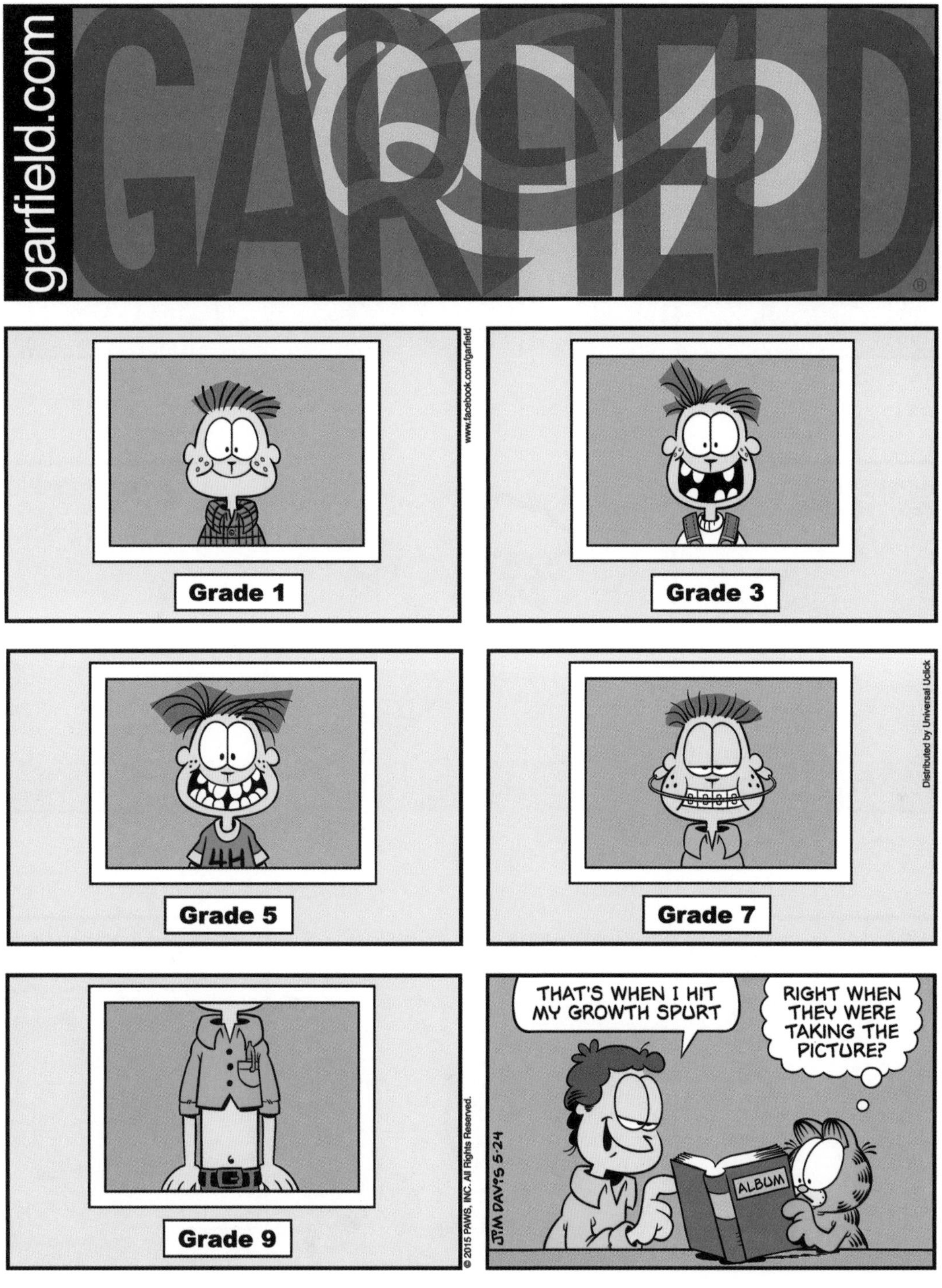
garfield.com
GARFIELD
www.facebook.com/garfield
Grade 1
Grade 3
Grade 5
Distributed by Universal Uclick
Grade 7
Grade 9
© 2015 PAWS, INC. All Rights Reserved.
THAT'S WHEN I HIT MY GROWTH SPURT
RIGHT WHEN THEY WERE TAKING THE PICTURE?
ALBUM
JPM DAVPS 5-24

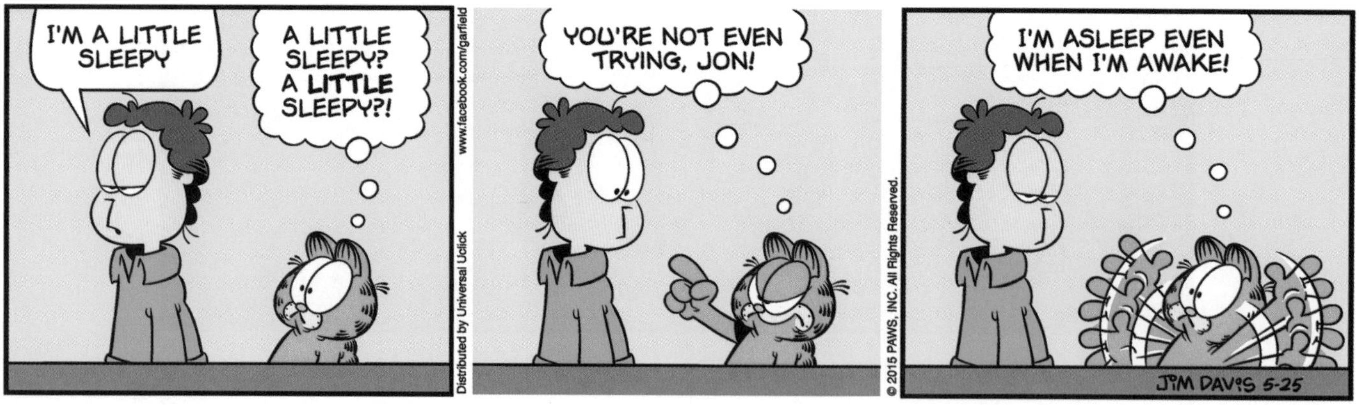
I'M A LITTLE SLEEPY
A LITTLE SLEEPY? A LITTLE SLEEPY?!
Distributed by Universal Uclick www.facebook.com/garfield
YOU'RE NOT EVEN TRYING, JON!
© 2015 PAWS, INC. All Rights Reserved.
I'M ASLEEP EVEN WHEN I'M AWAKE!
JIM DAVIS 5-25

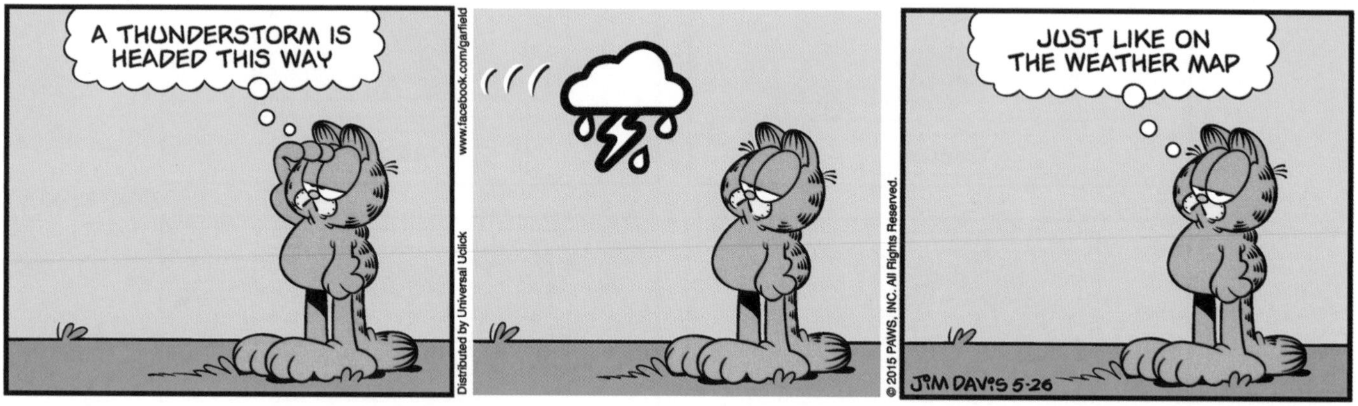
A THUNDERSTORM IS HEADED THIS WAY
Distributed by Universal Uclick www.facebook.com/garfield
© 2015 PAWS, INC. All Rights Reserved.
JUST LIKE ON THE WEATHER MAP
JIM DAVIS 5-26

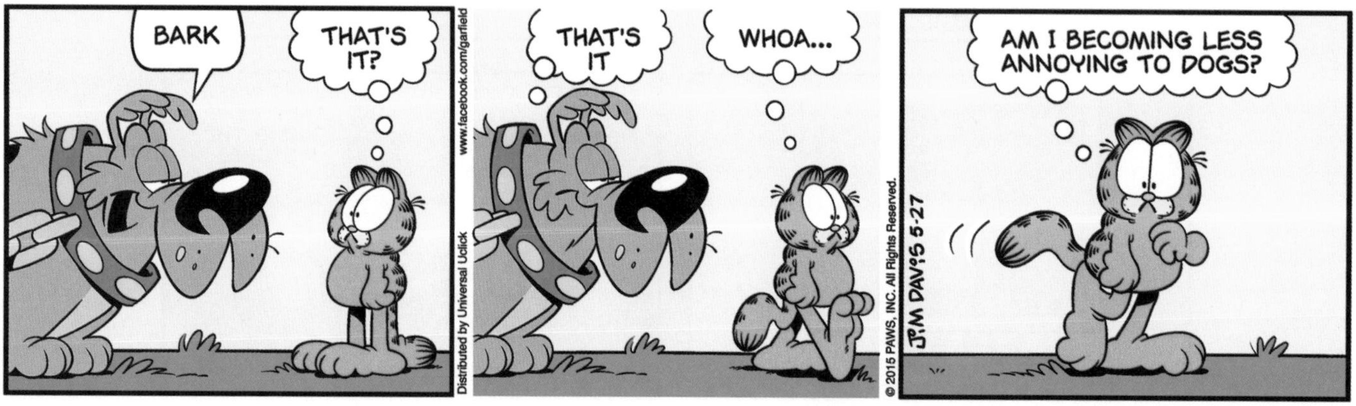
BARK
THAT'S IT?
Distributed by Universal Uclick www.facebook.com/garfield
THAT'S IT
WHOA...
© 2015 PAWS, INC. All Rights Reserved.
JIM DAVIS 5-27
AM I BECOMING LESS ANNOYING TO DOGS?

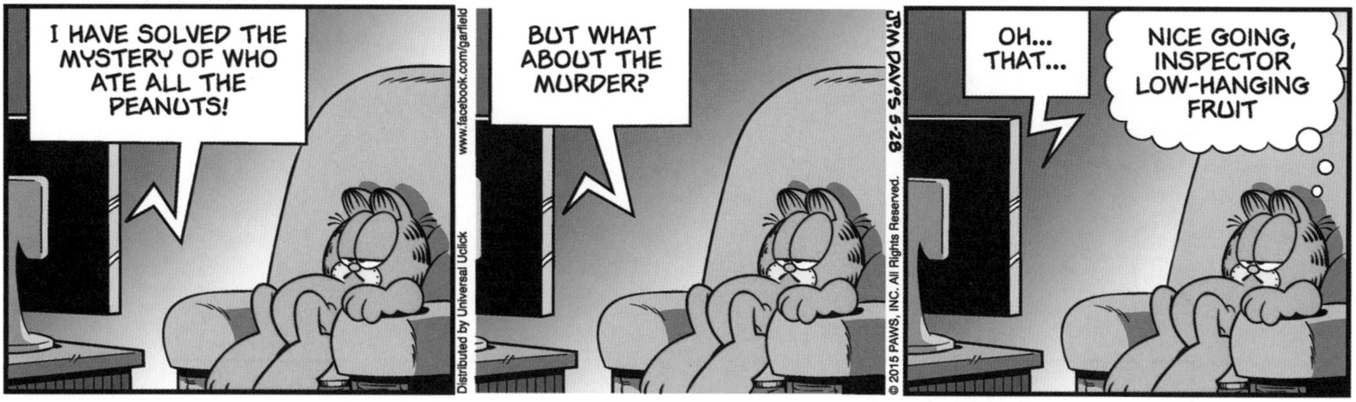
I HAVE SOLVED THE MYSTERY OF WHO ATE ALL THE PEANUTS!
Distributed by Universal Uclick www.facebook.com/garfield
BUT WHAT ABOUT THE MURDER?
JIM DAVIS 5-28
© 2015 PAWS, INC. All Rights Reserved.
OH... THAT...
NICE GOING, INSPECTOR LOW-HANGING FRUIT

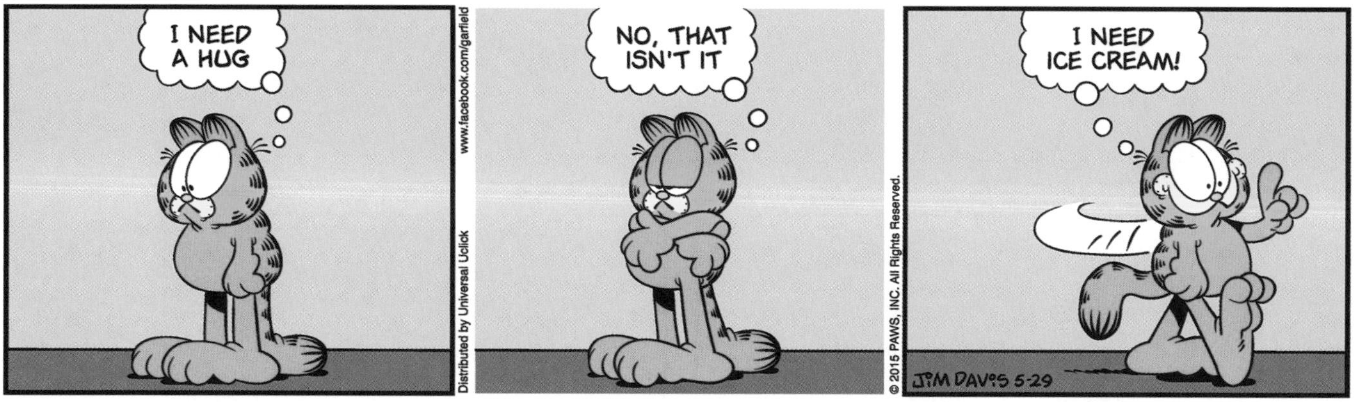
I NEED A HUG
Distributed by Universal Uclick www.facebook.com/garfield
NO, THAT ISN'T IT
© 2015 PAWS, INC. All Rights Reserved.
I NEED ICE CREAM!
JIM DAVIS 5-29

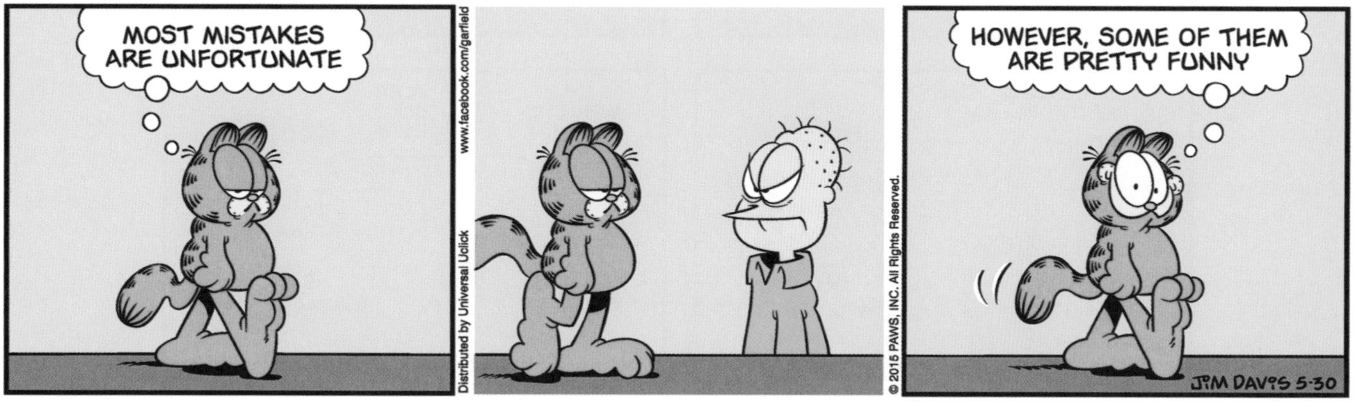
MOST MISTAKES ARE UNFORTUNATE
Distributed by Universal Uclick www.facebook.com/garfield
© 2015 PAWS, INC. All Rights Reserved.
HOWEVER, SOME OF THEM ARE PRETTY FUNNY
JIM DAVIS 5-30

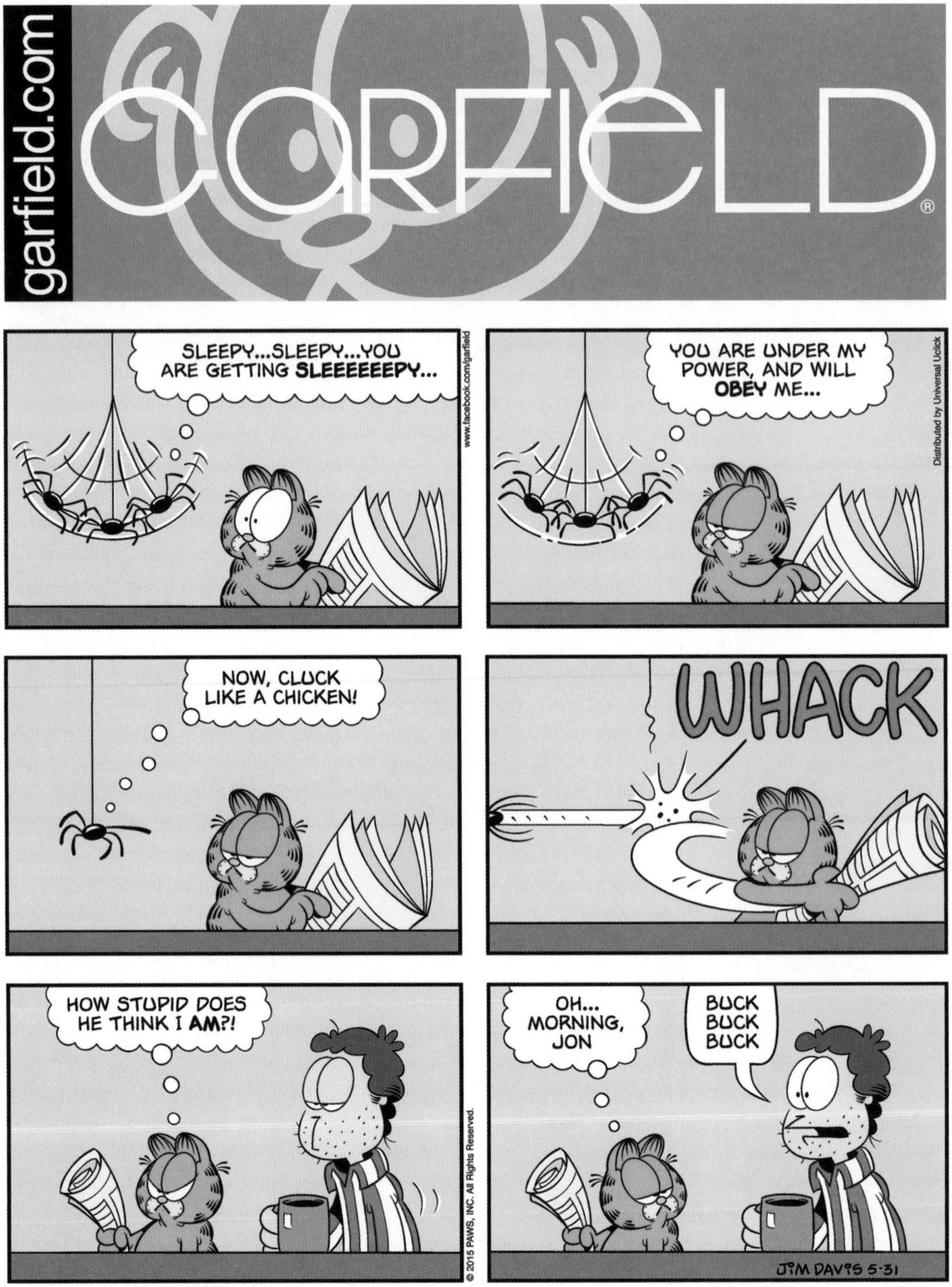
garfield.com
GARFIELD
SLEEPY...SLEEPY...YOU ARE GETTING SLEEEEEEPY...
www.facebook.com/garfield
YOU ARE UNDER MY POWER, AND WILL OBEY ME...
Distributed by Universal Uclick
NOW, CLUCK LIKE A CHICKEN!
WHACK
HOW STUPID DOES HE THINK I AM?!
© 2015 PAWS, INC. All Rights Reserved.
OH... MORNING, JON
BUCK BUCK BUCK
JIM DAVIS 5-31

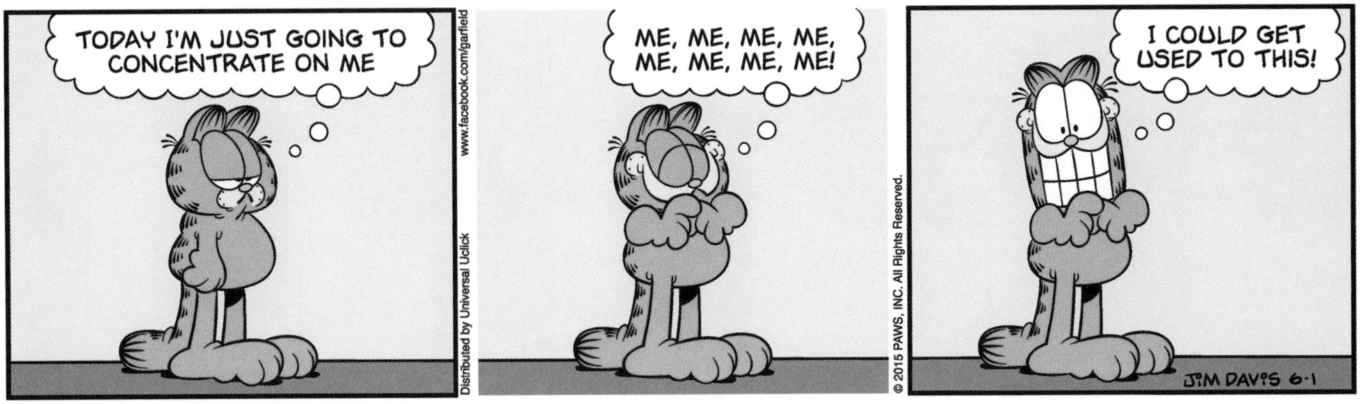
TODAY I'M JUST GOING TO CONCENTRATE ON ME
ME, ME, ME, ME, ME, ME, ME, ME!
I COULD GET USED TO THIS!
JIM DAVIS 6-1
Distributed by Universal Uclick www.facebook.com/garfield
© 2015 PAWS, INC. All Rights Reserved.

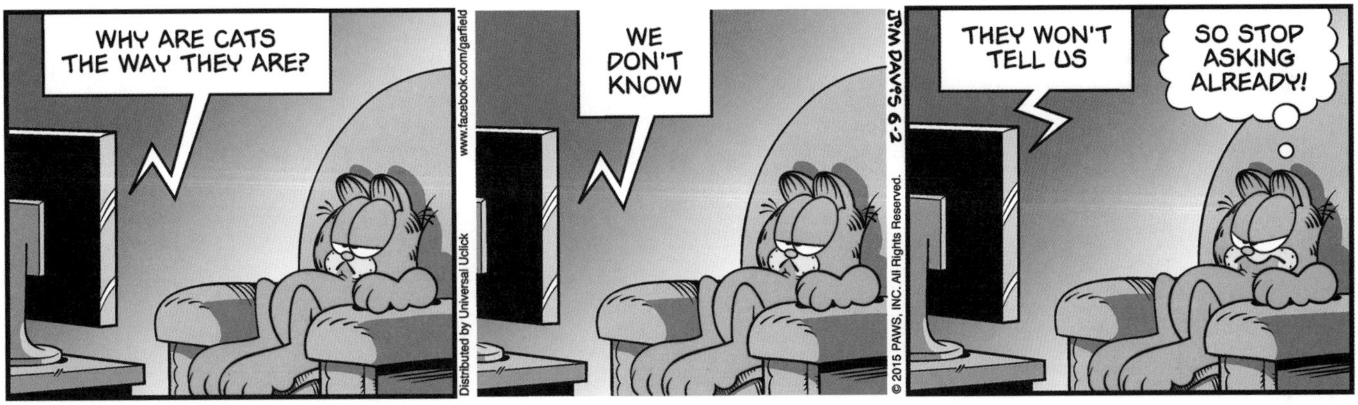
WHY ARE CATS THE WAY THEY ARE?
WE DON'T KNOW
THEY WON'T TELL US
SO STOP ASKING ALREADY!
JIM DAVIS 6-2
Distributed by Universal Uclick www.facebook.com/garfield
© 2015 PAWS, INC. All Rights Reserved.

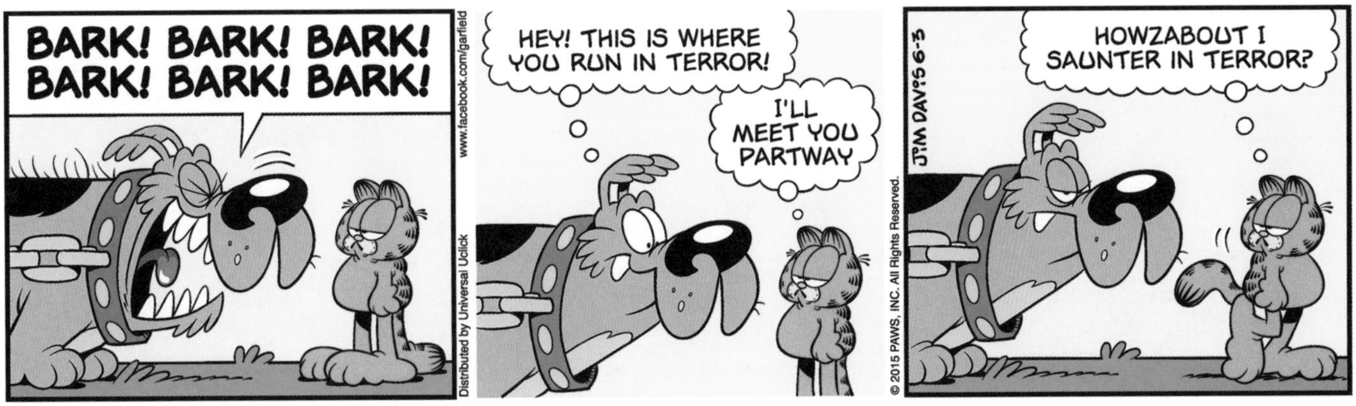
BARK! BARK! BARK! BARK! BARK! BARK!
HEY! THIS IS WHERE YOU RUN IN TERROR!
I'LL MEET YOU PARTWAY
HOWZABOUT I SAUNTER IN TERROR?
JIM DAVIS 6-3
Distributed by Universal Uclick www.facebook.com/garfield
© 2015 PAWS, INC. All Rights Reserved.

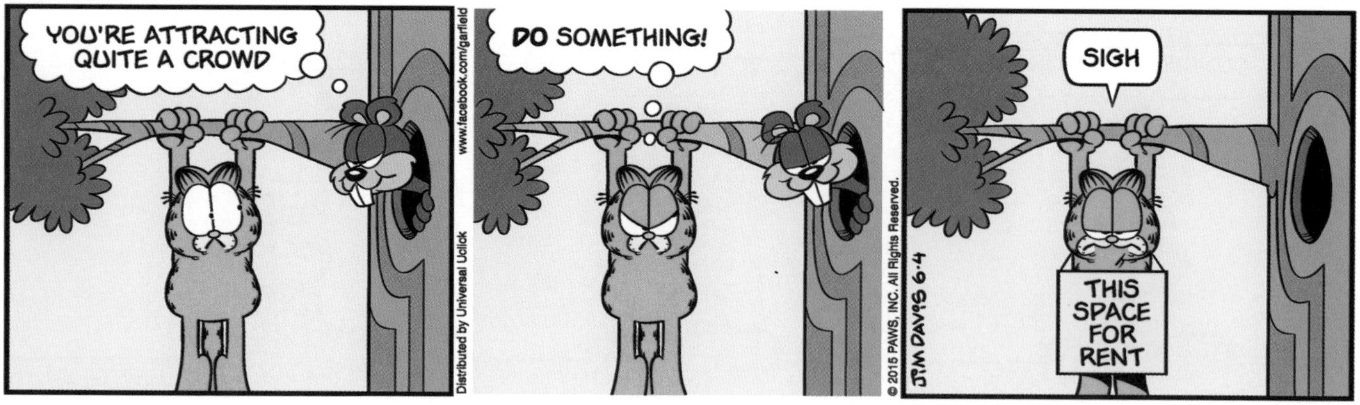
YOU'RE ATTRACTING QUITE A CROWD
www.facebook.com/garfield
Distributed by Universal Uclick
DO SOMETHING!
© 2015 PAWS, INC. All Rights Reserved.
JIM DAVIS 6-4
SIGH
THIS SPACE FOR RENT

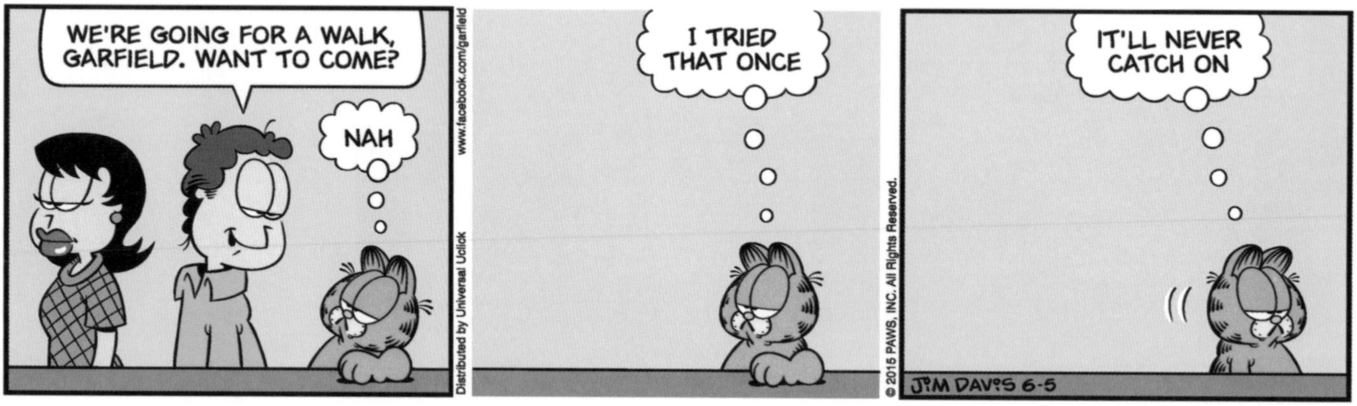
WE'RE GOING FOR A WALK, GARFIELD. WANT TO COME?
NAH
www.facebook.com/garfield
Distributed by Universal Uclick
I TRIED THAT ONCE
© 2015 PAWS, INC. All Rights Reserved.
IT'LL NEVER CATCH ON
JIM DAVIS 6-5

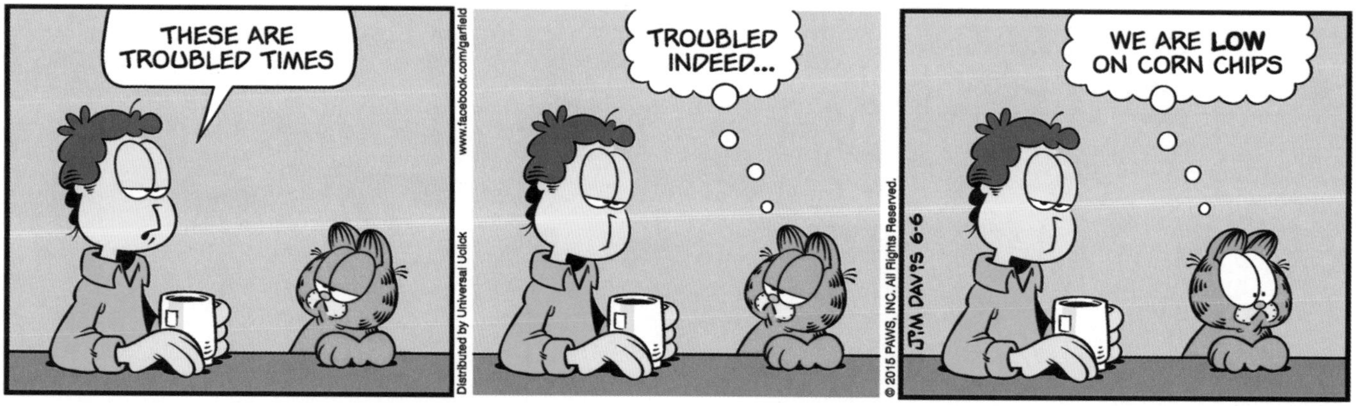
THESE ARE TROUBLED TIMES
www.facebook.com/garfield
Distributed by Universal Uclick
TROUBLED INDEED...
© 2015 PAWS, INC. All Rights Reserved.
JIM DAVIS 6-6
WE ARE LOW ON CORN CHIPS

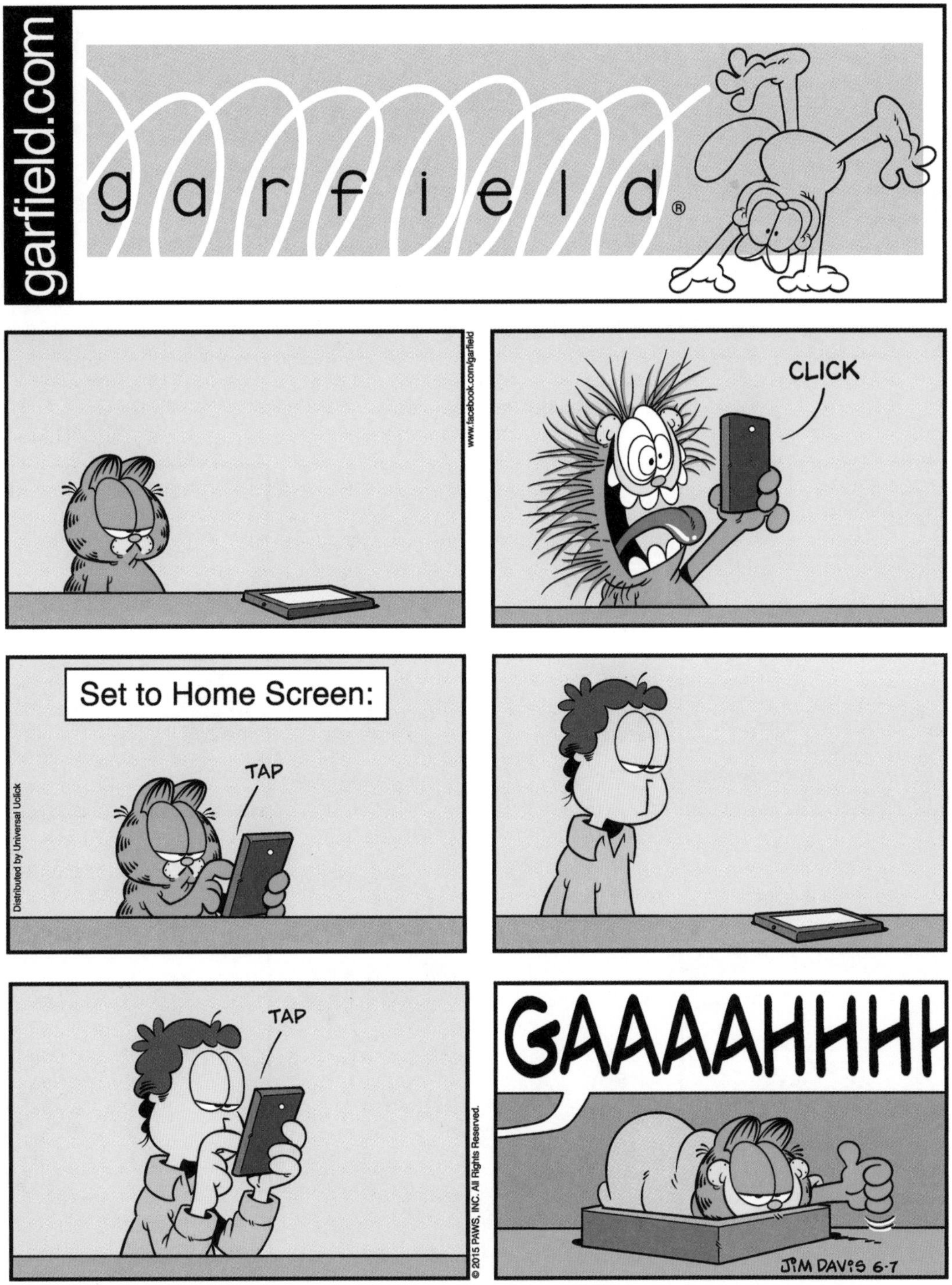
garfield.com
garfield®
www.facebook.com/garfield
CLICK
Set to Home Screen:
TAP
Distributed by Universal Uclick
TAP
© 2015 PAWS, INC. All Rights Reserved.
GAAAAHHHH
JIM DAVIS 6-7

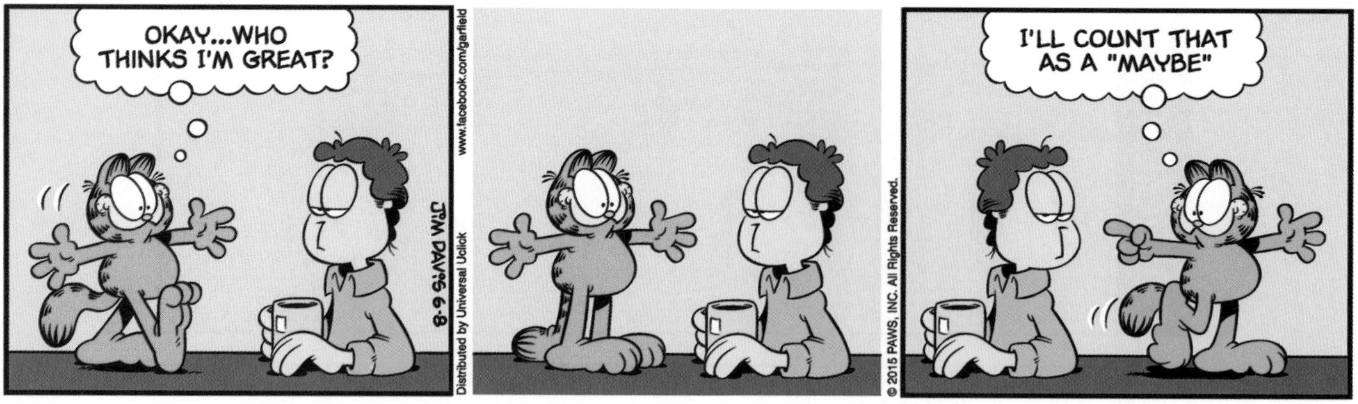
OKAY...WHO THINKS I'M GREAT?
JIM DAVIS 6-8
www.facebook.com/garfield
Distributed by Universal Uclick
I'LL COUNT THAT AS A "MAYBE"
© 2015 PAWS, INC. All Rights Reserved.

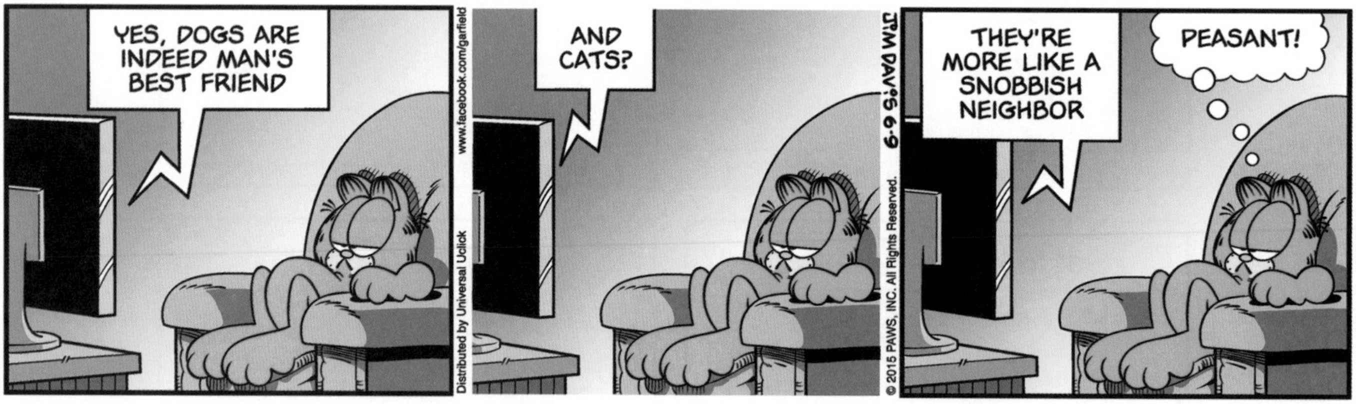
YES, DOGS ARE INDEED MAN'S BEST FRIEND
www.facebook.com/garfield
Distributed by Universal Uclick
AND CATS?
JIM DAVIS 6-9
© 2015 PAWS, INC. All Rights Reserved.
THEY'RE MORE LIKE A SNOBBISH NEIGHBOR
PEASANT!

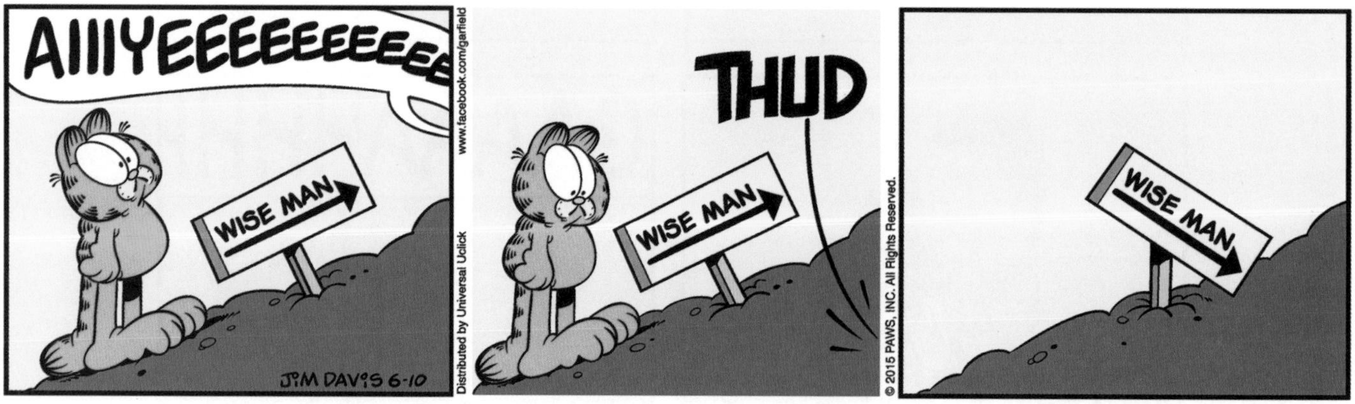
AIIIYEEEEEEEEEE
WISE MAN
JIM DAVIS 6-10
www.facebook.com/garfield
Distributed by Universal Uclick
THUD
WISE MAN
© 2015 PAWS, INC. All Rights Reserved.
WISE MAN

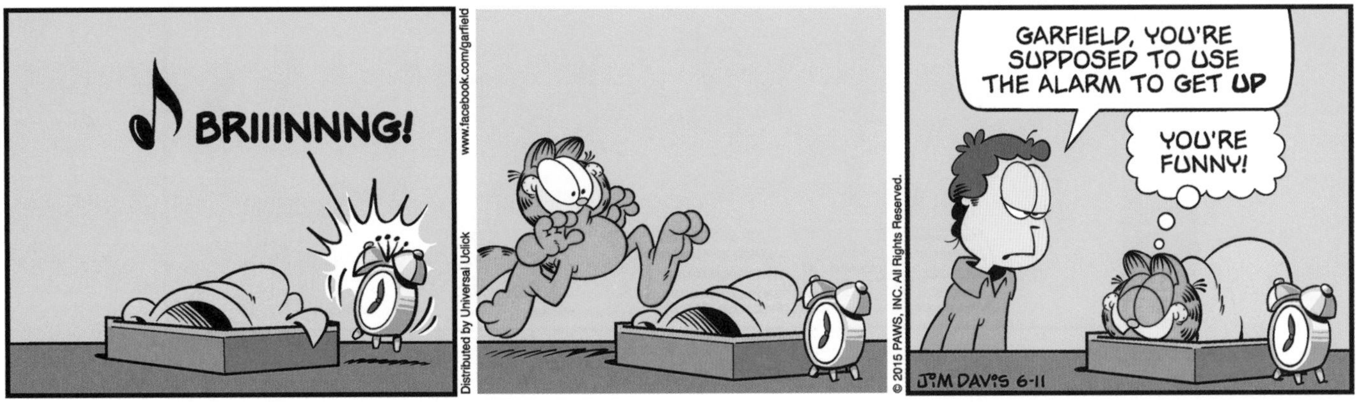
BRIIINNNG!
Distributed by Universal Uclick www.facebook.com/garfield
GARFIELD, YOU'RE SUPPOSED TO USE THE ALARM TO GET UP
YOU'RE FUNNY!
© 2015 PAWS, INC. All Rights Reserved.
JIM DAVIS 6-11

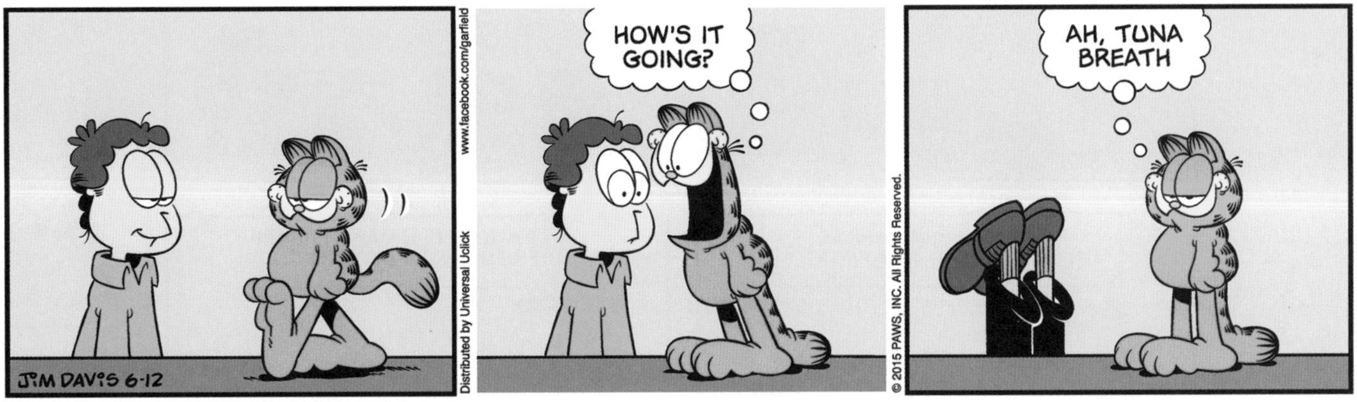
JIM DAVIS 6-12
Distributed by Universal Uclick www.facebook.com/garfield
HOW'S IT GOING?
© 2015 PAWS, INC. All Rights Reserved.
AH, TUNA BREATH

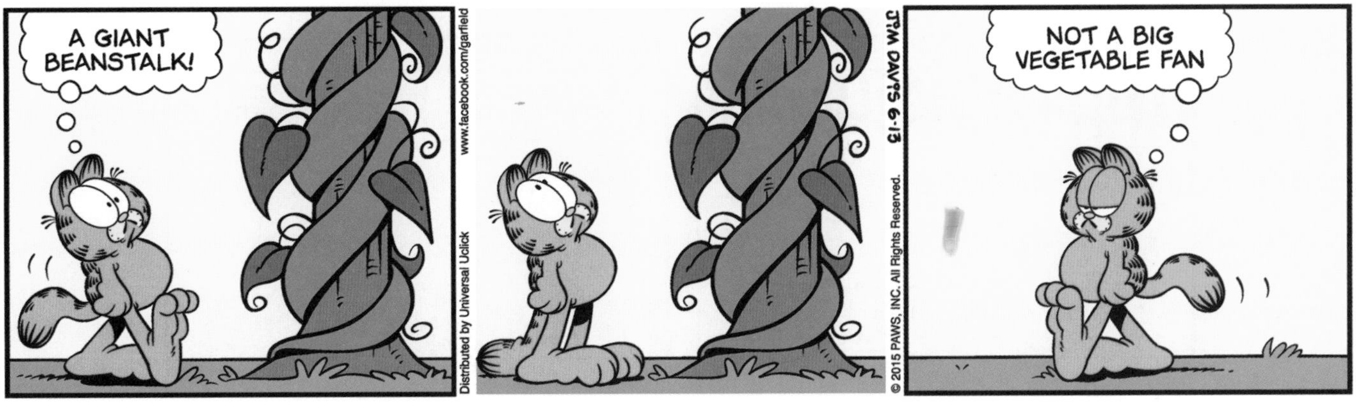
A GIANT BEANSTALK!
Distributed by Universal Uclick www.facebook.com/garfield
JIM DAVIS 6-13
© 2015 PAWS, INC. All Rights Reserved.
NOT A BIG VEGETABLE FAN

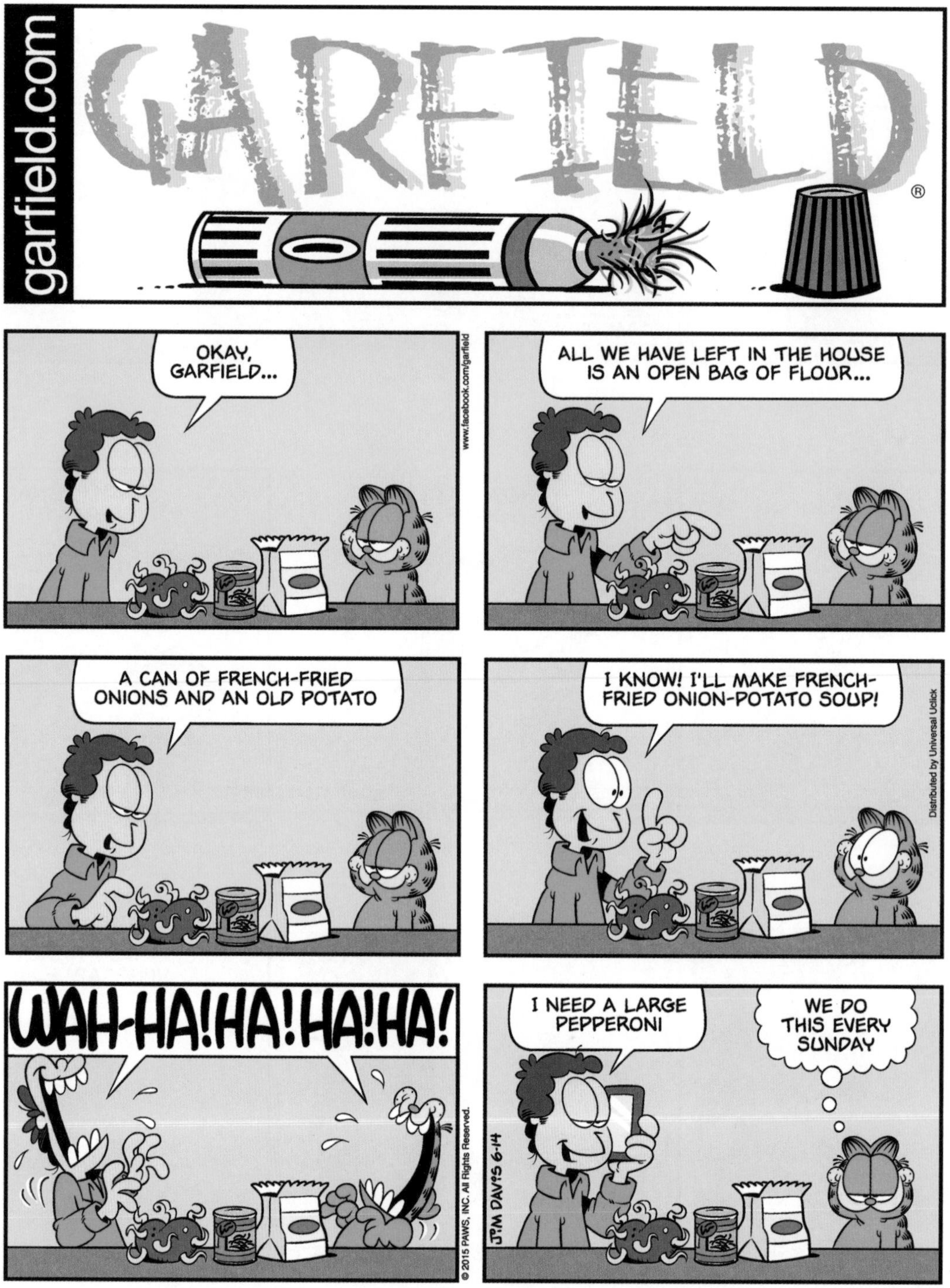
garfield.com
GARFIELD
OKAY, GARFIELD...
www.facebook.com/garfield
ALL WE HAVE LEFT IN THE HOUSE IS AN OPEN BAG OF FLOUR...
A CAN OF FRENCH-FRIED ONIONS AND AN OLD POTATO
I KNOW! I'LL MAKE FRENCH-FRIED ONION-POTATO SOUP!
Distributed by Universal Uclick
WAH-HA!HA!HA!HA!
© 2015 PAWS, INC. All Rights Reserved.
JIM DAVIS 6-14
I NEED A LARGE PEPPERONI
WE DO THIS EVERY SUNDAY

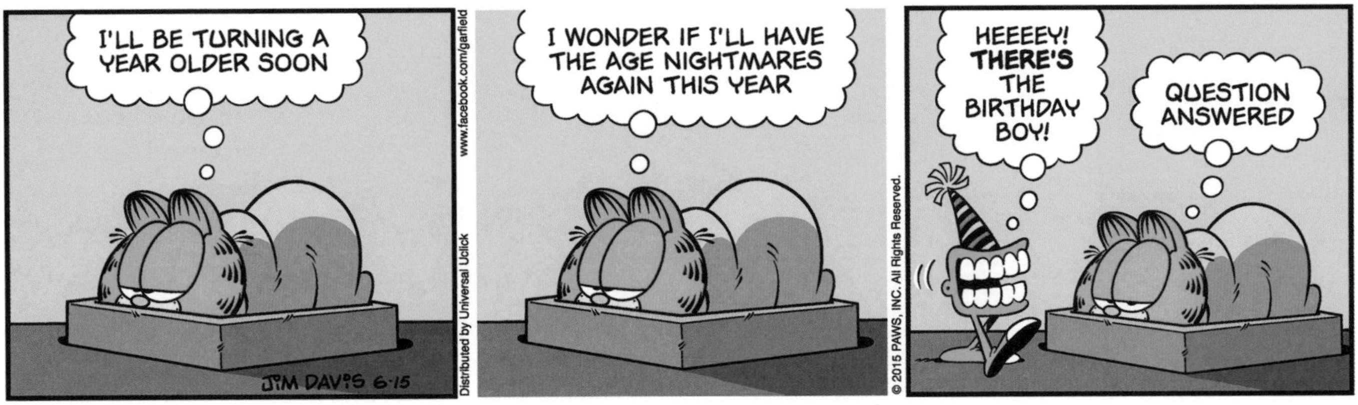
I'LL BE TURNING A YEAR OLDER SOON
JIM DAVIS 6-15
Distributed by Universal Uclick www.facebook.com/garfield
I WONDER IF I'LL HAVE THE AGE NIGHTMARES AGAIN THIS YEAR
© 2015 PAWS, INC. All Rights Reserved.
HEEEEY! **THERE'S** THE BIRTHDAY BOY!
QUESTION ANSWERED

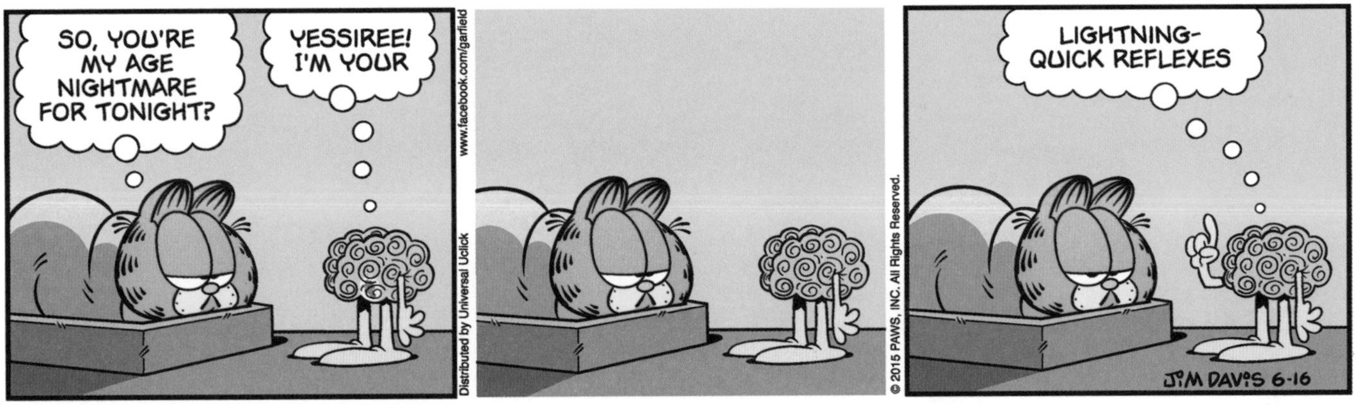
SO, YOU'RE MY AGE NIGHTMARE FOR TONIGHT?
YESSIREE! I'M YOUR
Distributed by Universal Uclick www.facebook.com/garfield
© 2015 PAWS, INC. All Rights Reserved.
LIGHTNING-QUICK REFLEXES
JIM DAVIS 6-16

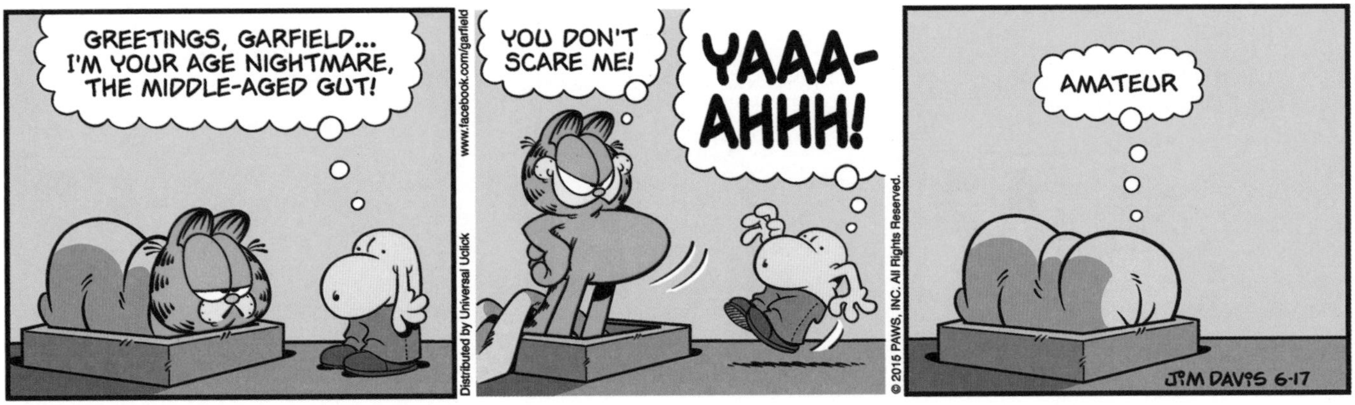
GREETINGS, GARFIELD... I'M YOUR AGE NIGHTMARE, THE MIDDLE-AGED GUT!
Distributed by Universal Uclick www.facebook.com/garfield
YOU DON'T SCARE ME!
YAAA-AHHH!
© 2015 PAWS, INC. All Rights Reserved.
AMATEUR
JIM DAVIS 6-17

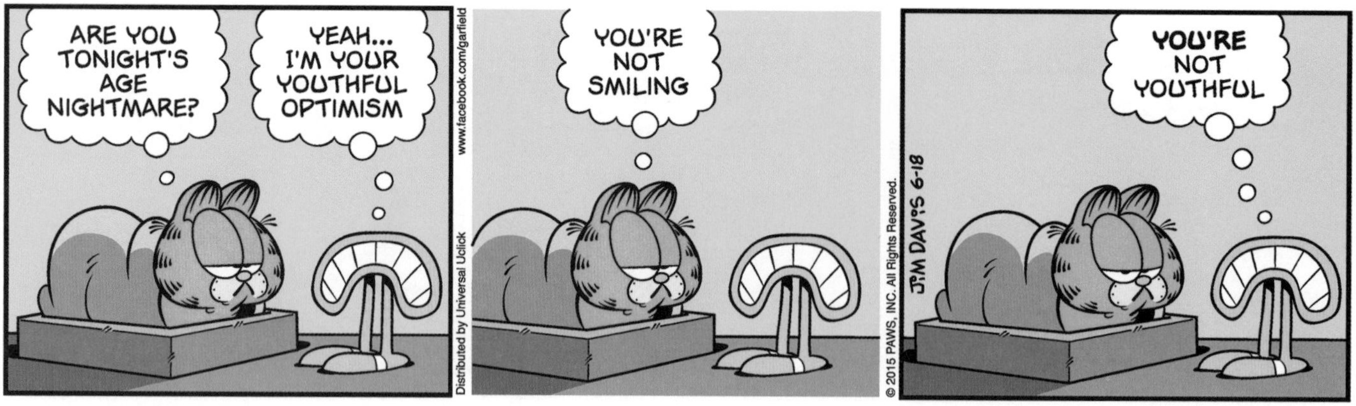
ARE YOU TONIGHT'S AGE NIGHTMARE?
YEAH... I'M YOUR YOUTHFUL OPTIMISM
www.facebook.com/garfield
Distributed by Universal Uclick
YOU'RE NOT SMILING
© 2015 PAWS, INC. All Rights Reserved.
JIM DAVIS 6-18
YOU'RE NOT YOUTHFUL

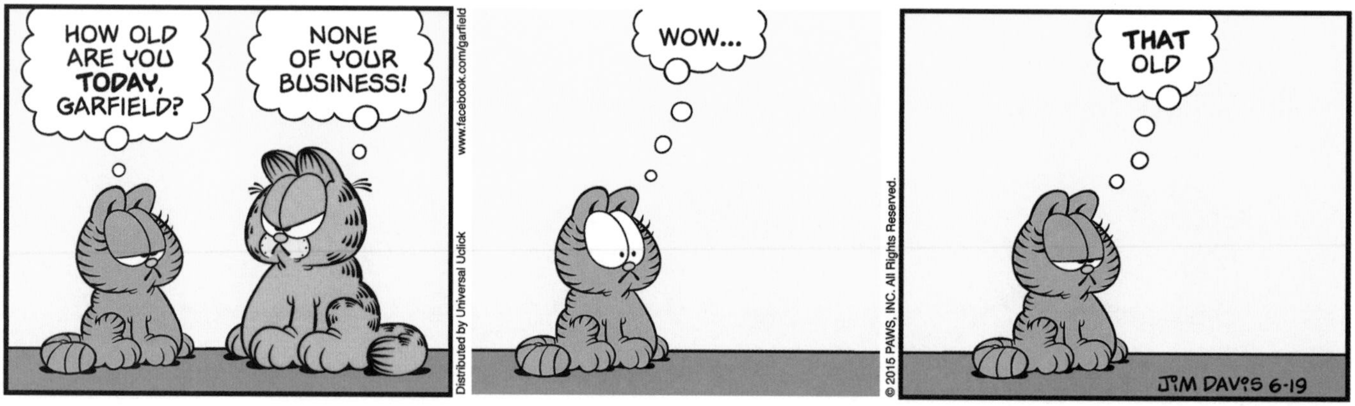
HOW OLD ARE YOU **TODAY**, GARFIELD?
NONE OF YOUR BUSINESS!
www.facebook.com/garfield
Distributed by Universal Uclick
WOW...
© 2015 PAWS, INC. All Rights Reserved.
THAT OLD
JIM DAVIS 6-19

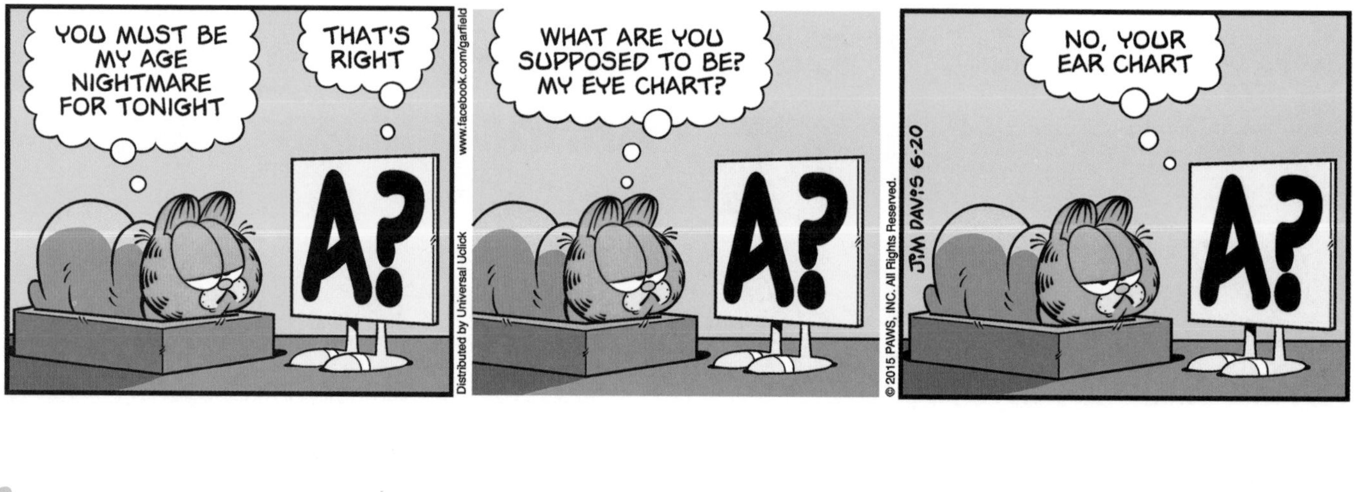
YOU MUST BE MY AGE NIGHTMARE FOR TONIGHT
THAT'S RIGHT
A?
www.facebook.com/garfield
Distributed by Universal Uclick
WHAT ARE YOU SUPPOSED TO BE? MY EYE CHART?
A?
© 2015 PAWS, INC. All Rights Reserved.
JIM DAVIS 6-20
NO, YOUR EAR CHART
A?

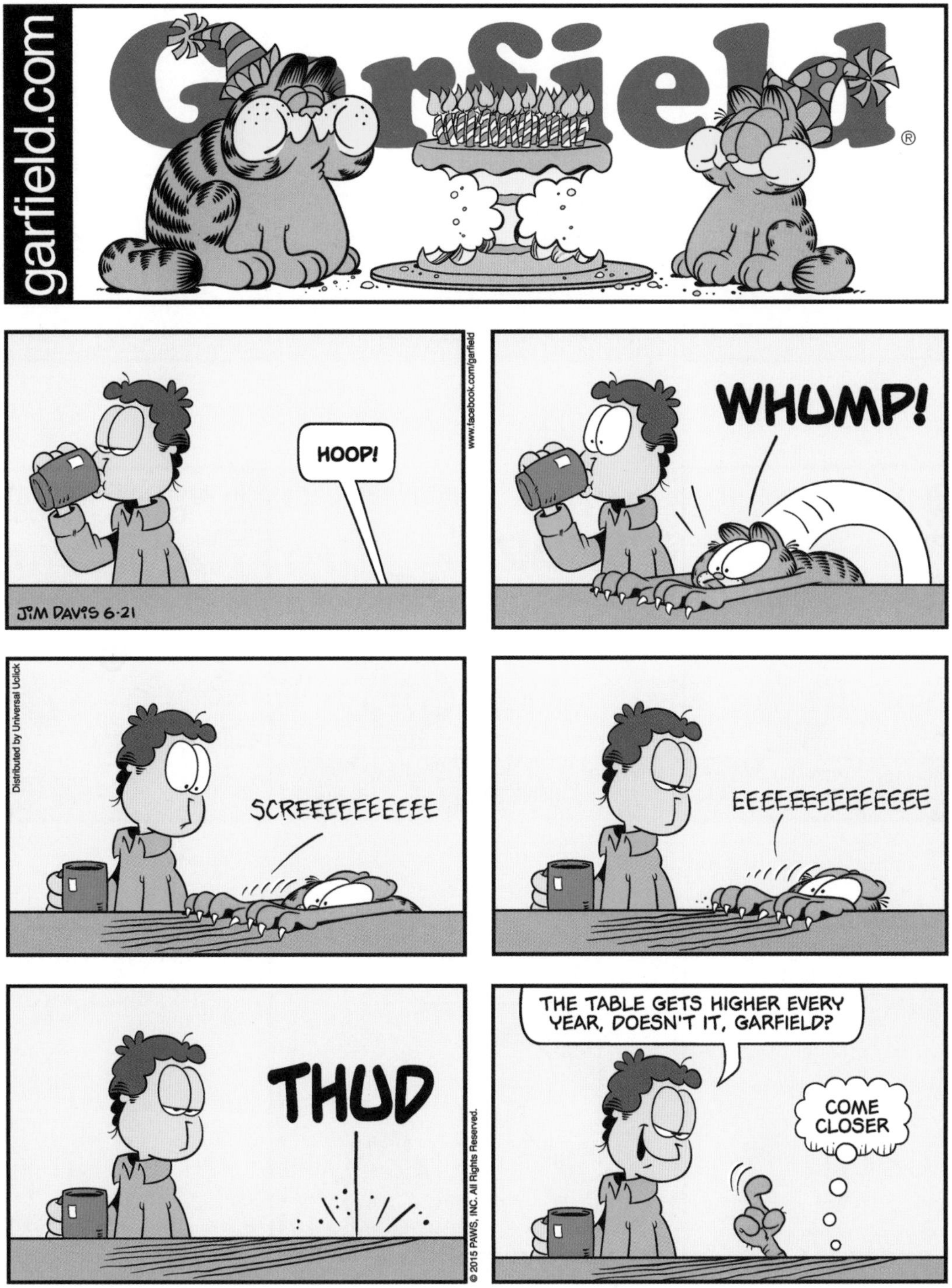
garfield.com
Garfield®
HOOP!
JIM DAVIS 6-21
www.facebook.com/garfield
WHUMP!
Distributed by Universal Uclick
SCREEEEEEEEEE
EEEEEEEEEEEEE
THUD
© 2015 PAWS, INC. All Rights Reserved.
THE TABLE GETS HIGHER EVERY YEAR, DOESN'T IT, GARFIELD?
COME CLOSER

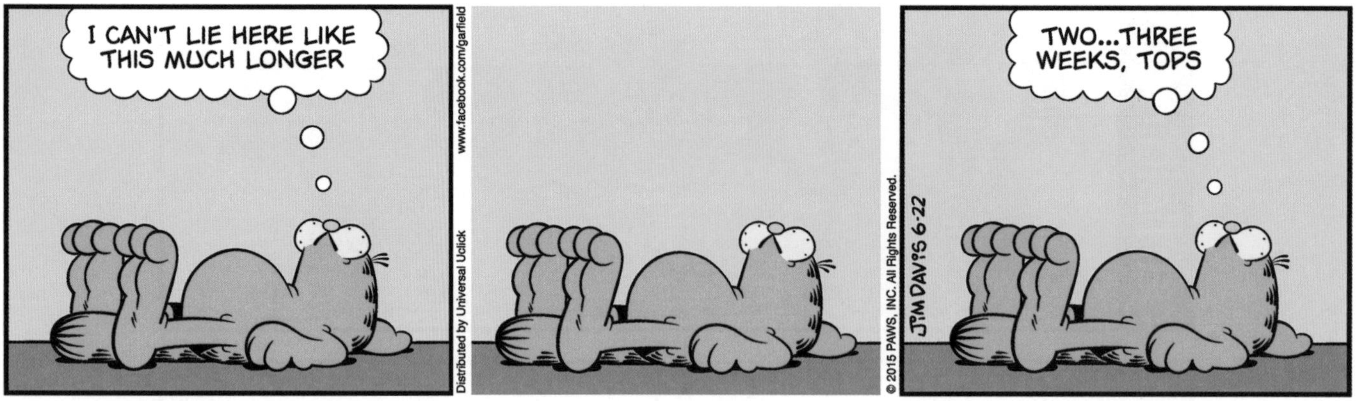
I CAN'T LIE HERE LIKE THIS MUCH LONGER
TWO...THREE WEEKS, TOPS
JIM DAVIS 6-22
www.facebook.com/garfield
Distributed by Universal Uclick
© 2015 PAWS, INC. All Rights Reserved.

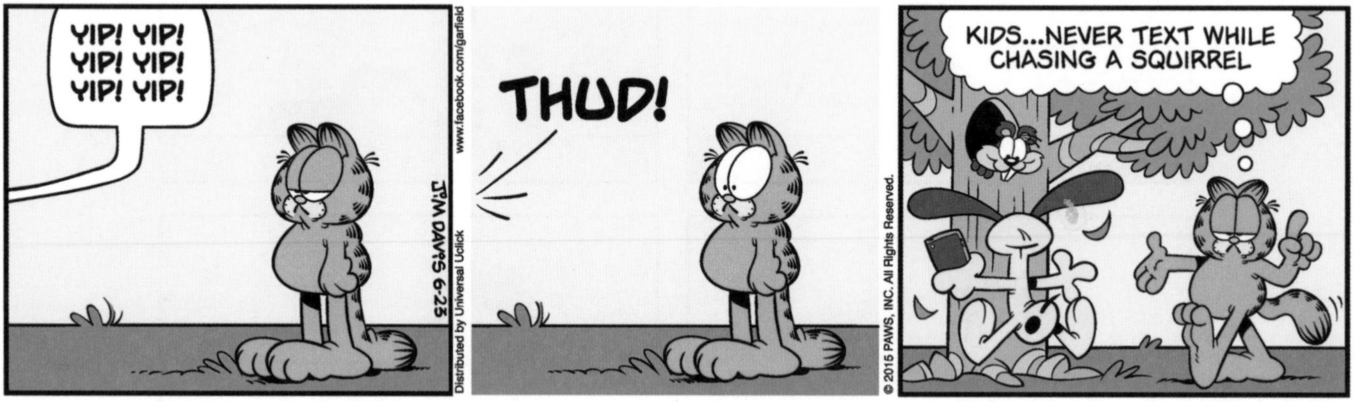
YIP! YIP! YIP! YIP! YIP! YIP!
JIM DAVIS 6-23
THUD!
KIDS...NEVER TEXT WHILE CHASING A SQUIRREL
www.facebook.com/garfield
Distributed by Universal Uclick
© 2015 PAWS, INC. All Rights Reserved.

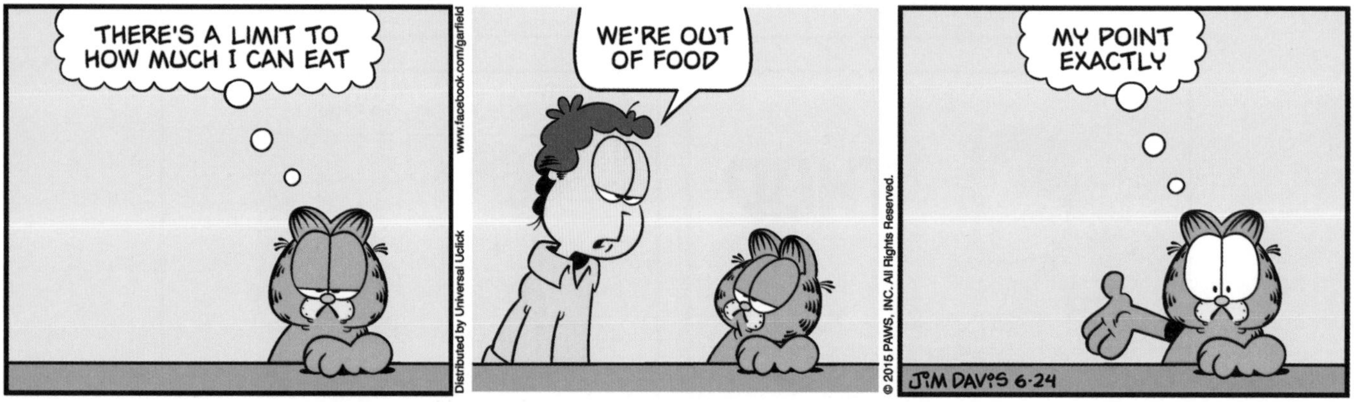
THERE'S A LIMIT TO HOW MUCH I CAN EAT
WE'RE OUT OF FOOD
MY POINT EXACTLY
JIM DAVIS 6-24
www.facebook.com/garfield
Distributed by Universal Uclick
© 2015 PAWS, INC. All Rights Reserved.

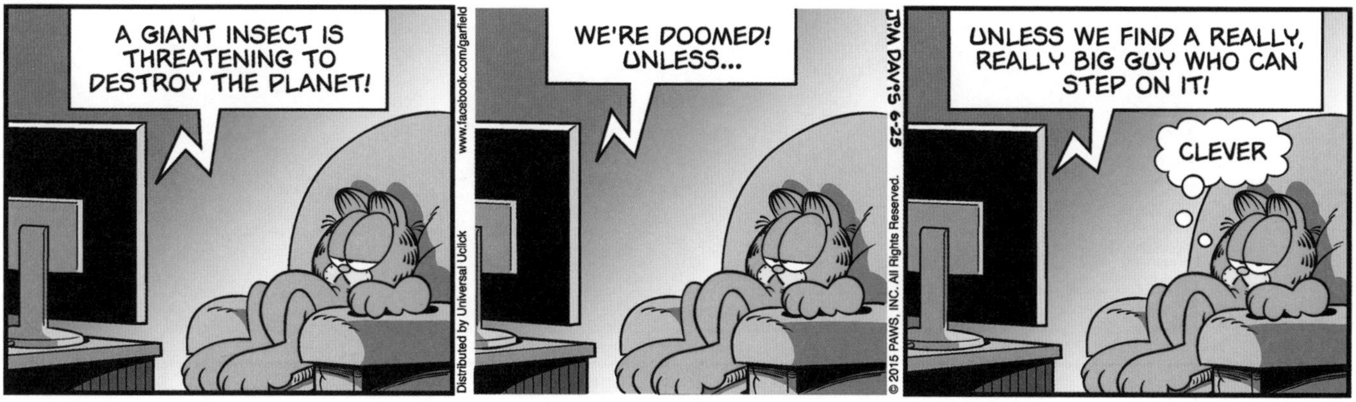
A GIANT INSECT IS THREATENING TO DESTROY THE PLANET!
WE'RE DOOMED! UNLESS...
UNLESS WE FIND A REALLY, REALLY BIG GUY WHO CAN STEP ON IT!
CLEVER
JIM DAVIS 6-25
Distributed by Universal Uclick www.facebook.com/garfield
© 2015 PAWS, INC. All Rights Reserved.

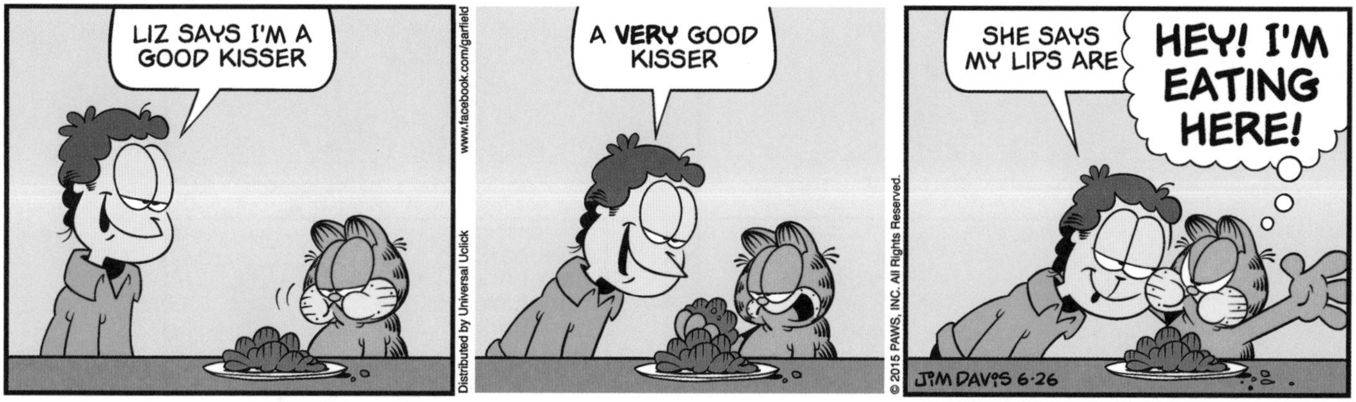
LIZ SAYS I'M A GOOD KISSER
A **VERY** GOOD KISSER
SHE SAYS MY LIPS ARE
HEY! I'M EATING HERE!
JIM DAVIS 6-26
Distributed by Universal Uclick www.facebook.com/garfield
© 2015 PAWS, INC. All Rights Reserved.

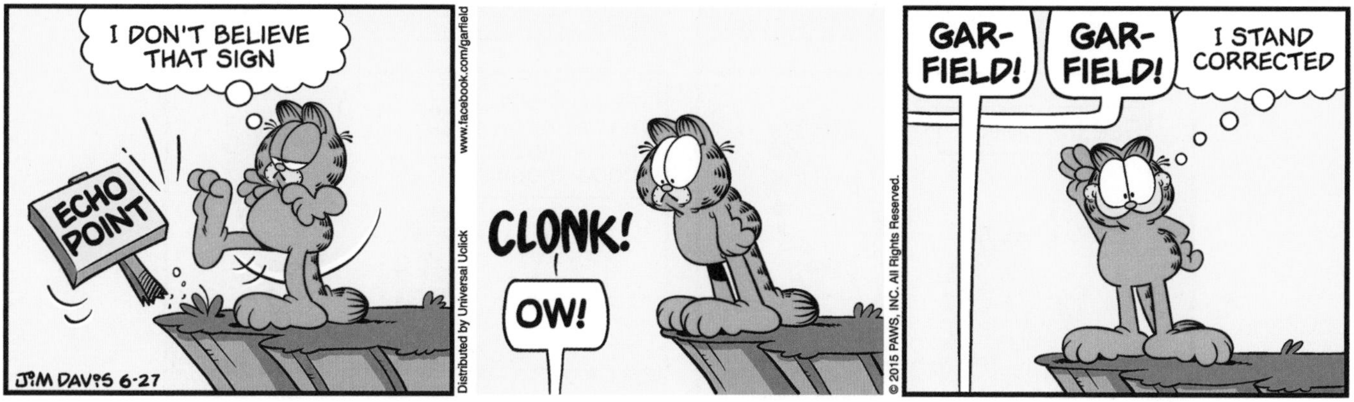
I DON'T BELIEVE THAT SIGN
ECHO POINT
JIM DAVIS 6-27
CLONK!
OW!
GAR-FIELD!
GAR-FIELD!
I STAND CORRECTED
Distributed by Universal Uclick www.facebook.com/garfield
© 2015 PAWS, INC. All Rights Reserved.

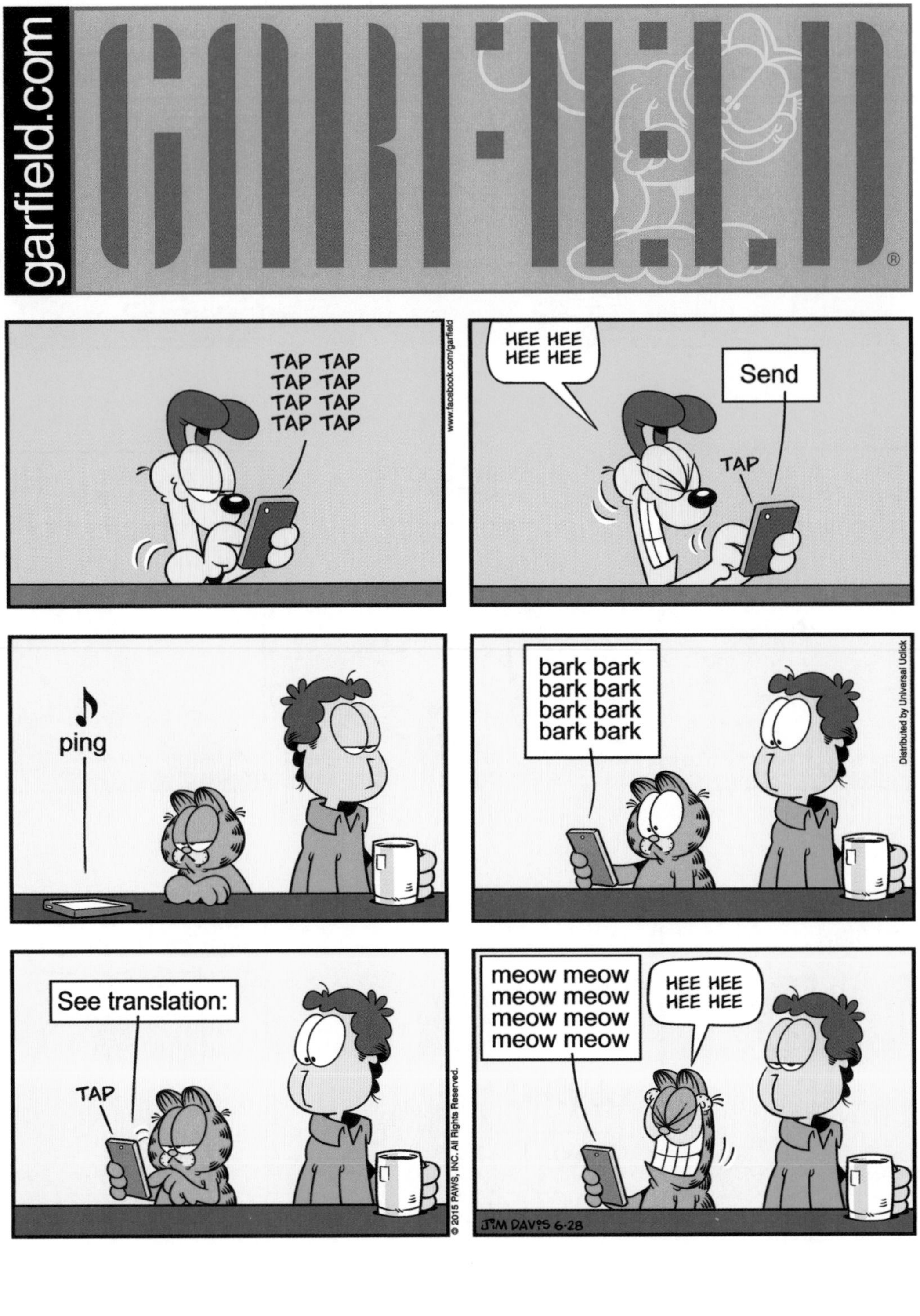

garfield.com
GARFIELD®
www.facebook.com/garfield
TAP TAP TAP TAP TAP TAP TAP TAP
HEE HEE HEE HEE
Send
TAP
ping
Distributed by Universal Uclick
bark bark bark bark bark bark bark bark
See translation:
TAP
© 2015 PAWS, INC. All Rights Reserved.
meow meow meow meow meow meow meow meow
HEE HEE HEE HEE
JIM DAVIS 6-28

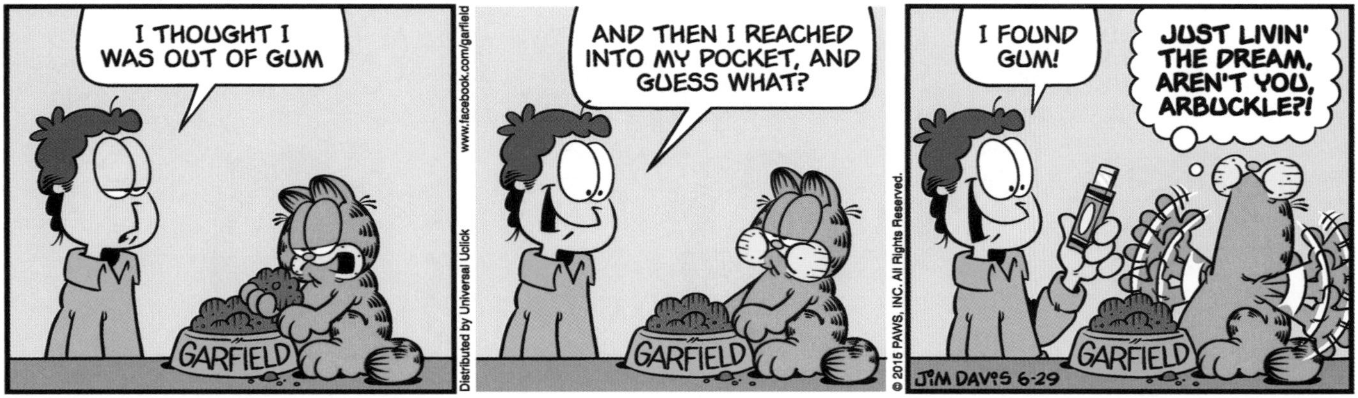
I THOUGHT I WAS OUT OF GUM
AND THEN I REACHED INTO MY POCKET, AND GUESS WHAT?
I FOUND GUM!
JUST LIVIN' THE DREAM, AREN'T YOU, ARBUCKLE?!
www.facebook.com/garfield
Distributed by Universal Uclick
© 2015 PAWS, INC. All Rights Reserved.
JIM DAVIS 6-29

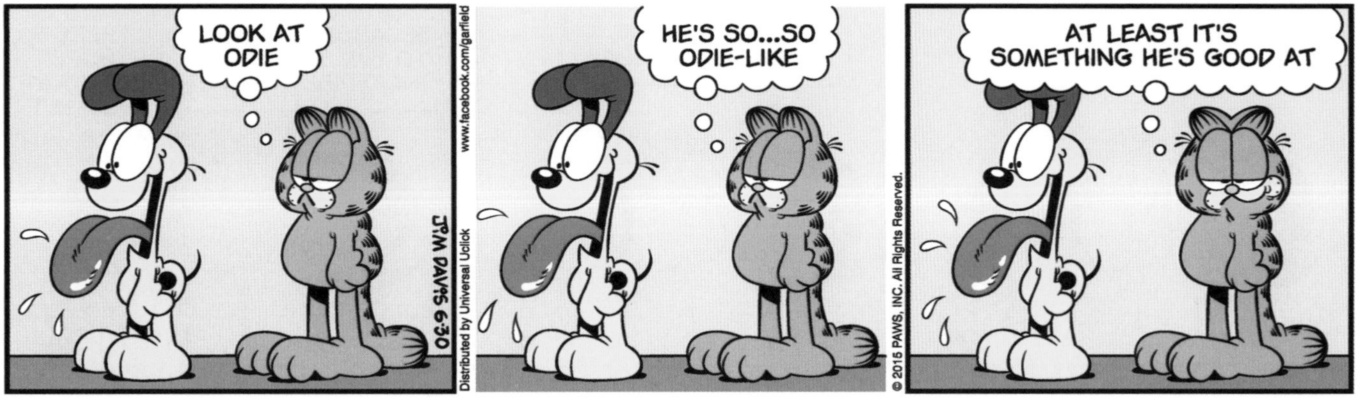
LOOK AT ODIE
HE'S SO...SO ODIE-LIKE
AT LEAST IT'S SOMETHING HE'S GOOD AT
JIM DAVIS 6-30
www.facebook.com/garfield
Distributed by Universal Uclick
© 2015 PAWS, INC. All Rights Reserved.

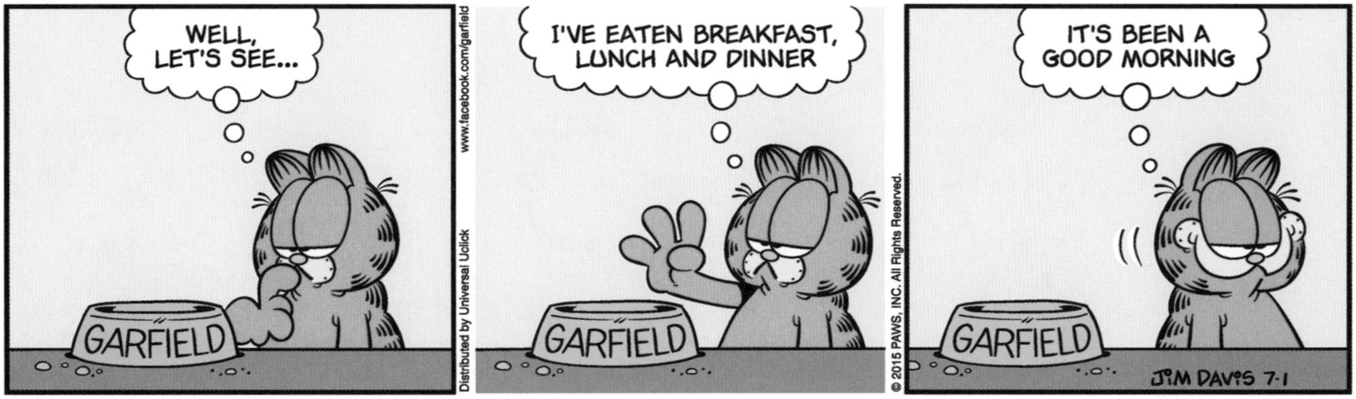
WELL, LET'S SEE...
I'VE EATEN BREAKFAST, LUNCH AND DINNER
IT'S BEEN A GOOD MORNING
www.facebook.com/garfield
Distributed by Universal Uclick
© 2015 PAWS, INC. All Rights Reserved.
JIM DAVIS 7-1

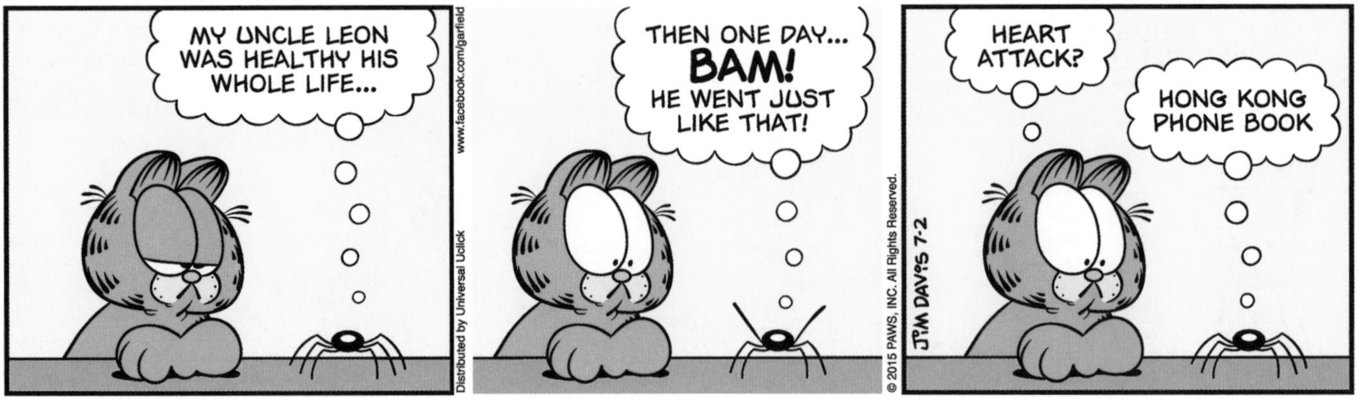
MY UNCLE LEON WAS HEALTHY HIS WHOLE LIFE...
www.facebook.com/garfield
Distributed by Universal Uclick
THEN ONE DAY... BAM! HE WENT JUST LIKE THAT!
© 2015 PAWS, INC. All Rights Reserved.
JIM DAVIS 7-2
HEART ATTACK?
HONG KONG PHONE BOOK

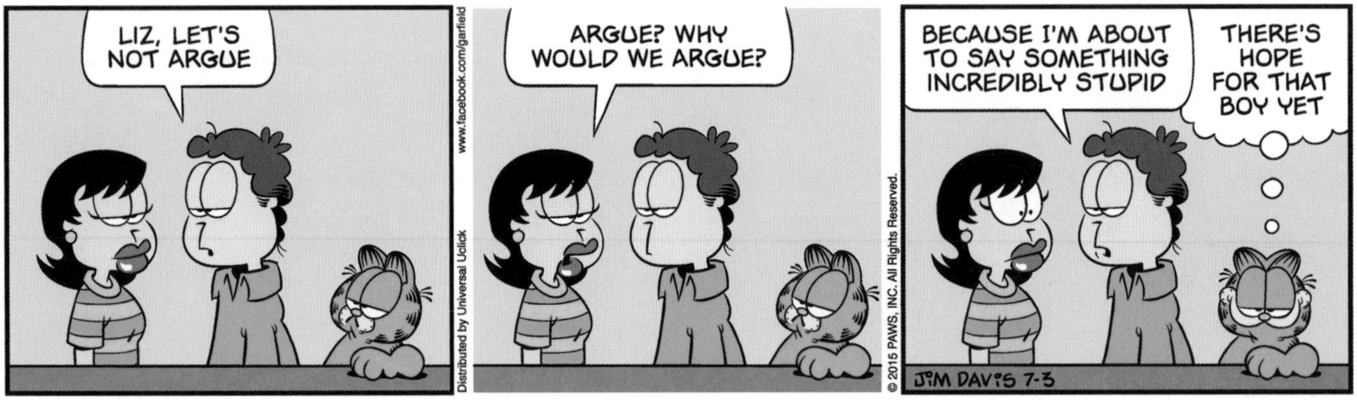
LIZ, LET'S NOT ARGUE
www.facebook.com/garfield
Distributed by Universal Uclick
ARGUE? WHY WOULD WE ARGUE?
© 2015 PAWS, INC. All Rights Reserved.
BECAUSE I'M ABOUT TO SAY SOMETHING INCREDIBLY STUPID
THERE'S HOPE FOR THAT BOY YET
JIM DAVIS 7-3

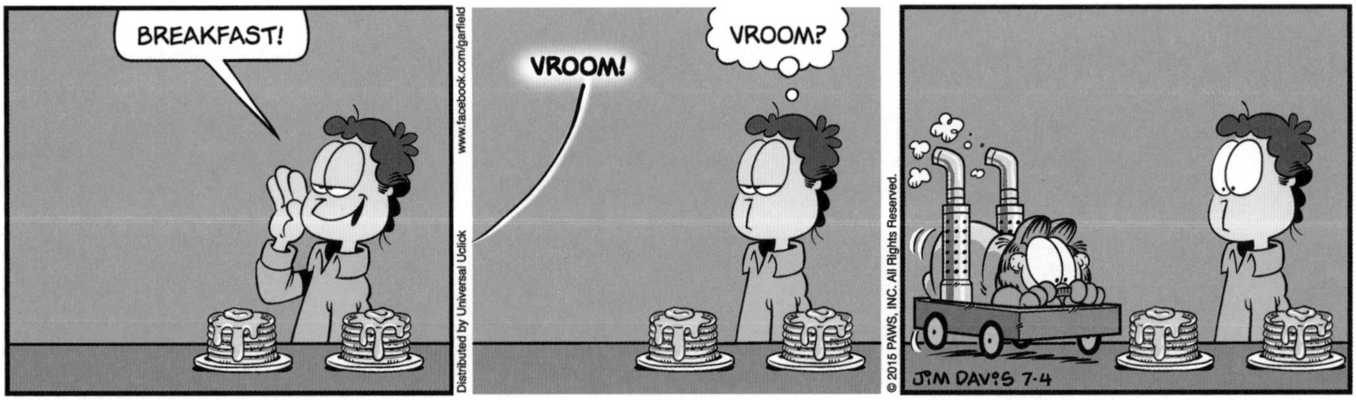
BREAKFAST!
www.facebook.com/garfield
Distributed by Universal Uclick
VROOM!
VROOM?
© 2015 PAWS, INC. All Rights Reserved.
JIM DAVIS 7-4

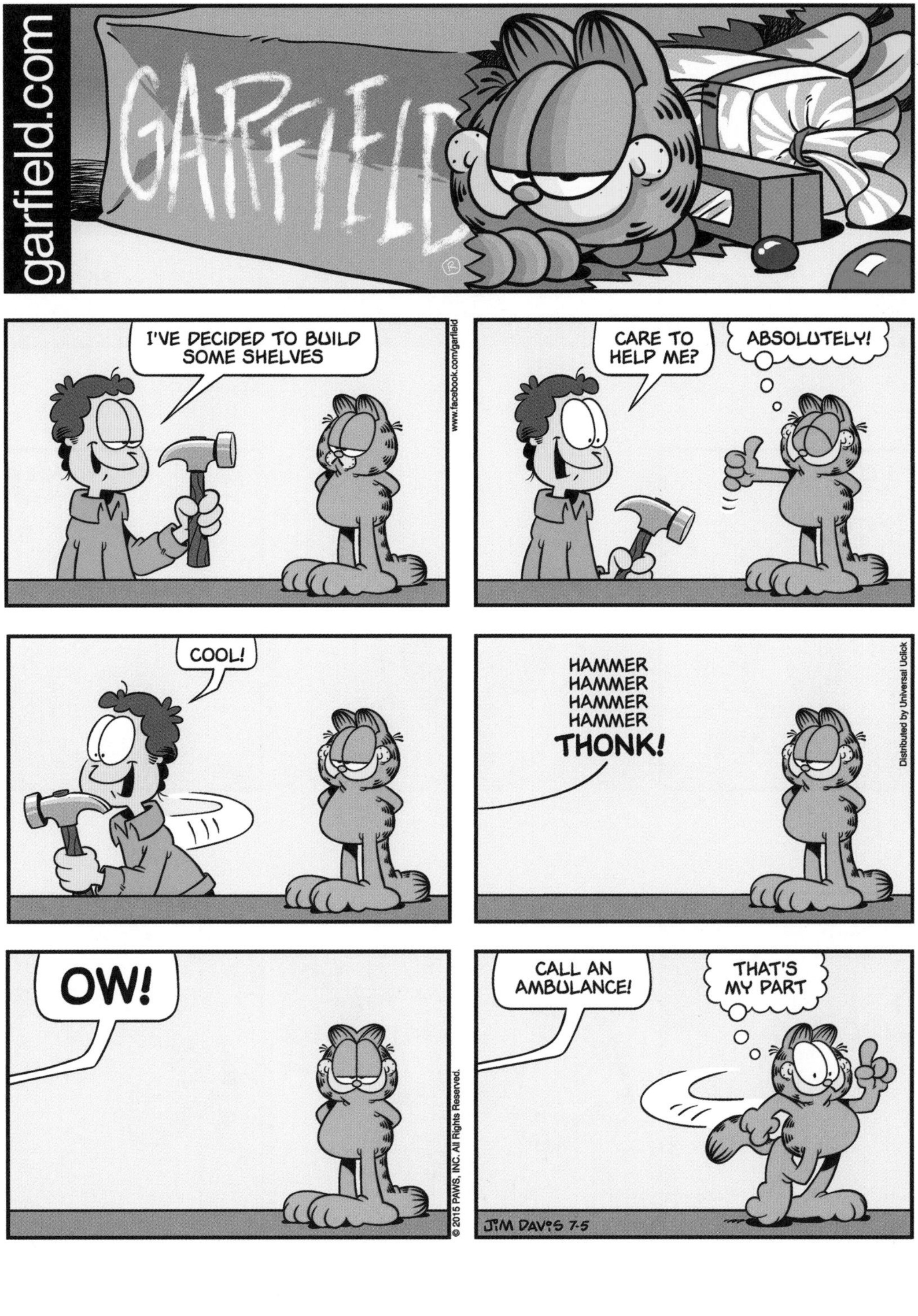
garfield.com
GARFIELD
I'VE DECIDED TO BUILD SOME SHELVES
www.facebook.com/garfield
CARE TO HELP ME?
ABSOLUTELY!
COOL!
HAMMER
HAMMER
HAMMER
HAMMER
THONK!
Distributed by Universal Uclick
OW!
© 2015 PAWS, INC. All Rights Reserved.
CALL AN AMBULANCE!
THAT'S MY PART
JIM DAVIS 7-5

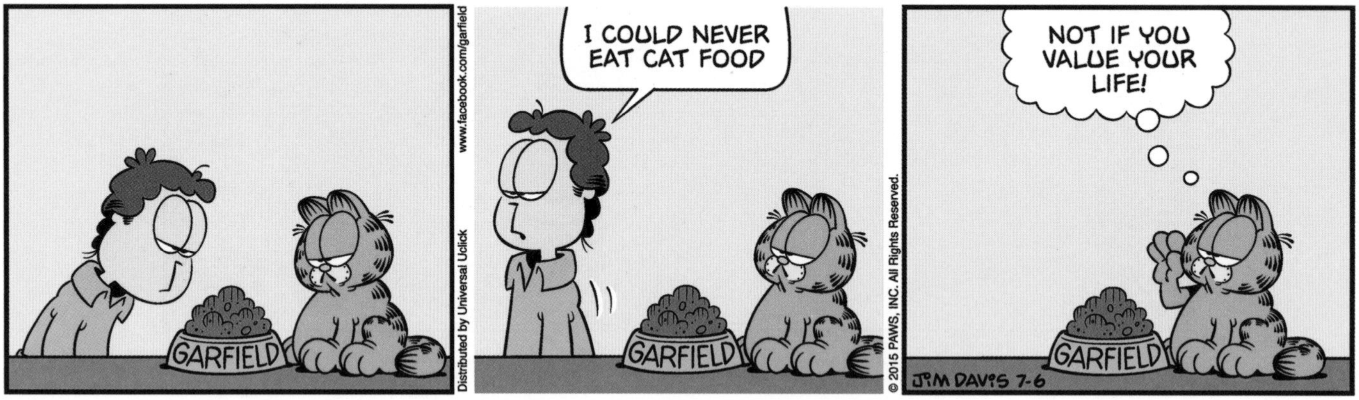
GARFIELD
www.facebook.com/garfield
Distributed by Universal Uclick
I COULD NEVER EAT CAT FOOD
GARFIELD
© 2015 PAWS, INC. All Rights Reserved.
NOT IF YOU VALUE YOUR LIFE!
GARFIELD
JIM DAVIS 7-6

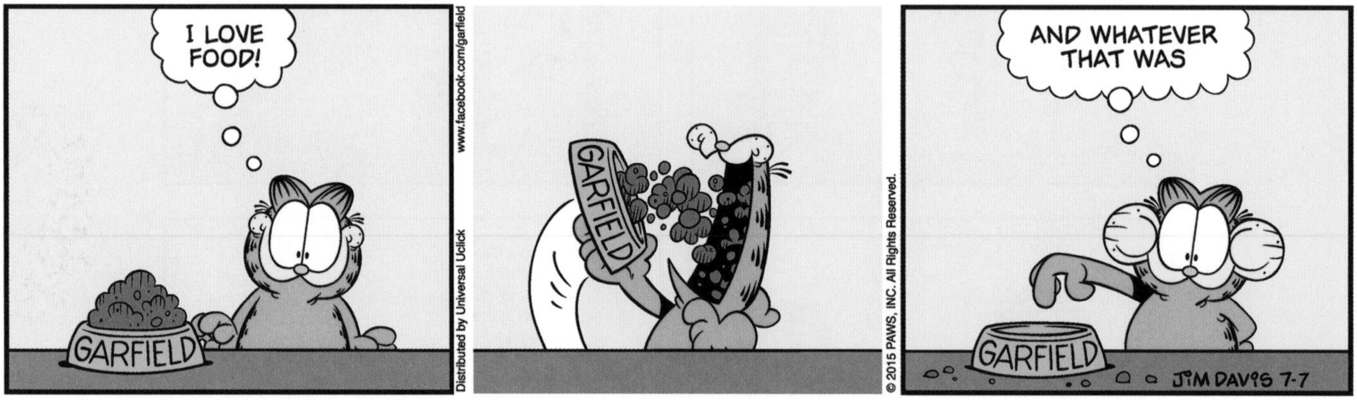
I LOVE FOOD!
GARFIELD
www.facebook.com/garfield
Distributed by Universal Uclick
GARFIELD
© 2015 PAWS, INC. All Rights Reserved.
AND WHATEVER THAT WAS
GARFIELD
JIM DAVIS 7-7

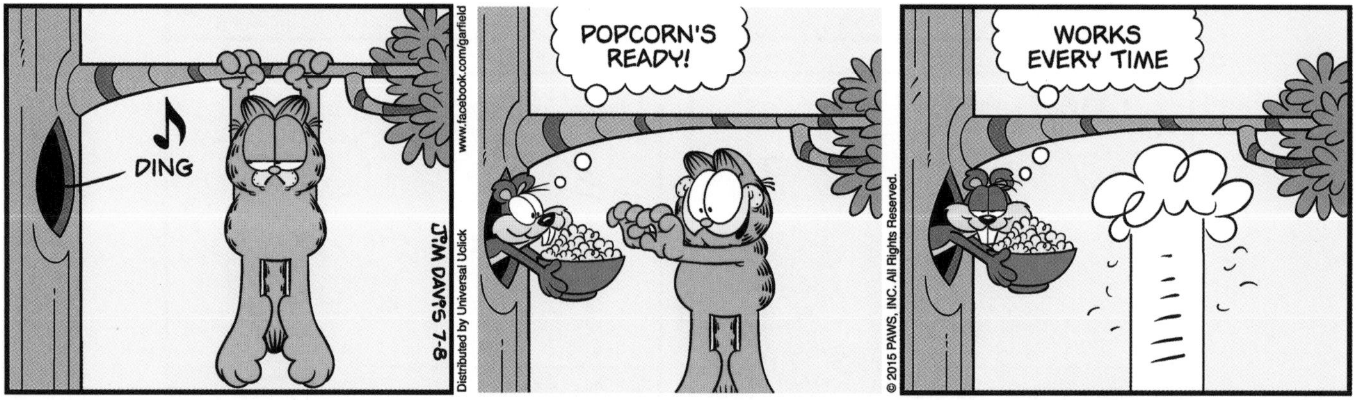
DING
JIM DAVIS 7-8
www.facebook.com/garfield
Distributed by Universal Uclick
POPCORN'S READY!
© 2015 PAWS, INC. All Rights Reserved.
WORKS EVERY TIME

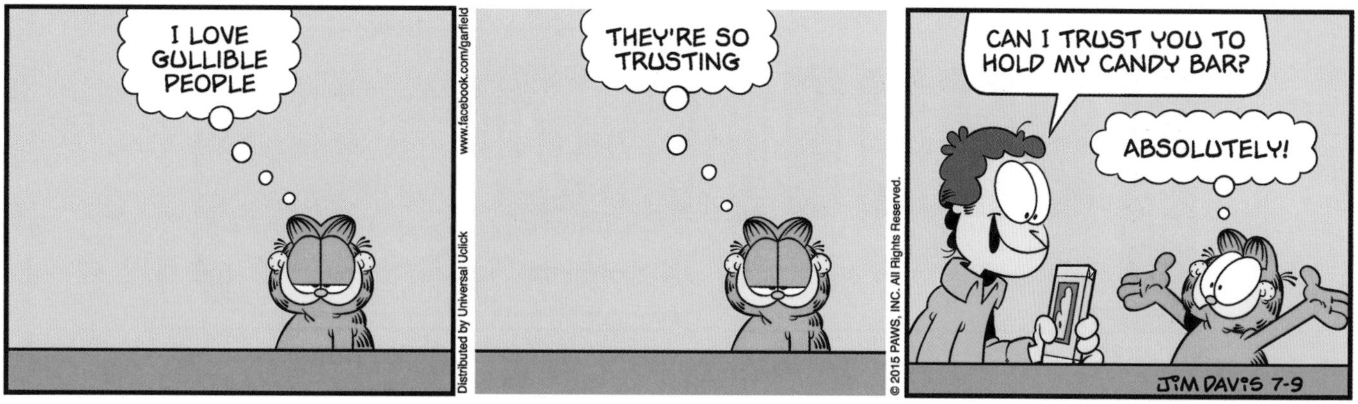
I LOVE GULLIBLE PEOPLE
Distributed by Universal Uclick www.facebook.com/garfield
THEY'RE SO TRUSTING
© 2015 PAWS, INC. All Rights Reserved.
CAN I TRUST YOU TO HOLD MY CANDY BAR?
ABSOLUTELY!
JIM DAVIS 7-9

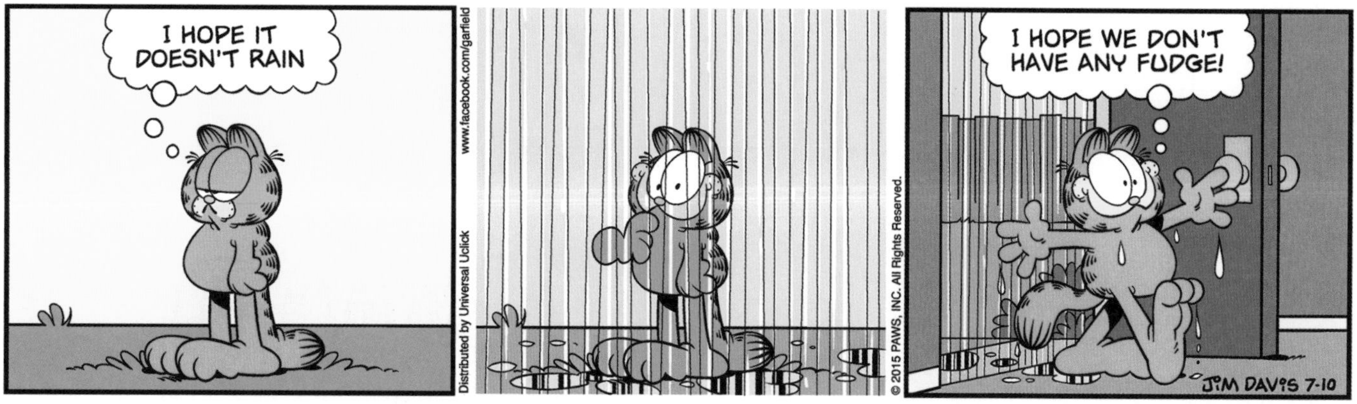
I HOPE IT DOESN'T RAIN
Distributed by Universal Uclick www.facebook.com/garfield
© 2015 PAWS, INC. All Rights Reserved.
I HOPE WE DON'T HAVE ANY FUDGE!
JIM DAVIS 7-10

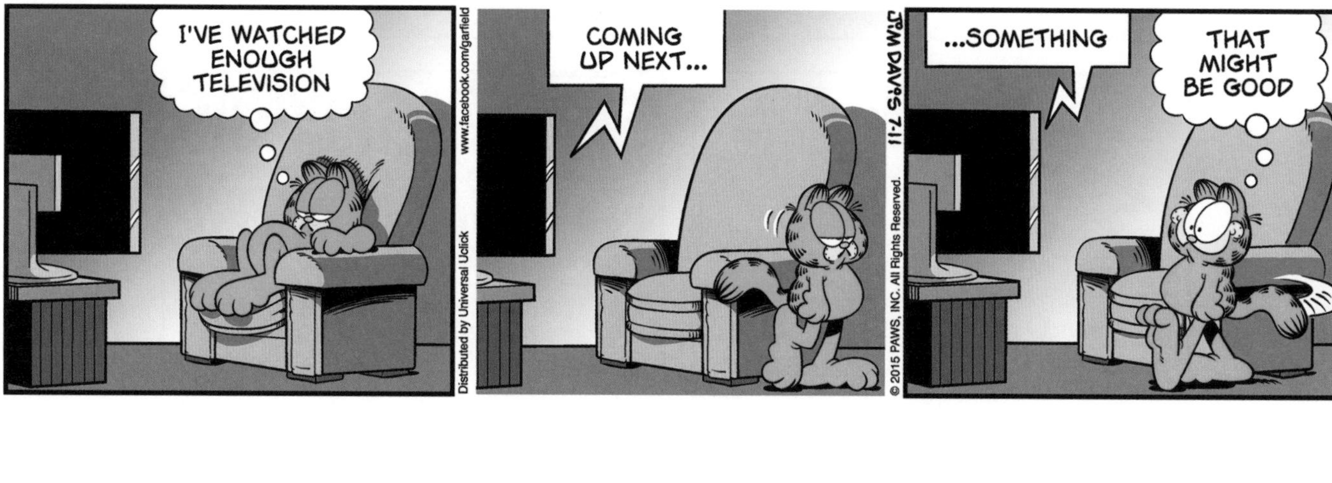
I'VE WATCHED ENOUGH TELEVISION
Distributed by Universal Uclick www.facebook.com/garfield
COMING UP NEXT...
JIM DAVIS 7-11
© 2015 PAWS, INC. All Rights Reserved.
...SOMETHING
THAT MIGHT BE GOOD

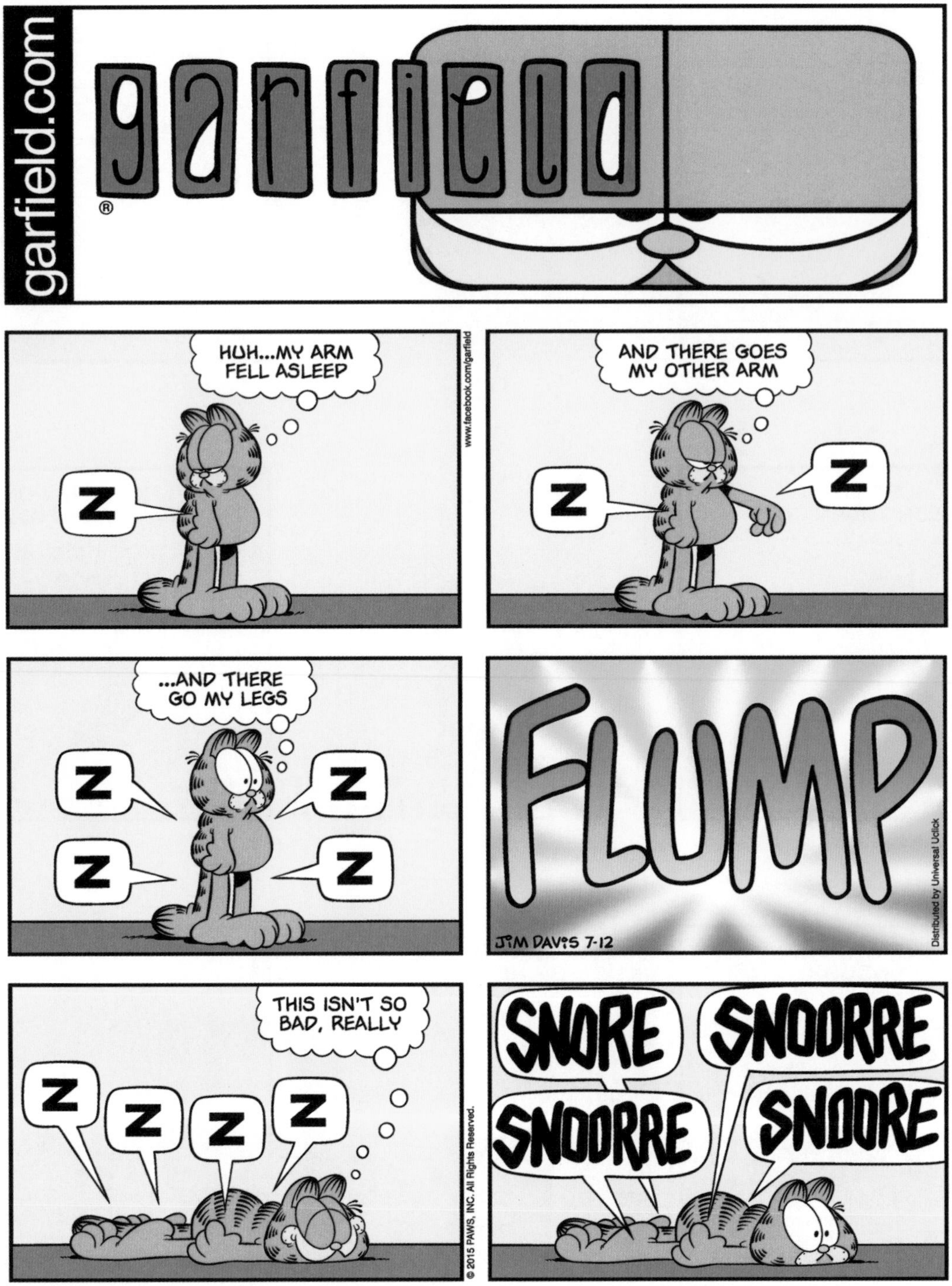
garfield.com
garfield
HUH...MY ARM FELL ASLEEP
Z
www.facebook.com/garfield
AND THERE GOES MY OTHER ARM
Z
Z
...AND THERE GO MY LEGS
Z
Z
Z
Z
FLUMP
JIM DAVIS 7-12
Distributed by Universal Uclick
THIS ISN'T SO BAD, REALLY
Z
Z
Z
Z
© 2015 PAWS, INC. All Rights Reserved.
SNORE
SNOORRE
SNOORRE
SNOORE

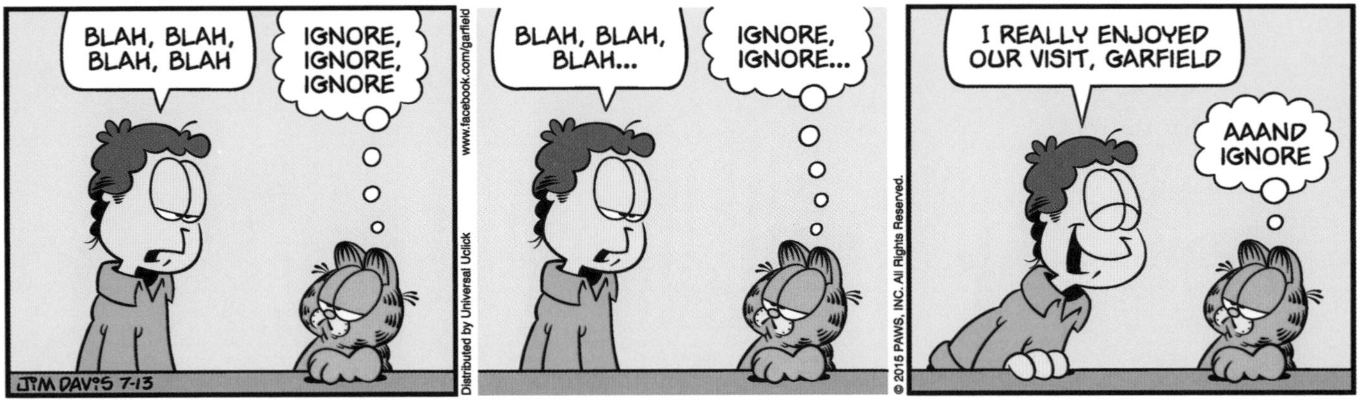
BLAH, BLAH, BLAH, BLAH
IGNORE, IGNORE, IGNORE
JIM DAVIS 7-13
www.facebook.com/garfield
Distributed by Universal Uclick
BLAH, BLAH, BLAH...
IGNORE, IGNORE...
© 2015 PAWS, INC. All Rights Reserved.
I REALLY ENJOYED OUR VISIT, GARFIELD
AAAND IGNORE

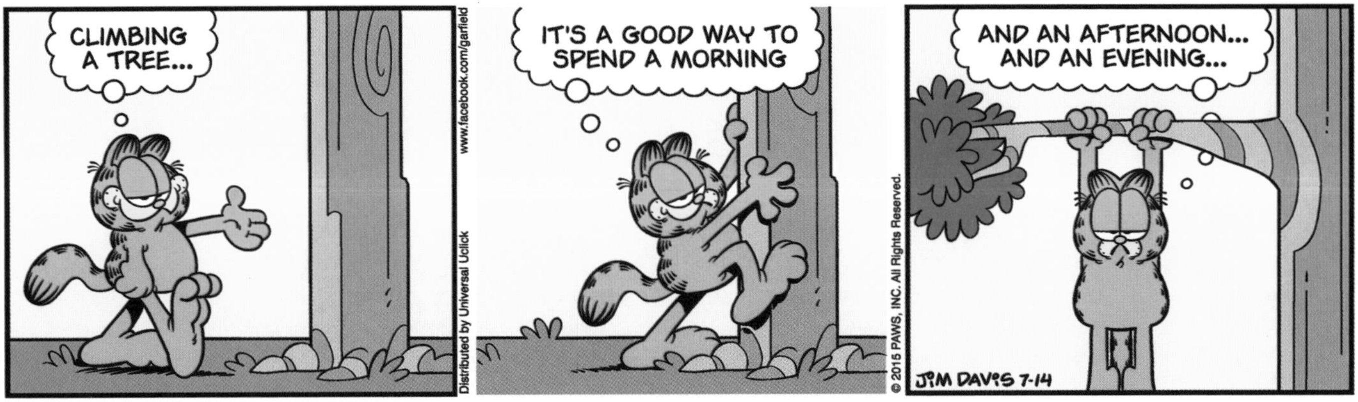
CLIMBING A TREE...
www.facebook.com/garfield
Distributed by Universal Uclick
IT'S A GOOD WAY TO SPEND A MORNING
© 2015 PAWS, INC. All Rights Reserved.
AND AN AFTERNOON... AND AN EVENING...
JIM DAVIS 7-14

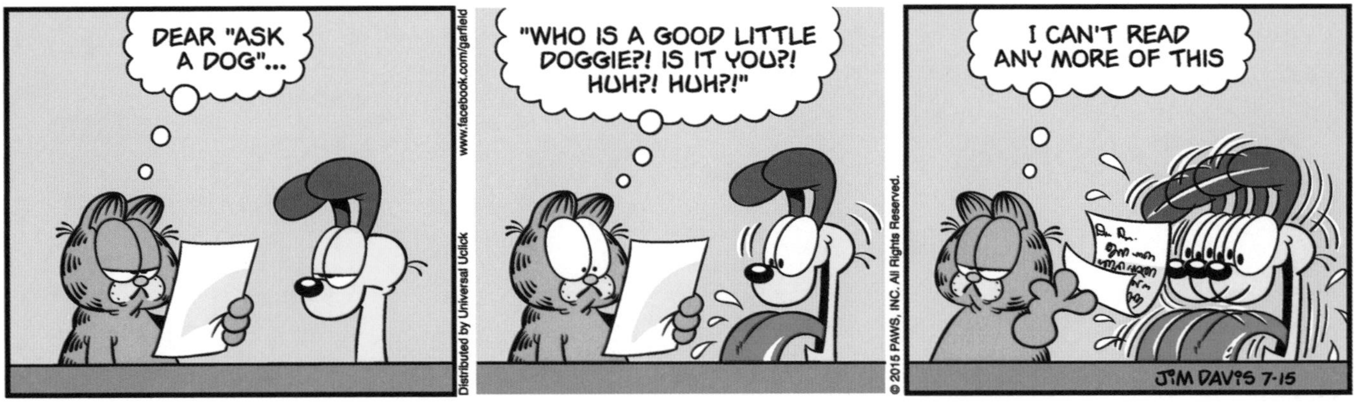
DEAR "ASK A DOG"...
www.facebook.com/garfield
Distributed by Universal Uclick
"WHO IS A GOOD LITTLE DOGGIE?! IS IT YOU?! HUH?! HUH?!"
© 2015 PAWS, INC. All Rights Reserved.
I CAN'T READ ANY MORE OF THIS
JIM DAVIS 7-15

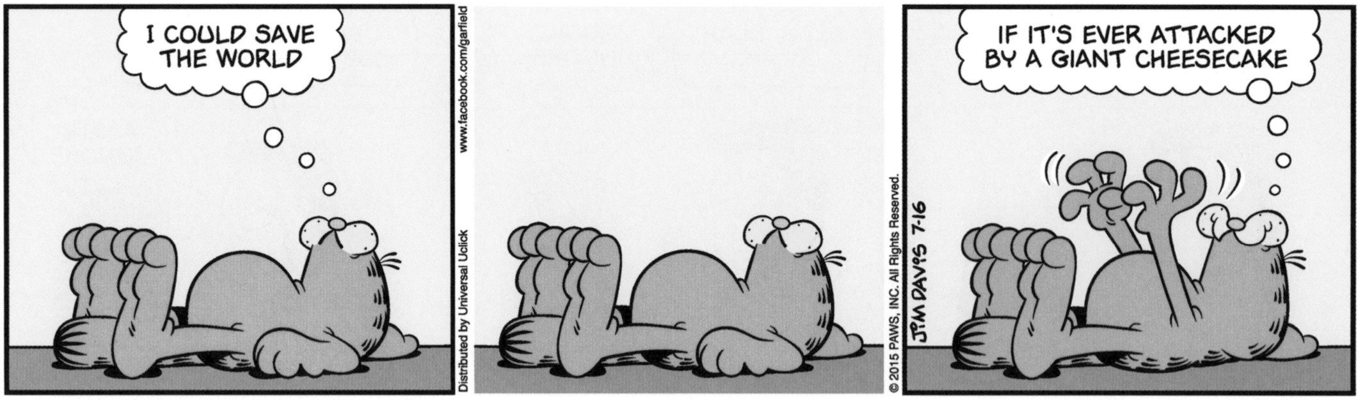
I COULD SAVE THE WORLD
IF IT'S EVER ATTACKED BY A GIANT CHEESECAKE
JIM DAVIS 7-16
www.facebook.com/garfield
Distributed by Universal Uclick
© 2015 PAWS, INC. All Rights Reserved.

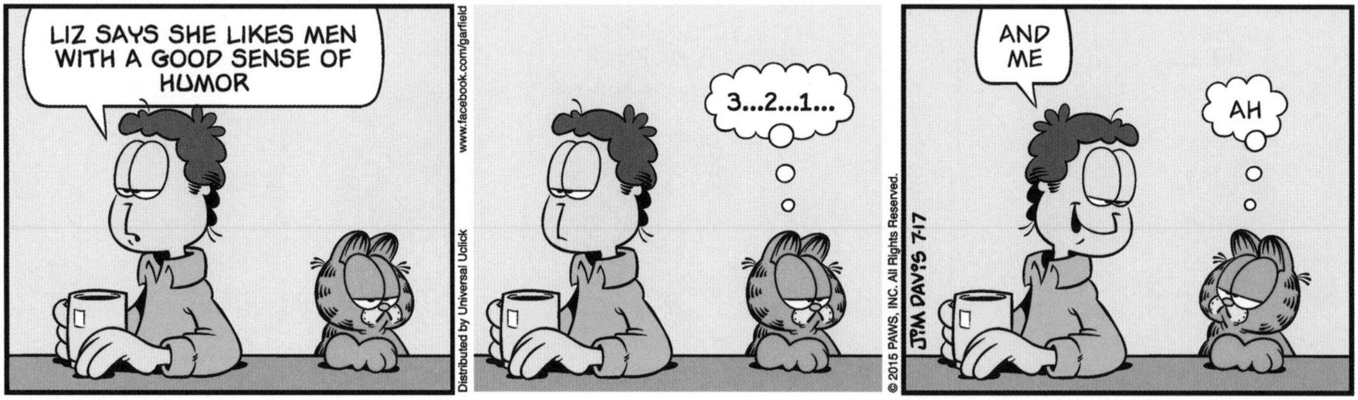
LIZ SAYS SHE LIKES MEN WITH A GOOD SENSE OF HUMOR
3...2...1...
AND ME
AH
JIM DAVIS 7-17
www.facebook.com/garfield
Distributed by Universal Uclick
© 2015 PAWS, INC. All Rights Reserved.

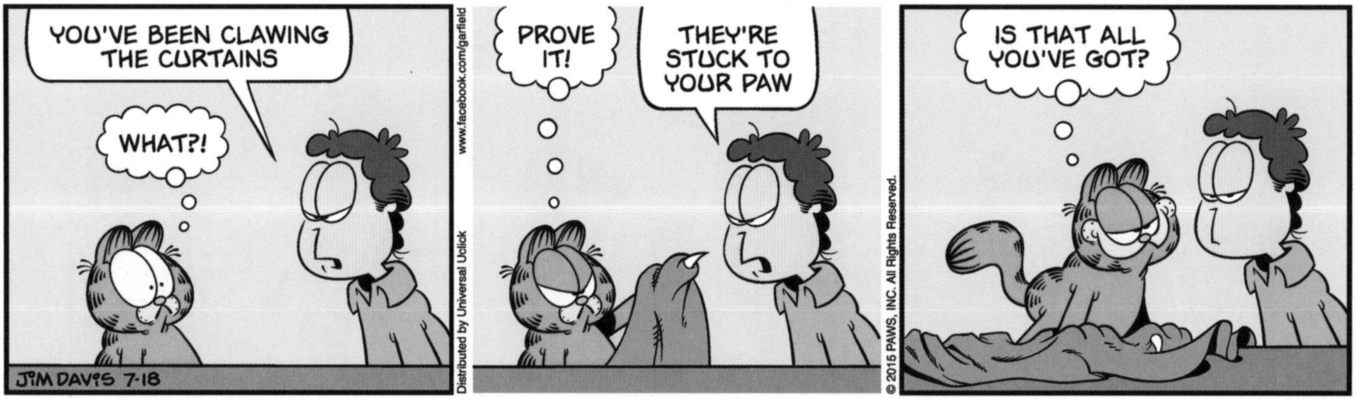
YOU'VE BEEN CLAWING THE CURTAINS
WHAT?!
PROVE IT!
THEY'RE STUCK TO YOUR PAW
IS THAT ALL YOU'VE GOT?
JIM DAVIS 7-18
www.facebook.com/garfield
Distributed by Universal Uclick
© 2015 PAWS, INC. All Rights Reserved.

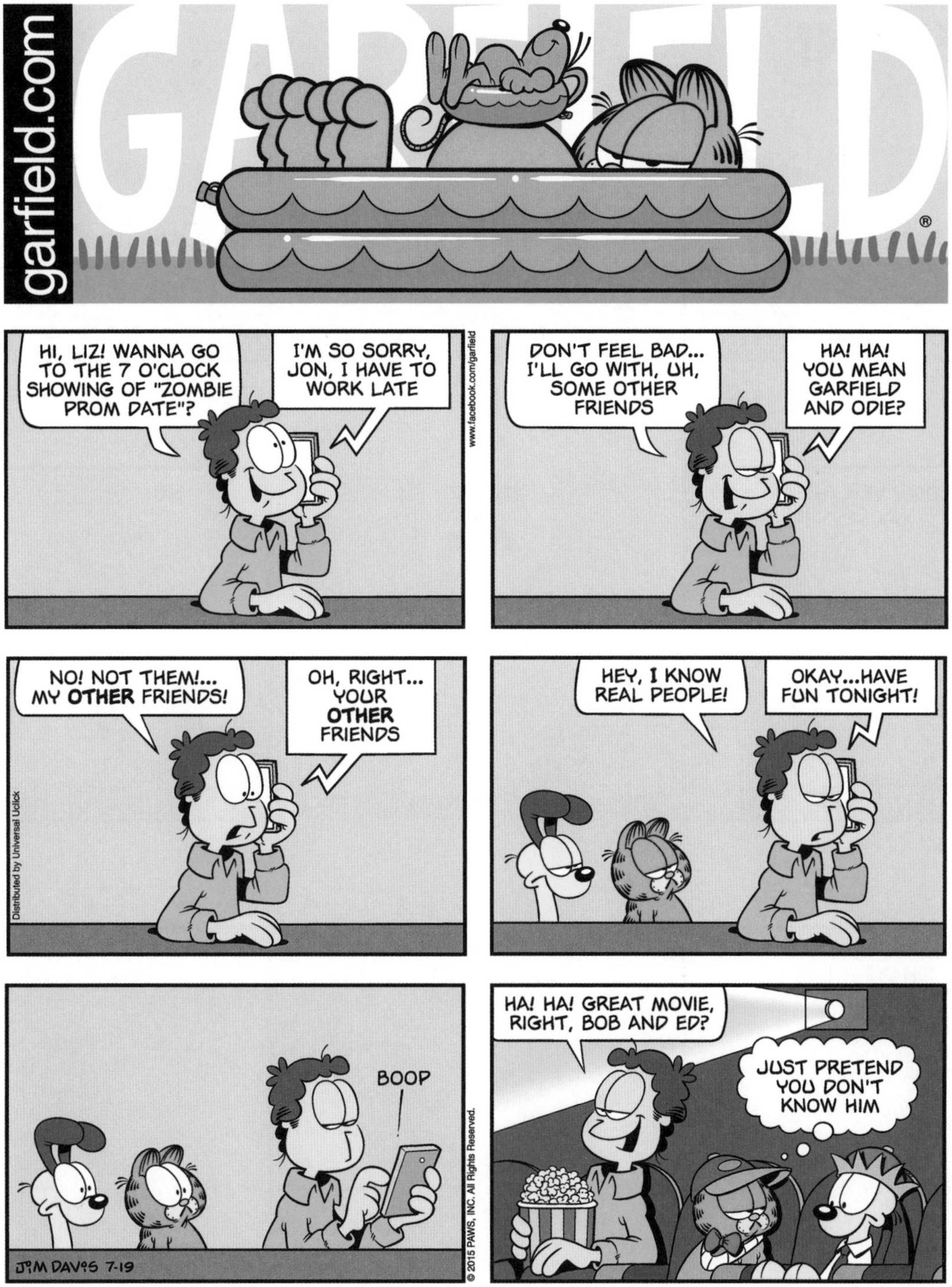

garfield.com
GARFIELD®
HI, LIZ! WANNA GO TO THE 7 O'CLOCK SHOWING OF "ZOMBIE PROM DATE"?
I'M SO SORRY, JON, I HAVE TO WORK LATE
www.facebook.com/garfield
DON'T FEEL BAD... I'LL GO WITH, UH, SOME OTHER FRIENDS
HA! HA! YOU MEAN GARFIELD AND ODIE?
NO! NOT THEM!... MY **OTHER** FRIENDS!
OH, RIGHT... YOUR **OTHER** FRIENDS
Distributed by Universal Uclick
HEY, I KNOW REAL PEOPLE!
OKAY...HAVE FUN TONIGHT!
BOOP
JIM DAVIS 7-19
© 2015 PAWS, INC. All Rights Reserved.
HA! HA! GREAT MOVIE, RIGHT, BOB AND ED?
JUST PRETEND YOU DON'T KNOW HIM

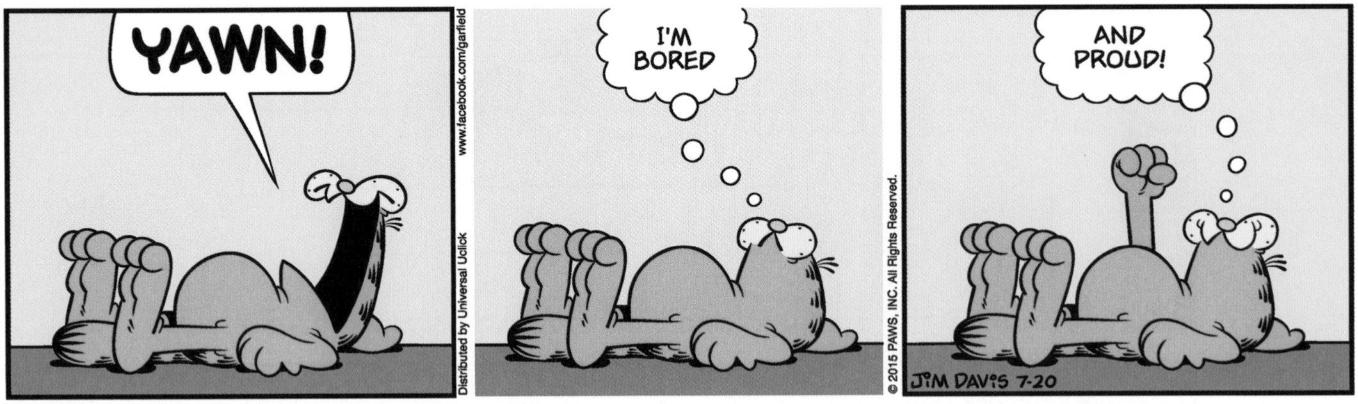
YAWN!
www.facebook.com/garfield
Distributed by Universal Uclick
I'M BORED
© 2015 PAWS, INC. All Rights Reserved.
AND PROUD!
JIM DAVIS 7-20

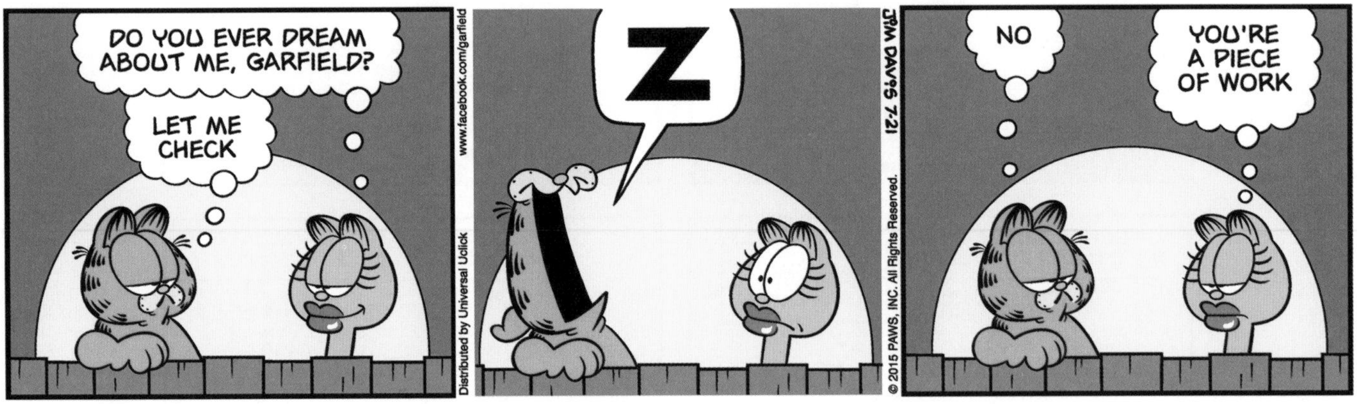
DO YOU EVER DREAM ABOUT ME, GARFIELD?
LET ME CHECK
www.facebook.com/garfield
Distributed by Universal Uclick
Z
JIM DAVIS 7-21
© 2015 PAWS, INC. All Rights Reserved.
NO
YOU'RE A PIECE OF WORK

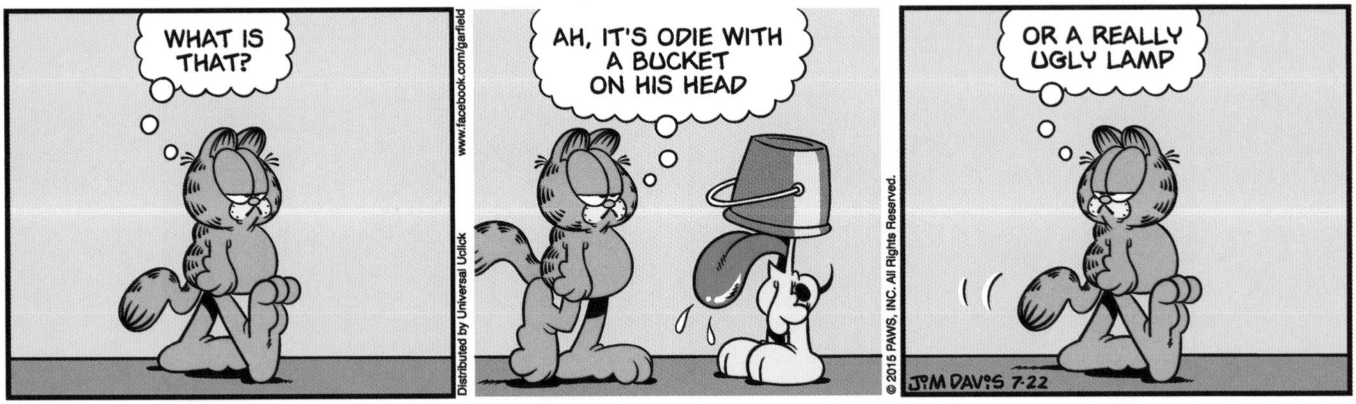
WHAT IS THAT?
www.facebook.com/garfield
Distributed by Universal Uclick
AH, IT'S ODIE WITH A BUCKET ON HIS HEAD
© 2015 PAWS, INC. All Rights Reserved.
OR A REALLY UGLY LAMP
JIM DAVIS 7-22

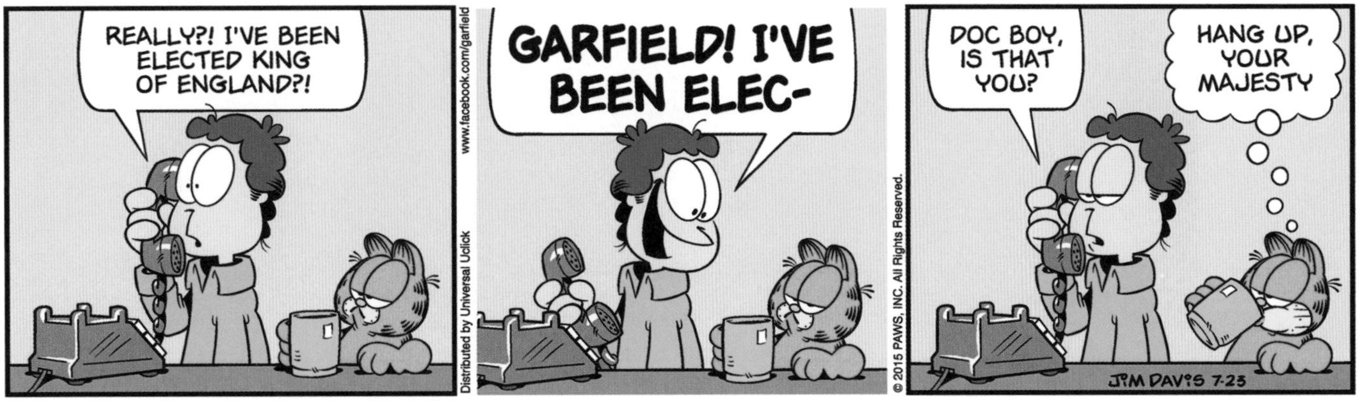
REALLY?! I'VE BEEN ELECTED KING OF ENGLAND?!
GARFIELD! I'VE BEEN ELEC-
DOC BOY, IS THAT YOU?
HANG UP, YOUR MAJESTY
JIM DAVIS 7-23
Distributed by Universal Uclick www.facebook.com/garfield
© 2015 PAWS, INC. All Rights Reserved.

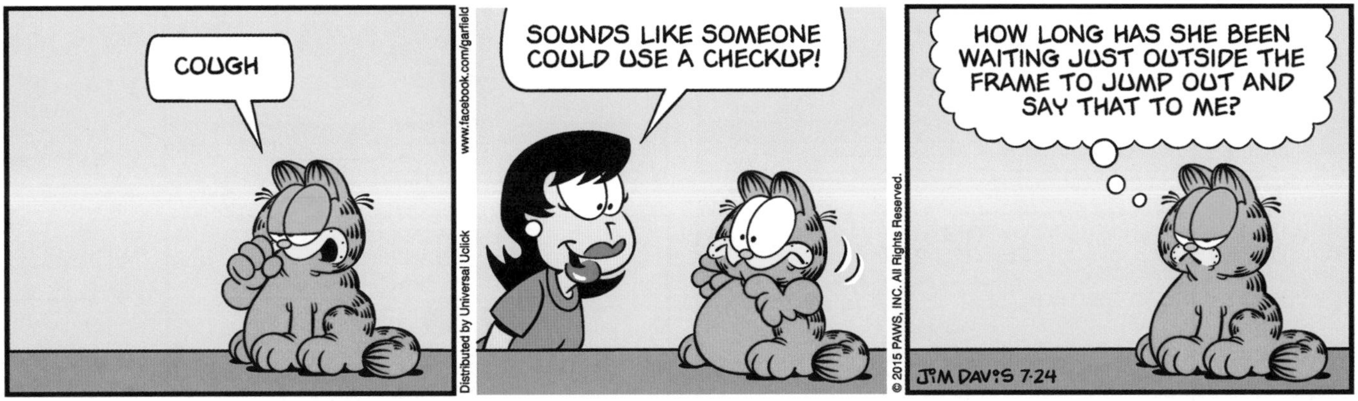
COUGH
SOUNDS LIKE SOMEONE COULD USE A CHECKUP!
HOW LONG HAS SHE BEEN WAITING JUST OUTSIDE THE FRAME TO JUMP OUT AND SAY THAT TO ME?
JIM DAVIS 7-24
Distributed by Universal Uclick www.facebook.com/garfield
© 2015 PAWS, INC. All Rights Reserved.

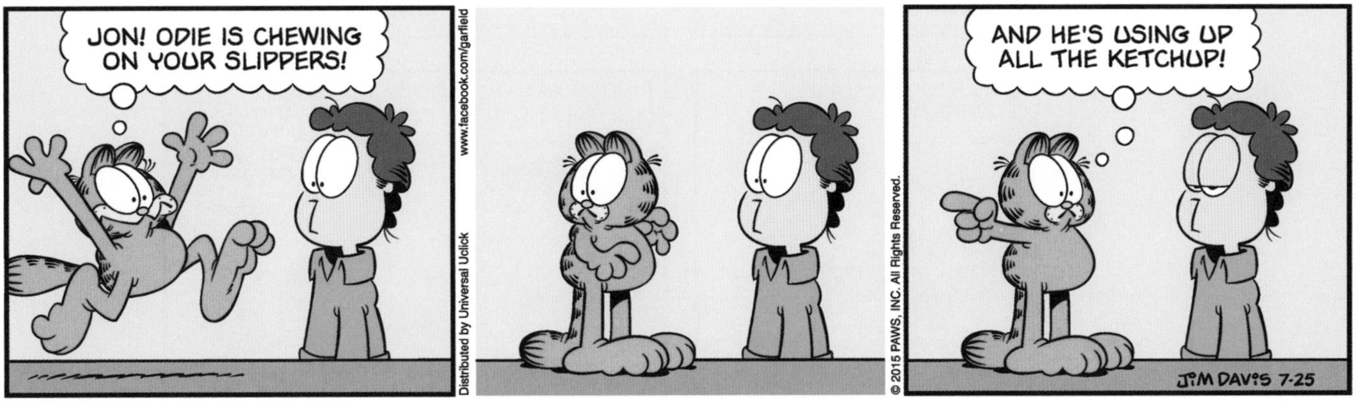
JON! ODIE IS CHEWING ON YOUR SLIPPERS!
AND HE'S USING UP ALL THE KETCHUP!
JIM DAVIS 7-25
Distributed by Universal Uclick www.facebook.com/garfield
© 2015 PAWS, INC. All Rights Reserved.

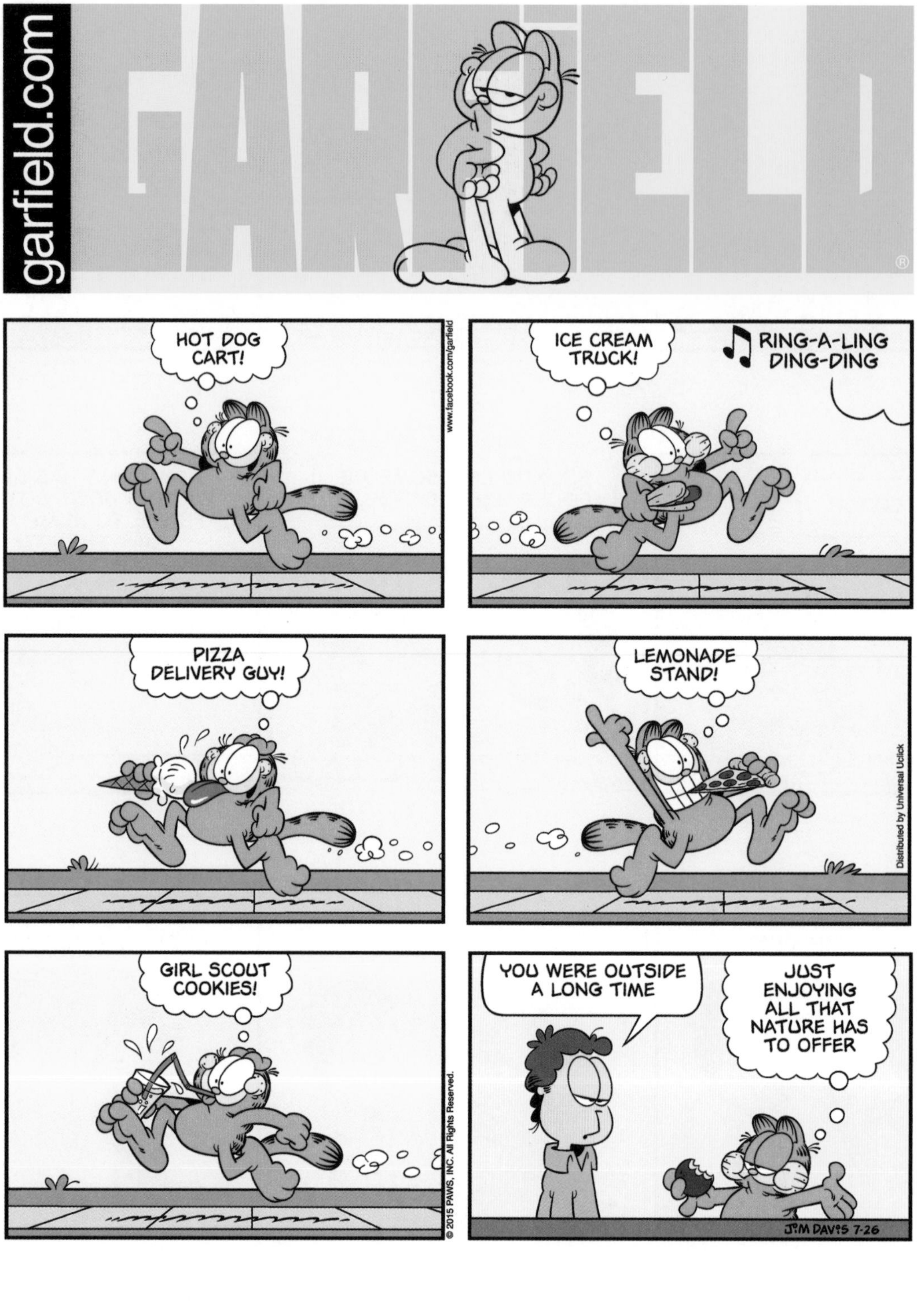

garfield.com
GARFIELD
HOT DOG CART!
www.facebook.com/garfield
ICE CREAM TRUCK!
RING-A-LING DING-DING
PIZZA DELIVERY GUY!
LEMONADE STAND!
Distributed by Universal Uclick
GIRL SCOUT COOKIES!
YOU WERE OUTSIDE A LONG TIME
JUST ENJOYING ALL THAT NATURE HAS TO OFFER
JIM DAVIS 7-26

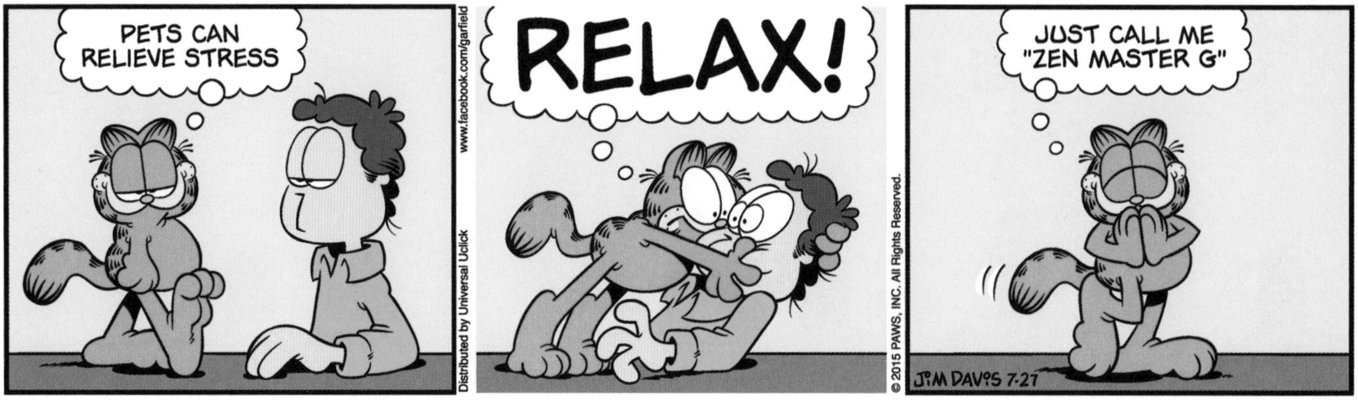
PETS CAN RELIEVE STRESS
RELAX!
JUST CALL ME "ZEN MASTER G"
Distributed by Universal Uclick
www.facebook.com/garfield
© 2015 PAWS, INC. All Rights Reserved.
JIM DAVIS 7-27

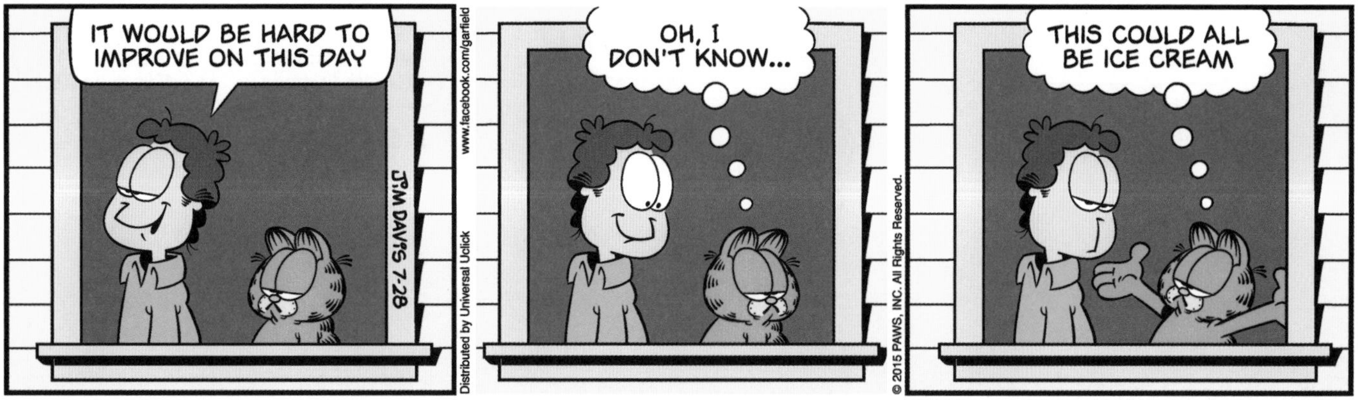
IT WOULD BE HARD TO IMPROVE ON THIS DAY
OH, I DON'T KNOW...
THIS COULD ALL BE ICE CREAM
JIM DAVIS 7-28
Distributed by Universal Uclick
www.facebook.com/garfield
© 2015 PAWS, INC. All Rights Reserved.

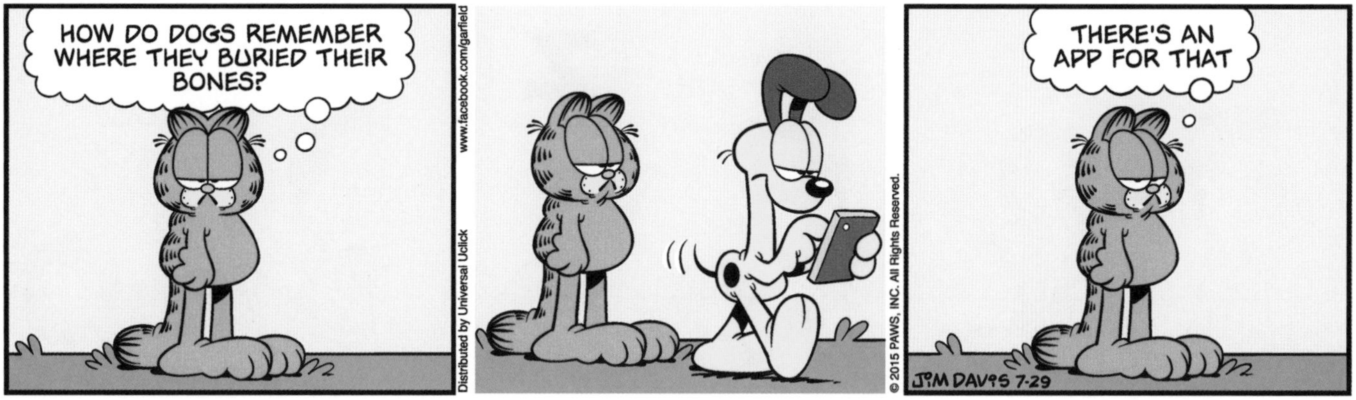
HOW DO DOGS REMEMBER WHERE THEY BURIED THEIR BONES?
THERE'S AN APP FOR THAT
Distributed by Universal Uclick
www.facebook.com/garfield
© 2015 PAWS, INC. All Rights Reserved.
JIM DAVIS 7-29

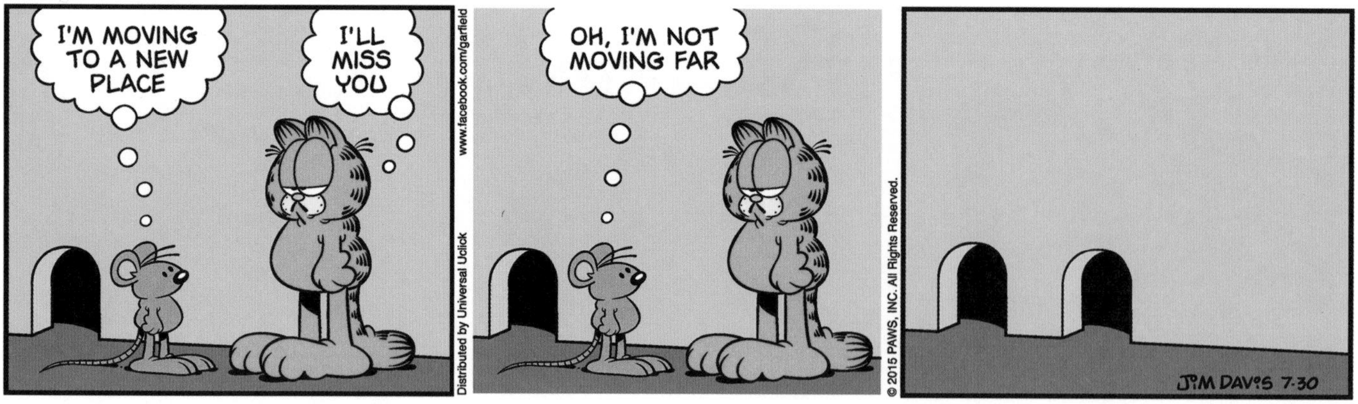
I'M MOVING TO A NEW PLACE
I'LL MISS YOU
OH, I'M NOT MOVING FAR
JIM DAVIS 7-30
Distributed by Universal Uclick www.facebook.com/garfield
© 2015 PAWS, INC. All Rights Reserved.

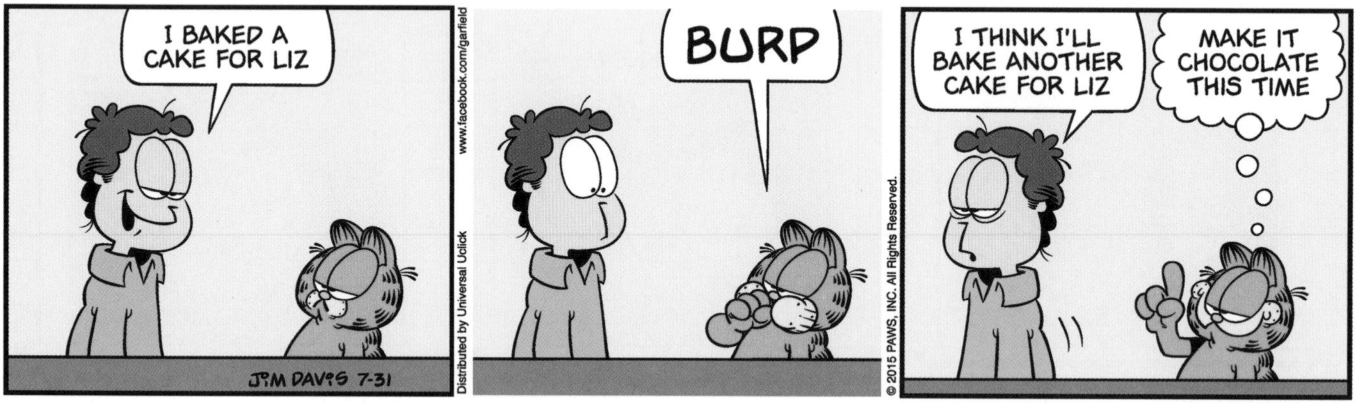
I BAKED A CAKE FOR LIZ
JIM DAVIS 7-31
BURP
I THINK I'LL BAKE ANOTHER CAKE FOR LIZ
MAKE IT CHOCOLATE THIS TIME
Distributed by Universal Uclick www.facebook.com/garfield
© 2015 PAWS, INC. All Rights Reserved.

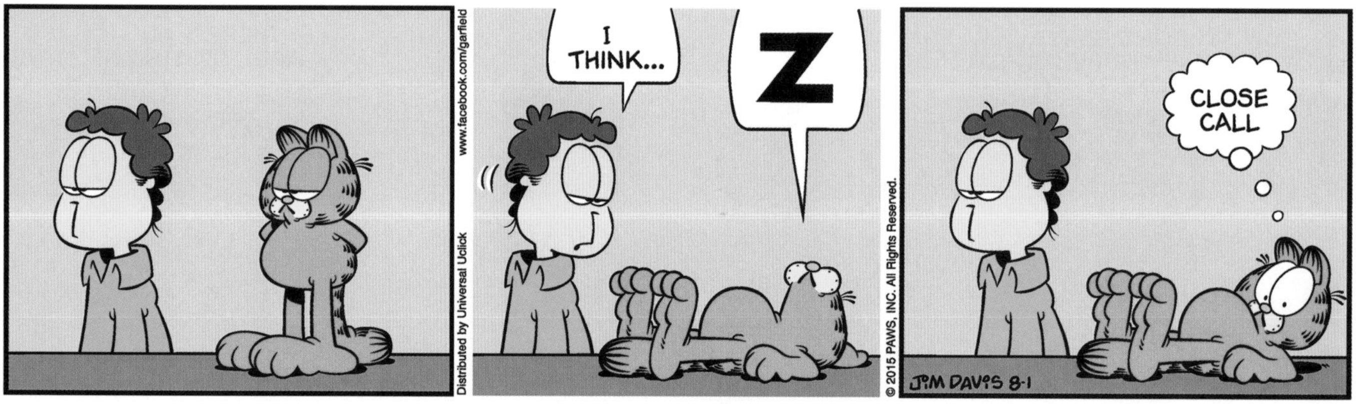
I THINK...
Z
CLOSE CALL
JIM DAVIS 8-1
Distributed by Universal Uclick www.facebook.com/garfield
© 2015 PAWS, INC. All Rights Reserved.

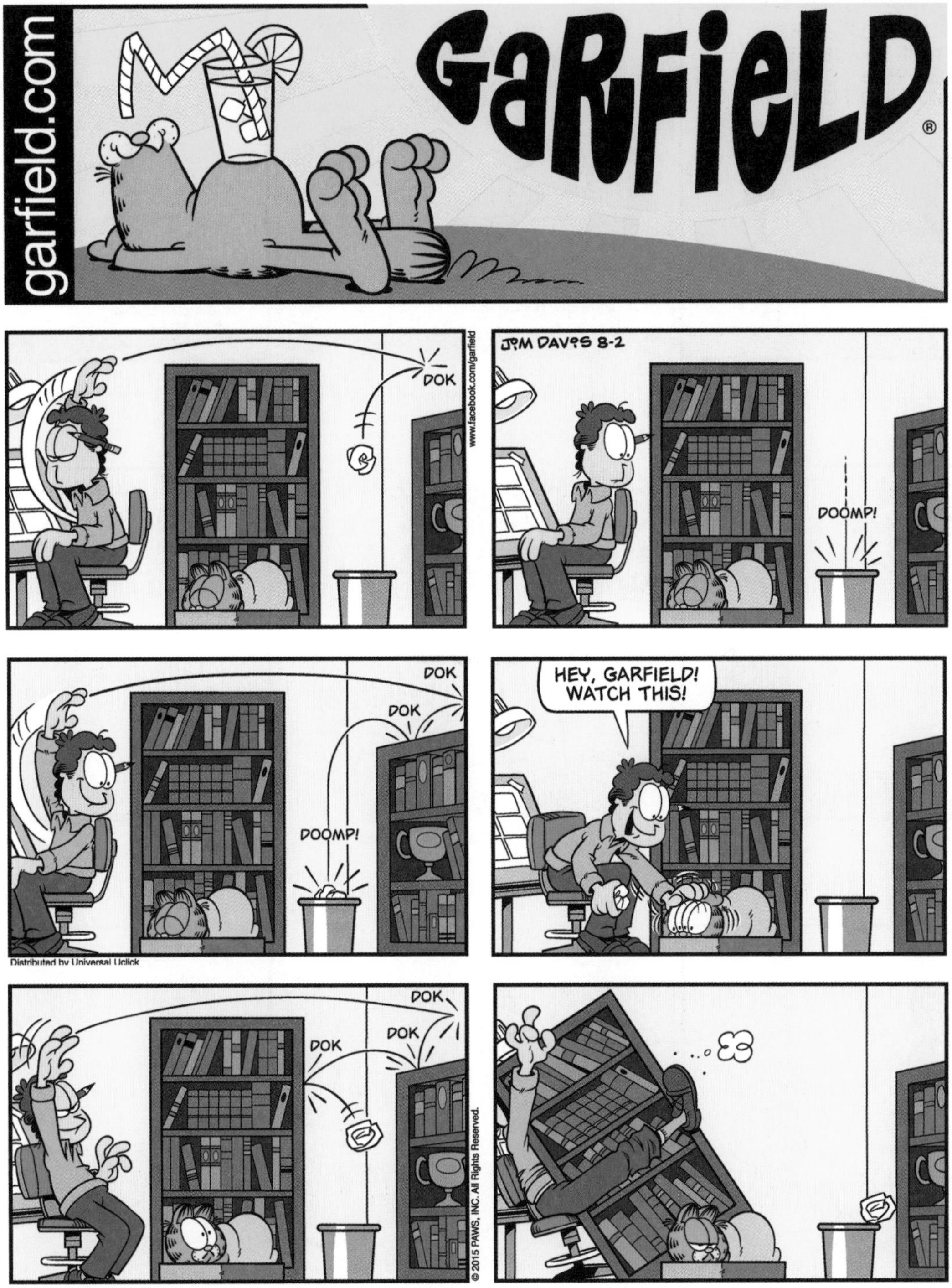
garfield.com
GARFIELD
DOK
www.facebook.com/garfield
JIM DAVIS 8-2
DOOMP!
DOK
DOK
DOOMP!
Distributed by Universal Uclick
HEY, GARFIELD! WATCH THIS!
DOK
DOK
DOK
© 2015 PAWS, INC. All Rights Reserved.

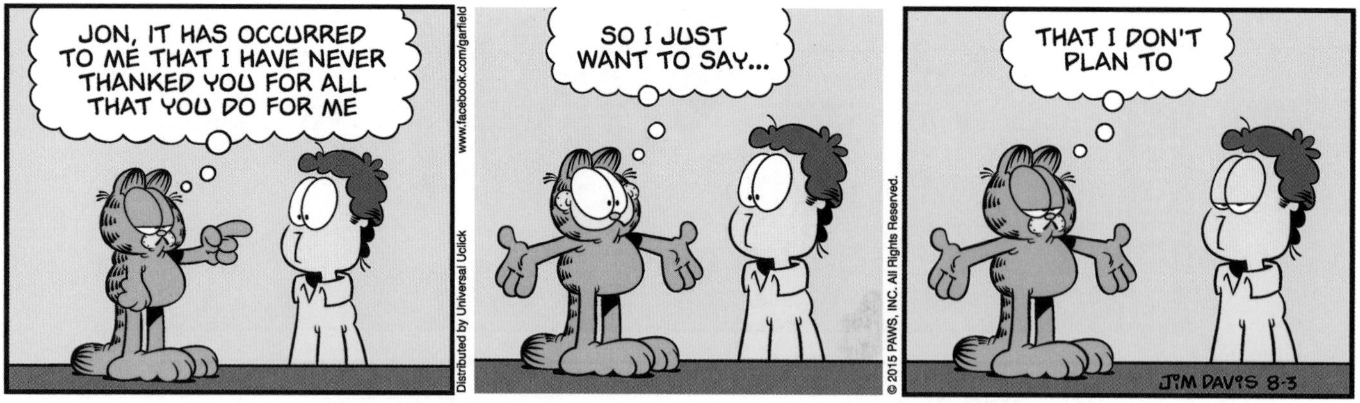
JON, IT HAS OCCURRED TO ME THAT I HAVE NEVER THANKED YOU FOR ALL THAT YOU DO FOR ME
SO I JUST WANT TO SAY...
THAT I DON'T PLAN TO
JIM DAVIS 8-3
Distributed by Universal Uclick www.facebook.com/garfield
© 2015 PAWS, INC. All Rights Reserved.

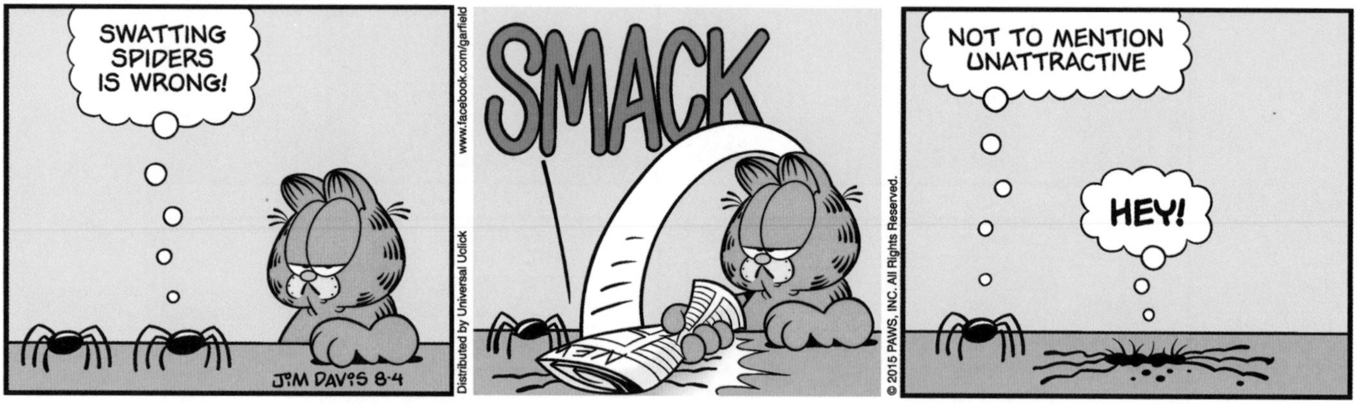
SWATTING SPIDERS IS WRONG!
JIM DAVIS 8-4
SMACK
NOT TO MENTION UNATTRACTIVE
HEY!
Distributed by Universal Uclick www.facebook.com/garfield
© 2015 PAWS, INC. All Rights Reserved.

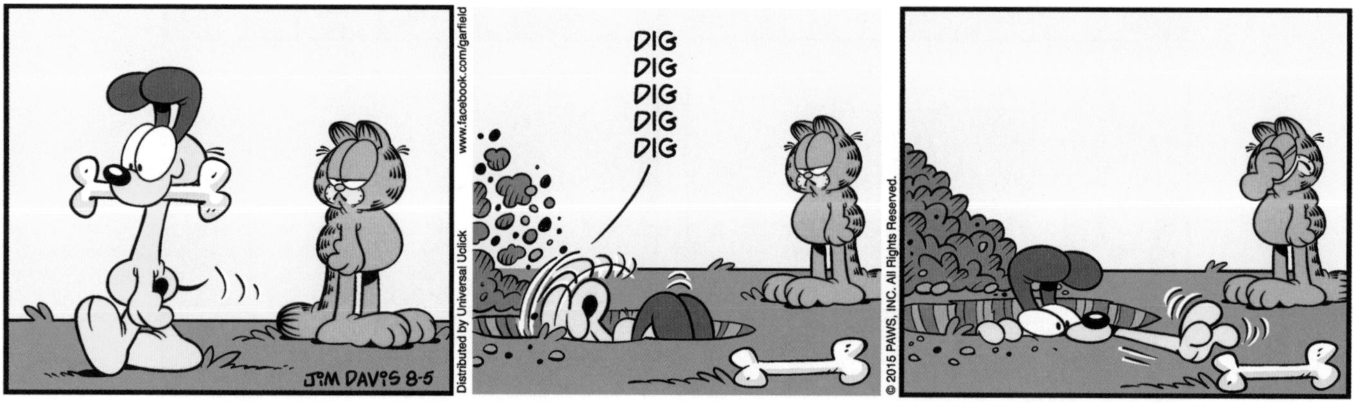
JIM DAVIS 8-5
DIG
DIG
DIG
DIG
DIG
Distributed by Universal Uclick www.facebook.com/garfield
© 2015 PAWS, INC. All Rights Reserved.

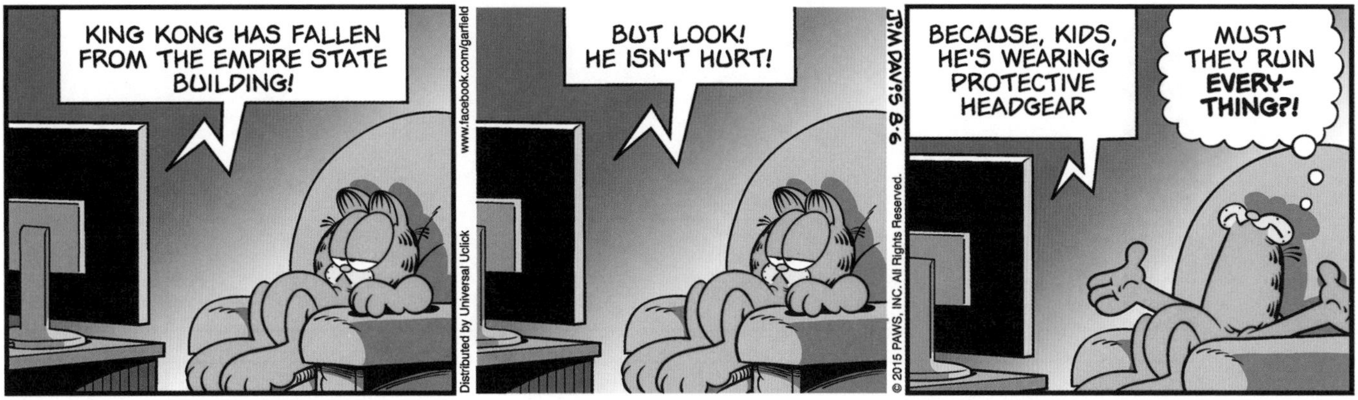
KING KONG HAS FALLEN FROM THE EMPIRE STATE BUILDING!
Distributed by Universal Uclick www.facebook.com/garfield
BUT LOOK! HE ISN'T HURT!
JIM DAVIS 8-6
© 2015 PAWS, INC. All Rights Reserved.
BECAUSE, KIDS, HE'S WEARING PROTECTIVE HEADGEAR
MUST THEY RUIN **EVERYTHING?!**

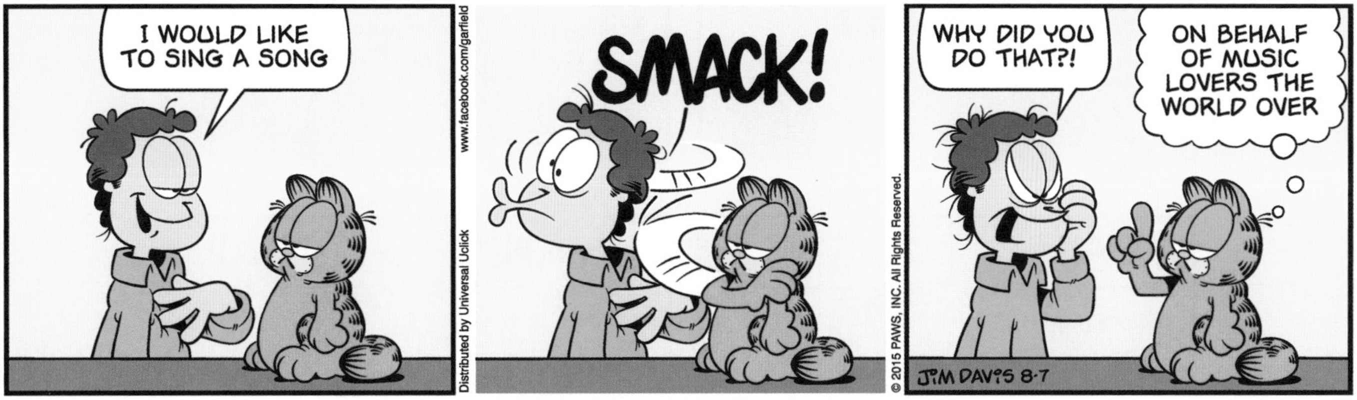
I WOULD LIKE TO SING A SONG
Distributed by Universal Uclick www.facebook.com/garfield
SMACK!
© 2015 PAWS, INC. All Rights Reserved.
WHY DID YOU DO THAT?!
ON BEHALF OF MUSIC LOVERS THE WORLD OVER
JIM DAVIS 8-7

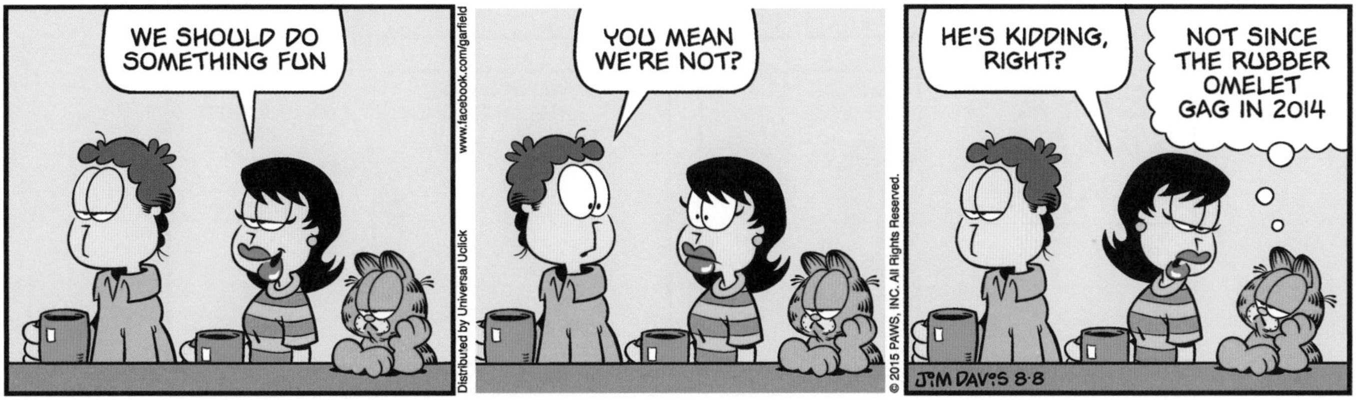
WE SHOULD DO SOMETHING FUN
Distributed by Universal Uclick www.facebook.com/garfield
YOU MEAN WE'RE NOT?
© 2015 PAWS, INC. All Rights Reserved.
HE'S KIDDING, RIGHT?
NOT SINCE THE RUBBER OMELET GAG IN 2014
JIM DAVIS 8-8

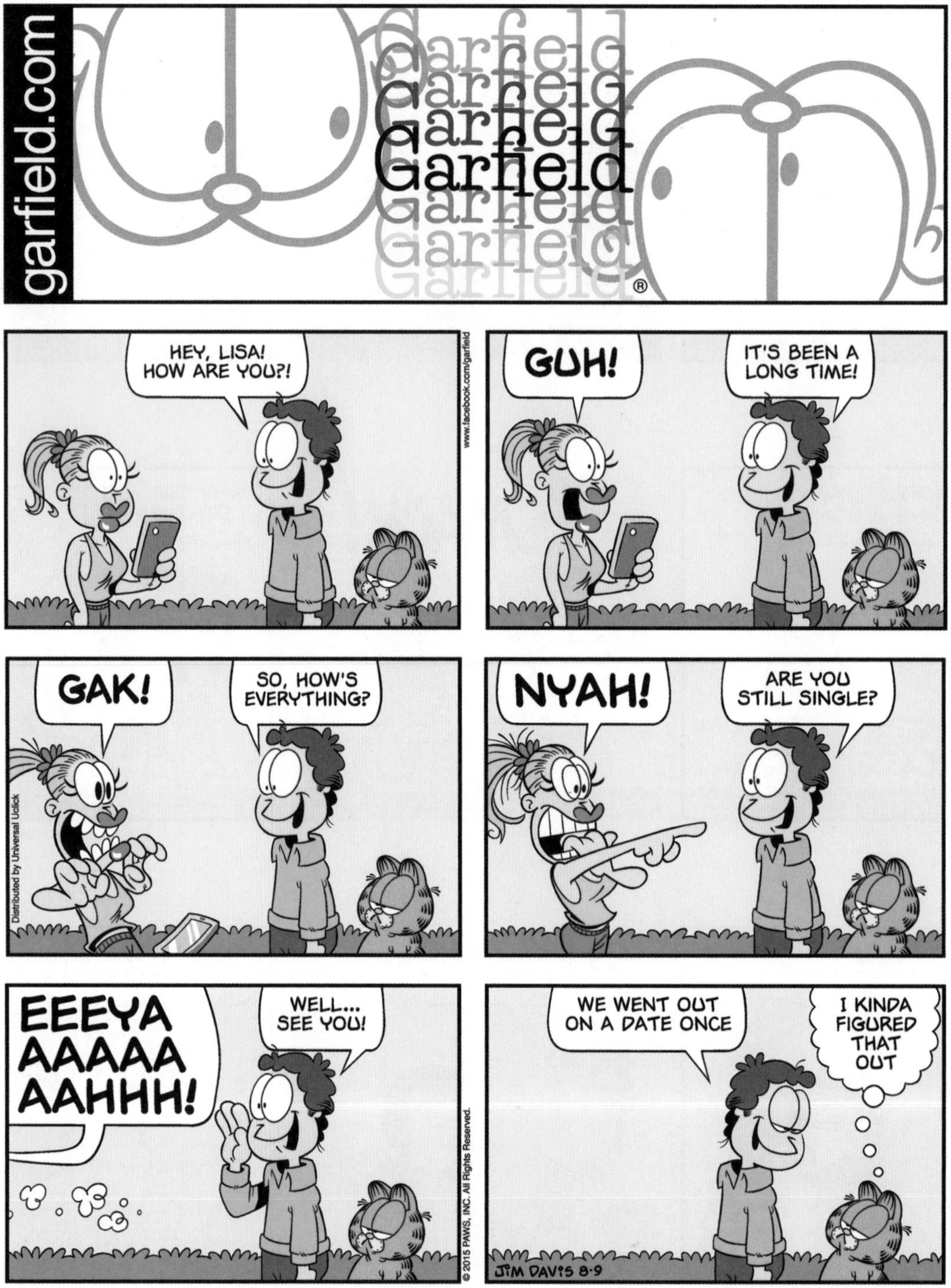
garfield.com
Garfield
HEY, LISA! HOW ARE YOU?!
www.facebook.com/garfield
GUH!
IT'S BEEN A LONG TIME!
GAK!
SO, HOW'S EVERYTHING?
Distributed by Universal Uclick
NYAH!
ARE YOU STILL SINGLE?
EEEYA AAAAA AAHHH!
WELL... SEE YOU!
© 2015 PAWS, INC. All Rights Reserved.
WE WENT OUT ON A DATE ONCE
I KINDA FIGURED THAT OUT
JIM DAVIS 8-9

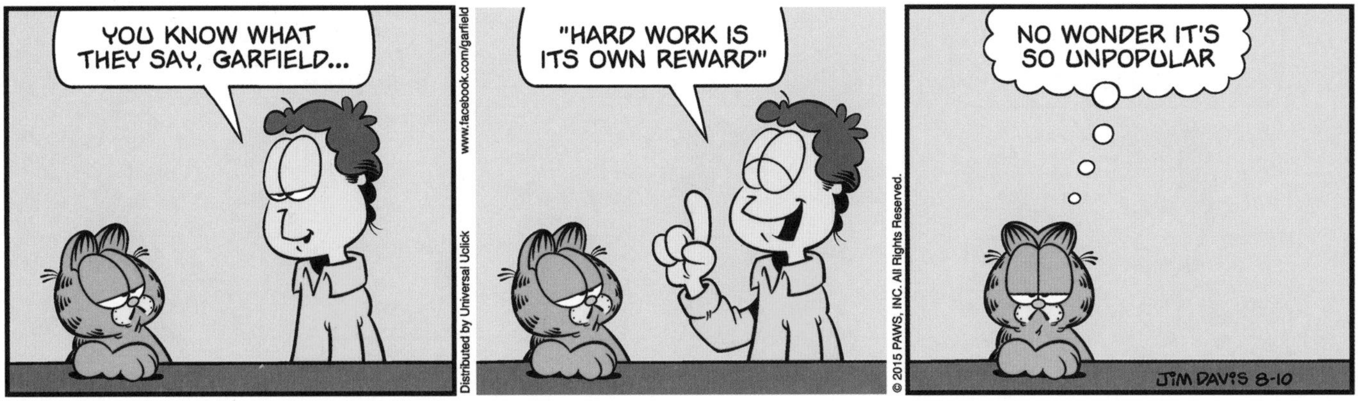
YOU KNOW WHAT THEY SAY, GARFIELD...
"HARD WORK IS ITS OWN REWARD"
NO WONDER IT'S SO UNPOPULAR
JIM DAVIS 8-10
Distributed by Universal Uclick www.facebook.com/garfield
© 2015 PAWS, INC. All Rights Reserved.

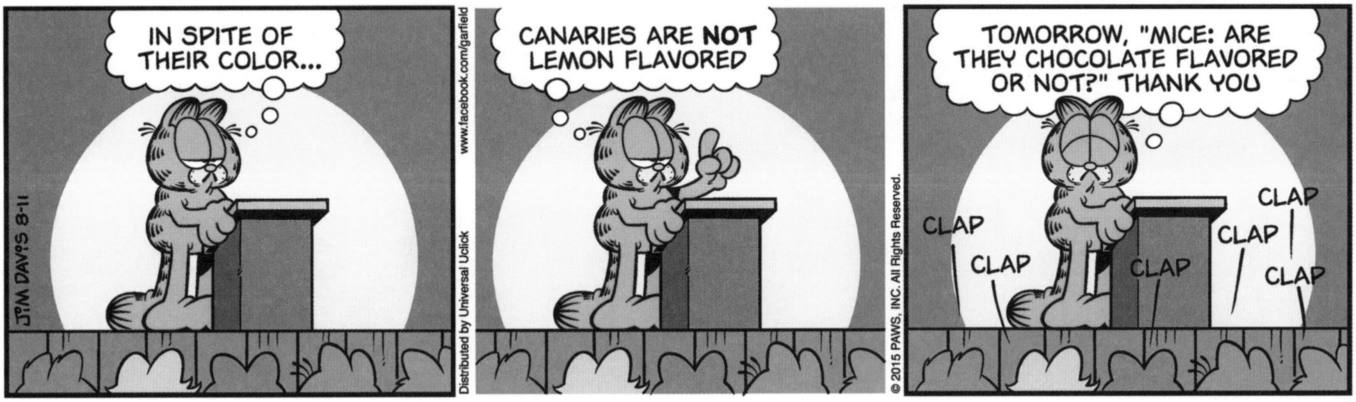
JIM DAVIS 8-11
IN SPITE OF THEIR COLOR...
CANARIES ARE **NOT** LEMON FLAVORED
TOMORROW, "MICE: ARE THEY CHOCOLATE FLAVORED OR NOT?" THANK YOU
CLAP
CLAP
CLAP
CLAP
CLAP
CLAP
Distributed by Universal Uclick www.facebook.com/garfield
© 2015 PAWS, INC. All Rights Reserved.

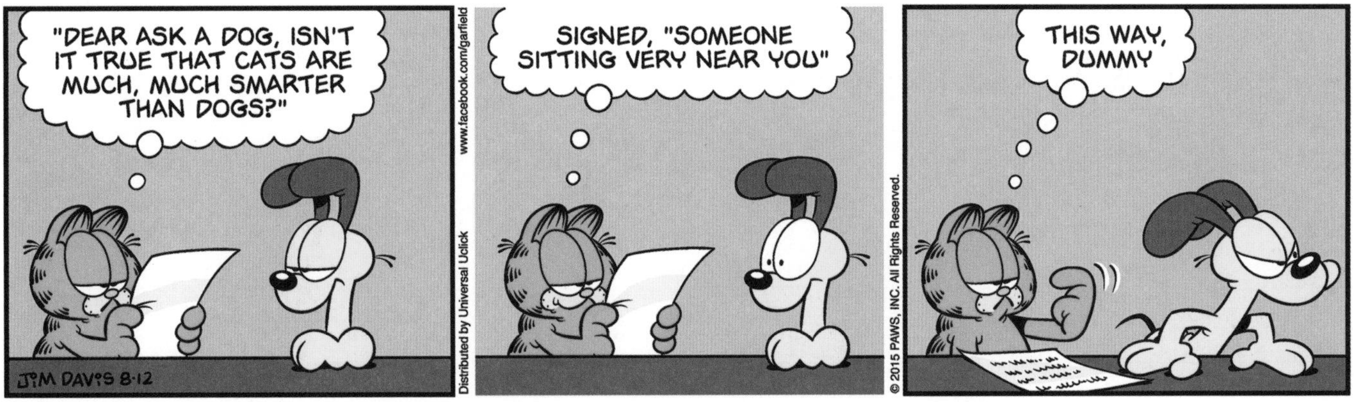
"DEAR ASK A DOG, ISN'T IT TRUE THAT CATS ARE MUCH, MUCH SMARTER THAN DOGS?"
JIM DAVIS 8-12
SIGNED, "SOMEONE SITTING VERY NEAR YOU"
THIS WAY, DUMMY
Distributed by Universal Uclick www.facebook.com/garfield
© 2015 PAWS, INC. All Rights Reserved.

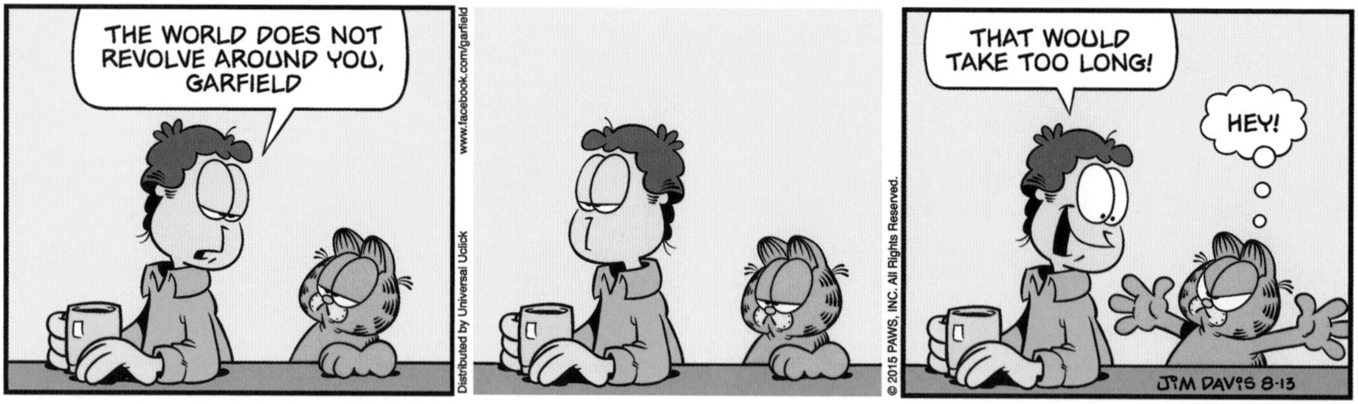
THE WORLD DOES NOT REVOLVE AROUND YOU, GARFIELD
THAT WOULD TAKE TOO LONG!
HEY!
JIM DAVIS 8-13
www.facebook.com/garfield
Distributed by Universal Uclick
© 2015 PAWS, INC. All Rights Reserved.

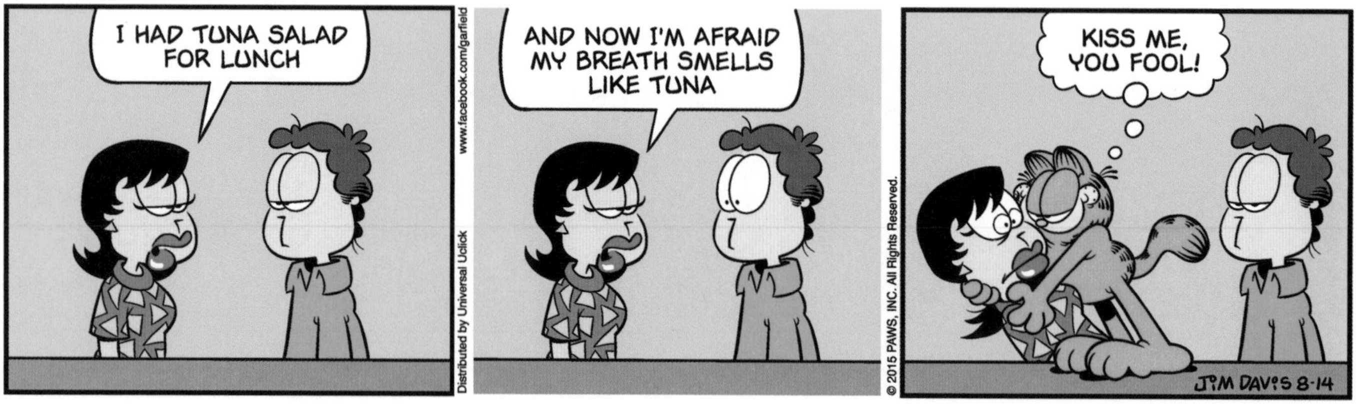
I HAD TUNA SALAD FOR LUNCH
AND NOW I'M AFRAID MY BREATH SMELLS LIKE TUNA
KISS ME, YOU FOOL!
JIM DAVIS 8-14
www.facebook.com/garfield
Distributed by Universal Uclick
© 2015 PAWS, INC. All Rights Reserved.

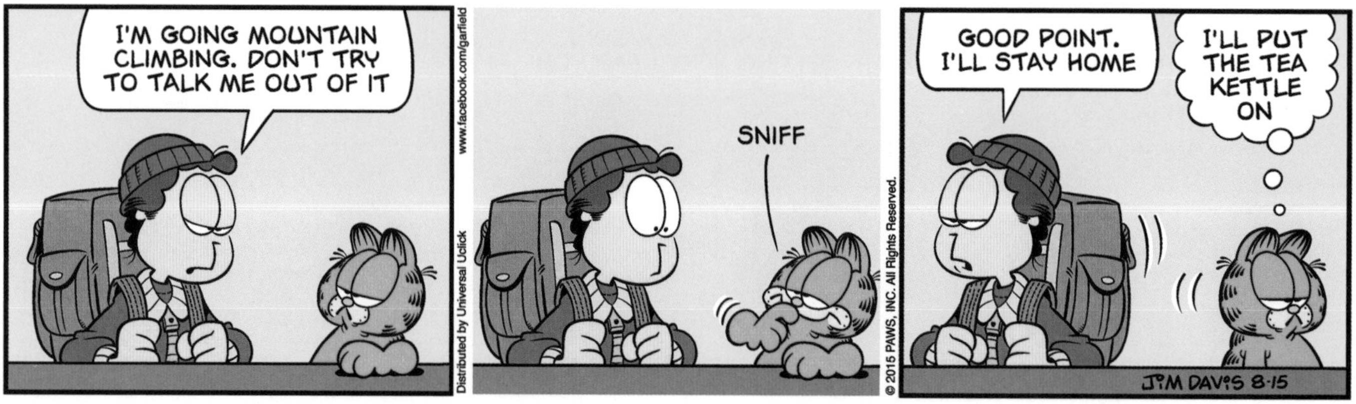
I'M GOING MOUNTAIN CLIMBING. DON'T TRY TO TALK ME OUT OF IT
SNIFF
GOOD POINT. I'LL STAY HOME
I'LL PUT THE TEA KETTLE ON
JIM DAVIS 8-15
www.facebook.com/garfield
Distributed by Universal Uclick
© 2015 PAWS, INC. All Rights Reserved.

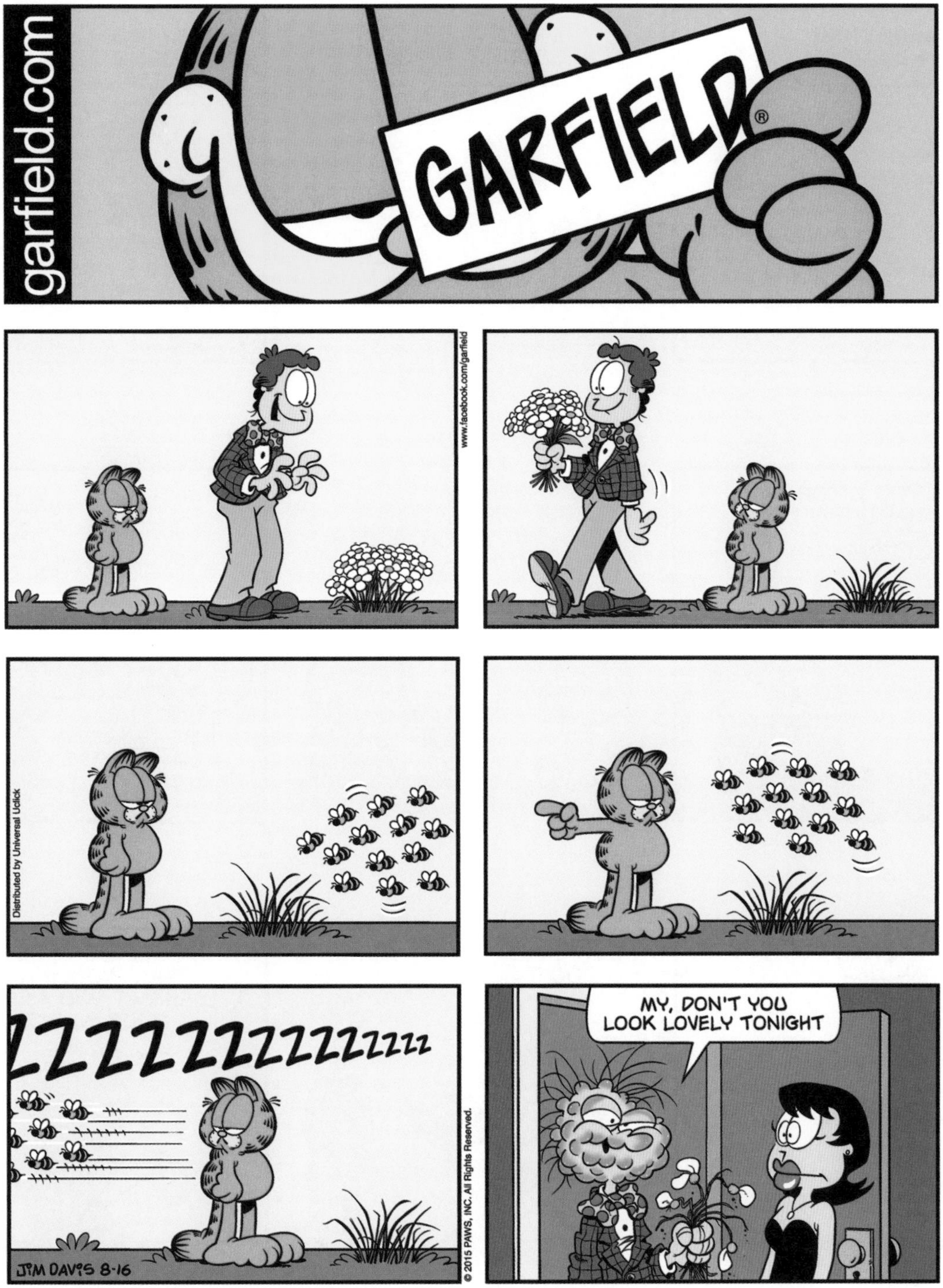
garfield.com
GARFIELD®
www.facebook.com/garfield
Distributed by Universal Uclick
ZZZZZZZZZZZzzzz
JIM DAVIS 8-16
© 2015 PAWS, INC. All Rights Reserved.
MY, DON'T YOU LOOK LOVELY TONIGHT

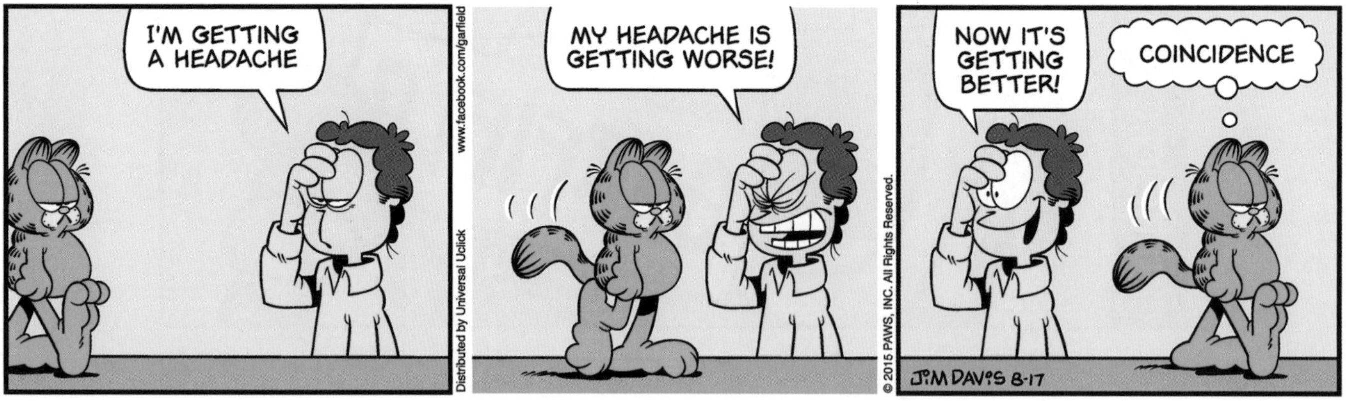
I'M GETTING A HEADACHE
www.facebook.com/garfield
Distributed by Universal Uclick
MY HEADACHE IS GETTING WORSE!
© 2015 PAWS, INC. All Rights Reserved.
NOW IT'S GETTING BETTER!
COINCIDENCE
JIM DAVIS 8-17

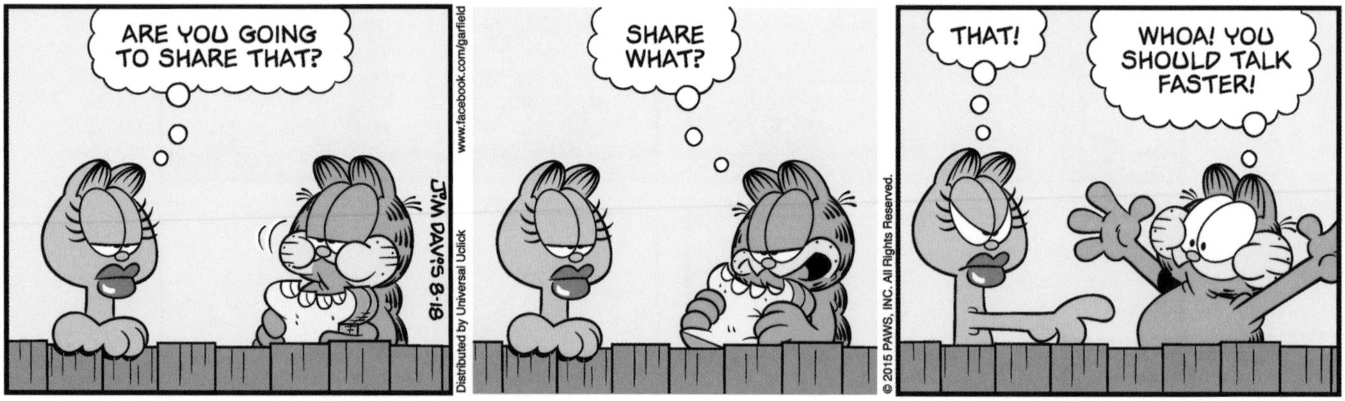
ARE YOU GOING TO SHARE THAT?
JIM DAVIS 8-18
www.facebook.com/garfield
Distributed by Universal Uclick
SHARE WHAT?
© 2015 PAWS, INC. All Rights Reserved.
THAT!
WHOA! YOU SHOULD TALK FASTER!

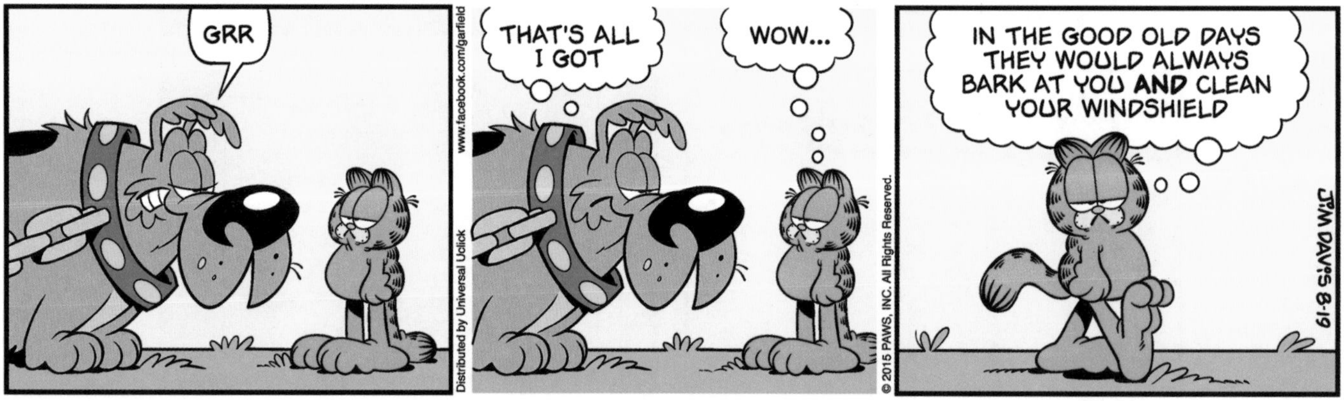
GRR
www.facebook.com/garfield
Distributed by Universal Uclick
THAT'S ALL I GOT
WOW...
© 2015 PAWS, INC. All Rights Reserved.
IN THE GOOD OLD DAYS THEY WOULD ALWAYS BARK AT YOU **AND** CLEAN YOUR WINDSHIELD
JIM DAVIS 8-19

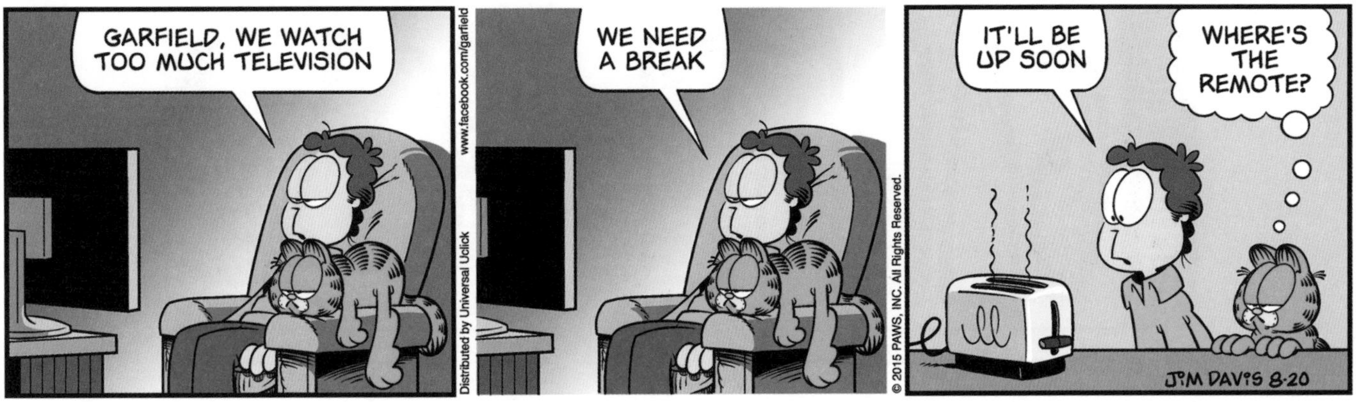
GARFIELD, WE WATCH TOO MUCH TELEVISION
Distributed by Universal Uclick www.facebook.com/garfield
WE NEED A BREAK
© 2015 PAWS, INC. All Rights Reserved.
IT'LL BE UP SOON
WHERE'S THE REMOTE?
JIM DAVIS 8-20

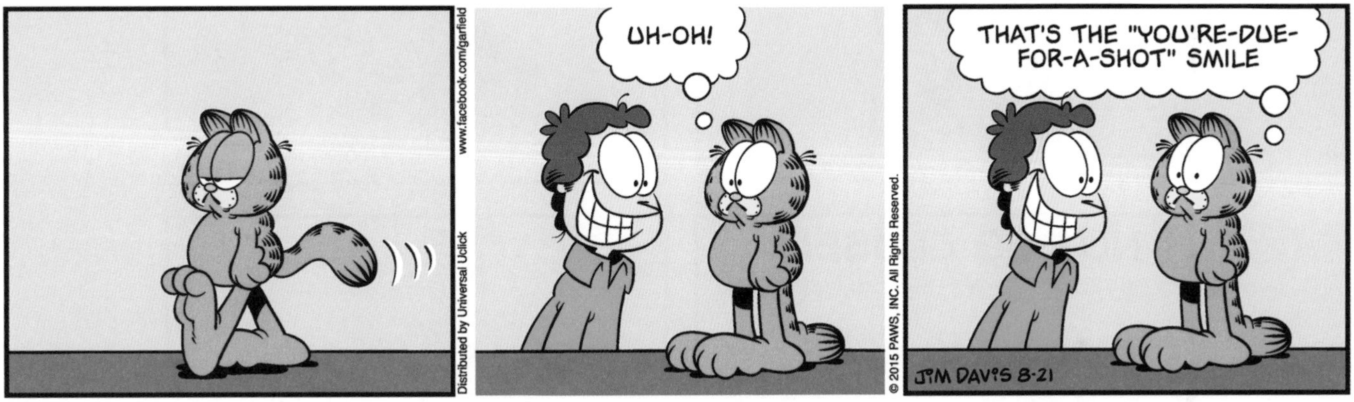
Distributed by Universal Uclick www.facebook.com/garfield
UH-OH!
© 2015 PAWS, INC. All Rights Reserved.
THAT'S THE "YOU'RE-DUE-FOR-A-SHOT" SMILE
JIM DAVIS 8-21

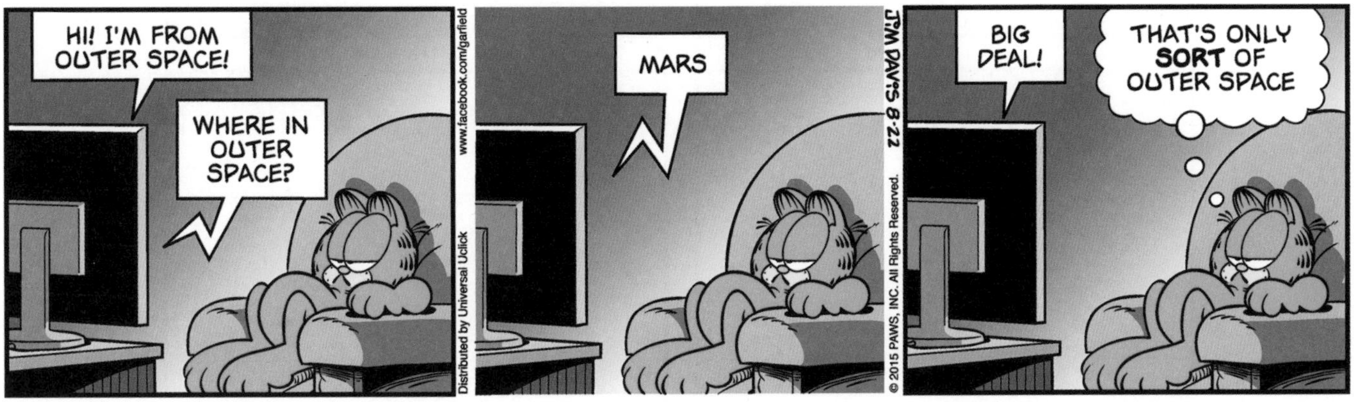
HI! I'M FROM OUTER SPACE!
WHERE IN OUTER SPACE?
Distributed by Universal Uclick www.facebook.com/garfield
MARS
JIM DAVIS 8-22
© 2015 PAWS, INC. All Rights Reserved.
BIG DEAL!
THAT'S ONLY **SORT** OF OUTER SPACE

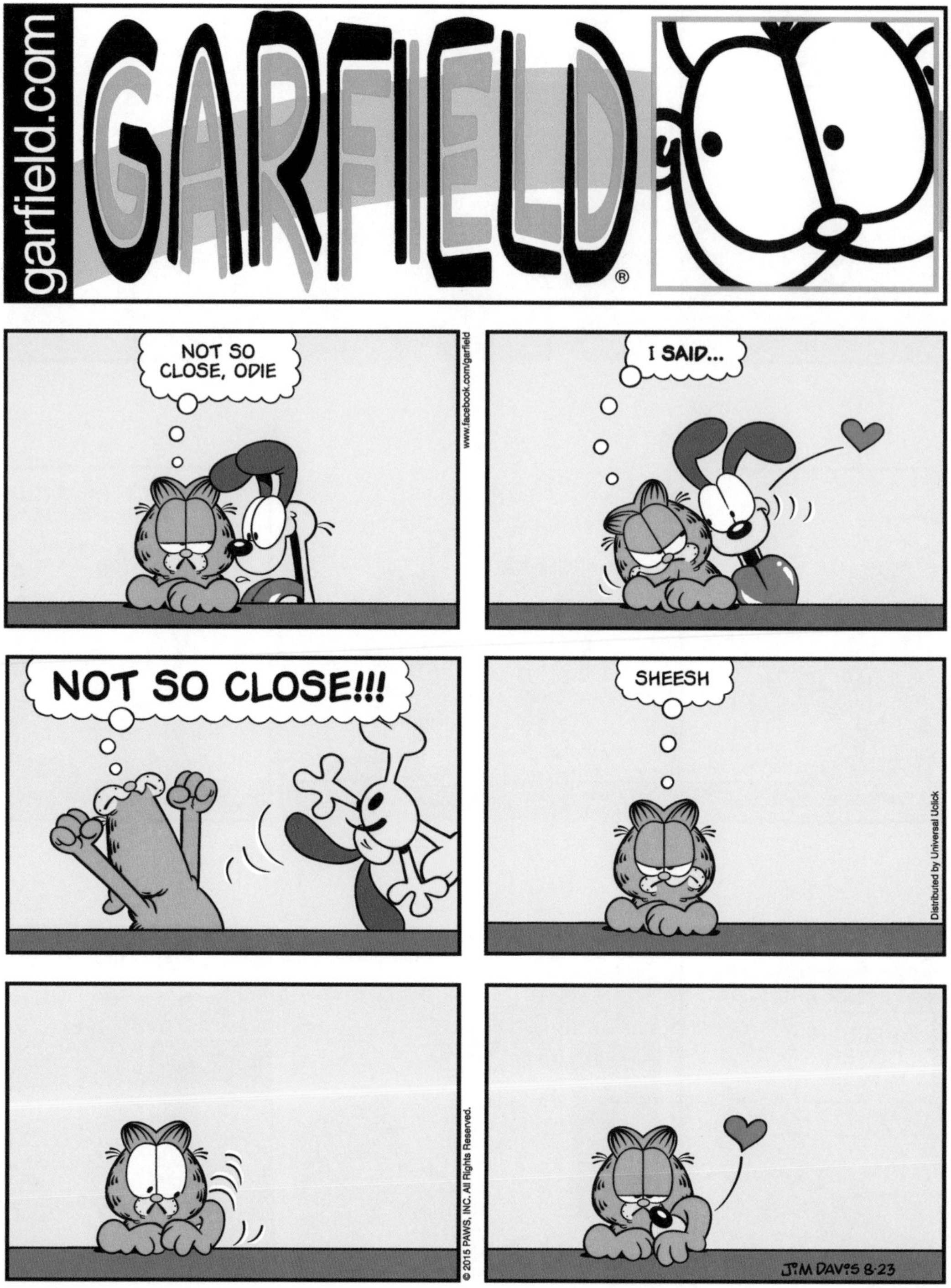
garfield.com
GARFIELD®
NOT SO CLOSE, ODIE
www.facebook.com/garfield
I SAID...
NOT SO CLOSE!!!
SHEESH
Distributed by Universal Uclick
© 2015 PAWS, INC. All Rights Reserved.
JIM DAVIS 8-23

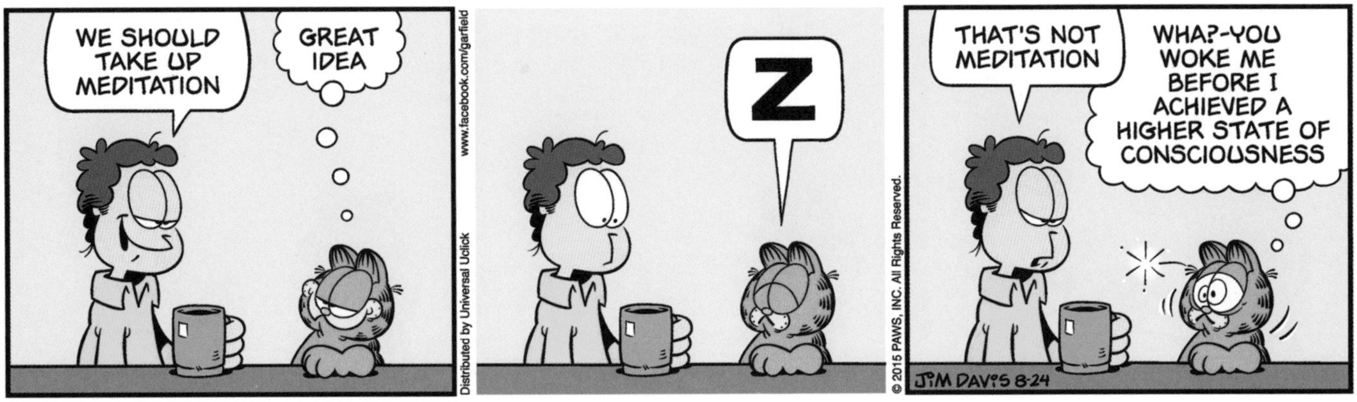
WE SHOULD TAKE UP MEDITATION
GREAT IDEA
Distributed by Universal Uclick www.facebook.com/garfield
Z
THAT'S NOT MEDITATION
WHA?-YOU WOKE ME BEFORE I ACHIEVED A HIGHER STATE OF CONSCIOUSNESS
© 2015 PAWS, INC. All Rights Reserved.
JIM DAVIS 8-24

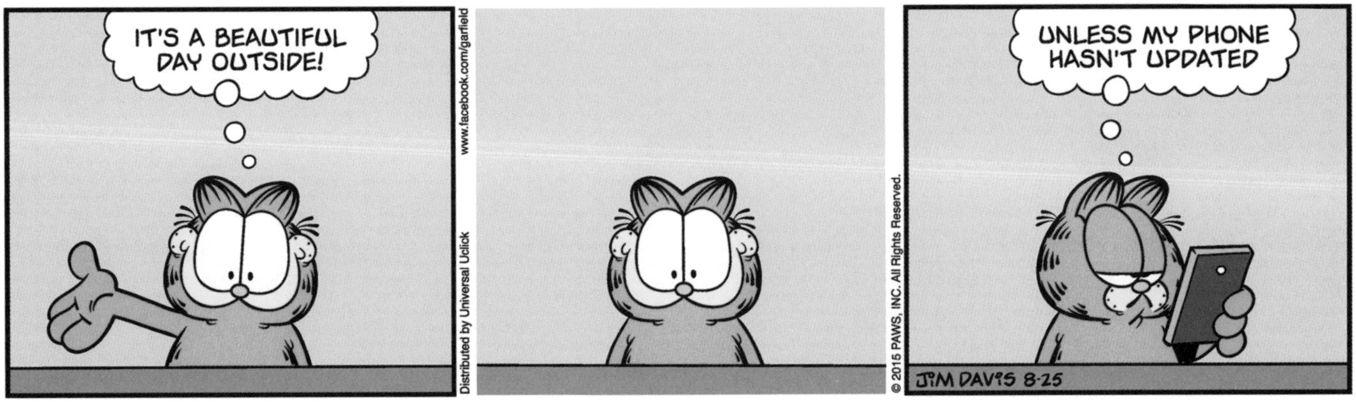
IT'S A BEAUTIFUL DAY OUTSIDE!
Distributed by Universal Uclick www.facebook.com/garfield
UNLESS MY PHONE HASN'T UPDATED
© 2015 PAWS, INC. All Rights Reserved.
JIM DAVIS 8-25

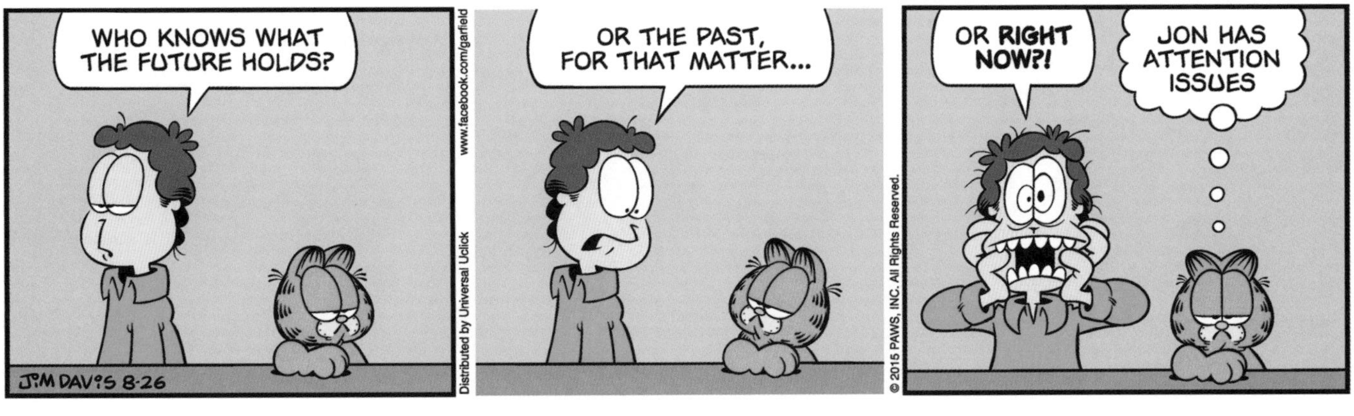
WHO KNOWS WHAT THE FUTURE HOLDS?
JIM DAVIS 8-26
Distributed by Universal Uclick www.facebook.com/garfield
OR THE PAST, FOR THAT MATTER...
OR **RIGHT NOW?!**
JON HAS ATTENTION ISSUES
© 2015 PAWS, INC. All Rights Reserved.

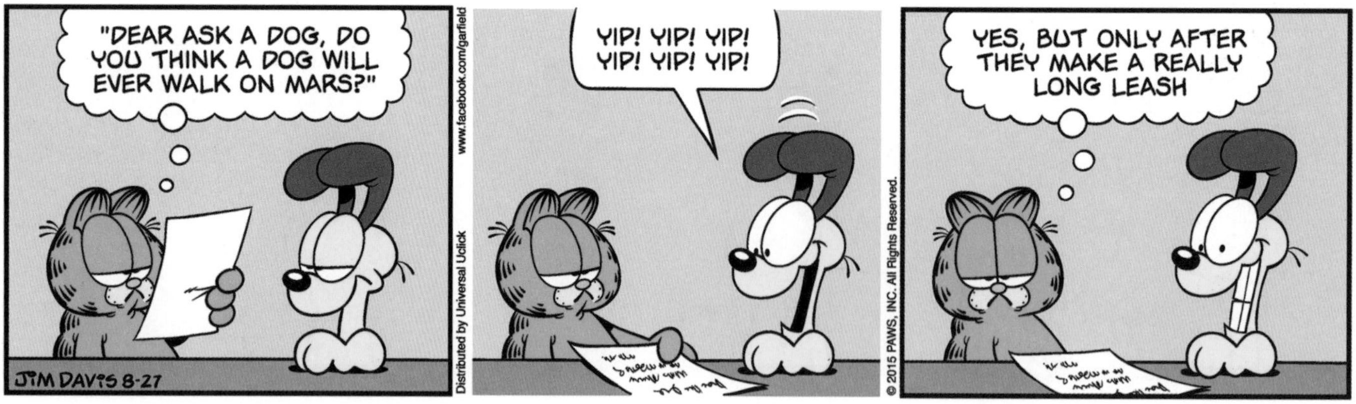
"DEAR ASK A DOG, DO YOU THINK A DOG WILL EVER WALK ON MARS?"
JIM DAVIS 8-27
Distributed by Universal Uclick www.facebook.com/garfield
YIP! YIP! YIP! YIP! YIP! YIP!
© 2015 PAWS, INC. All Rights Reserved.
YES, BUT ONLY AFTER THEY MAKE A REALLY LONG LEASH

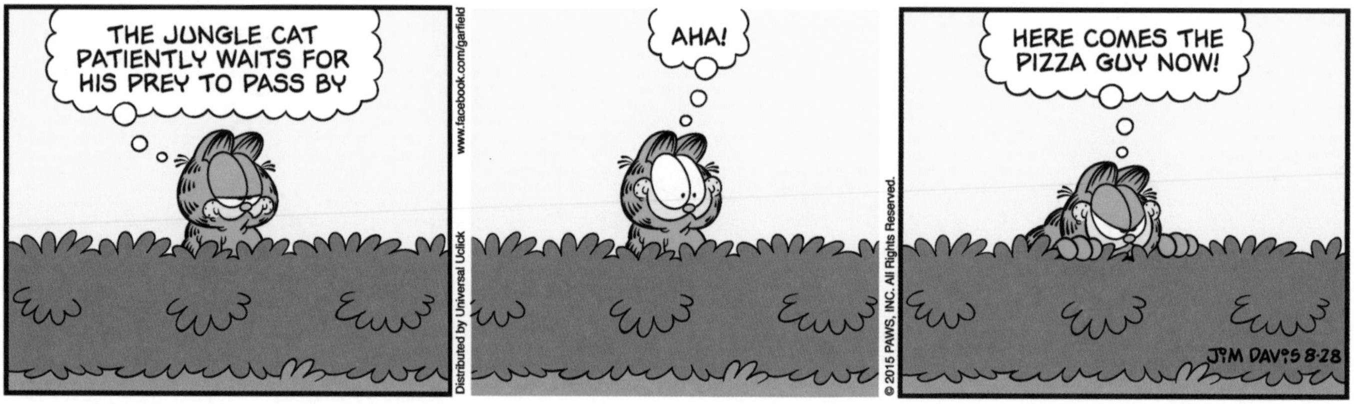
THE JUNGLE CAT PATIENTLY WAITS FOR HIS PREY TO PASS BY
Distributed by Universal Uclick www.facebook.com/garfield
AHA!
© 2015 PAWS, INC. All Rights Reserved.
HERE COMES THE PIZZA GUY NOW!
JIM DAVIS 8-28

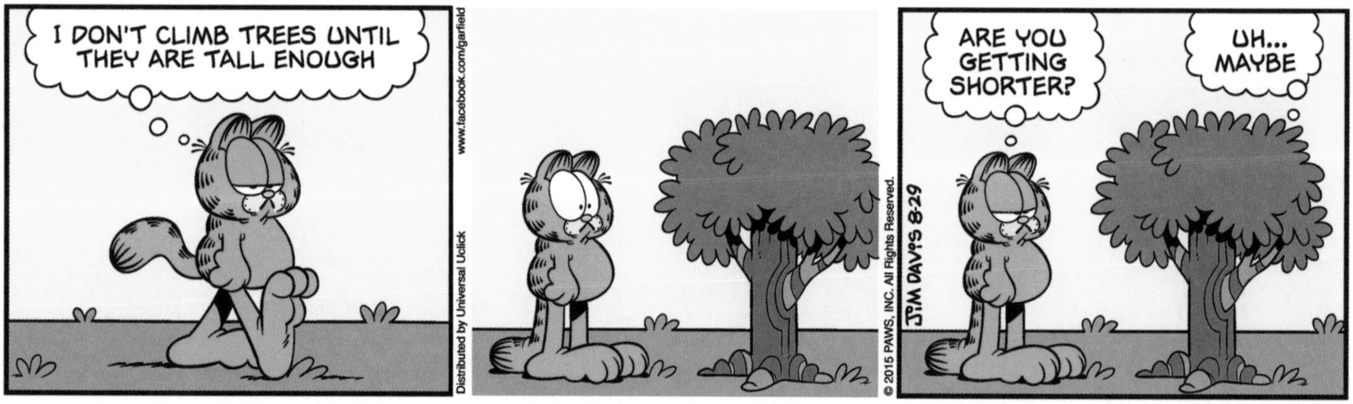
I DON'T CLIMB TREES UNTIL THEY ARE TALL ENOUGH
Distributed by Universal Uclick www.facebook.com/garfield
© 2015 PAWS, INC. All Rights Reserved.
JIM DAVIS 8-29
ARE YOU GETTING SHORTER?
UH... MAYBE

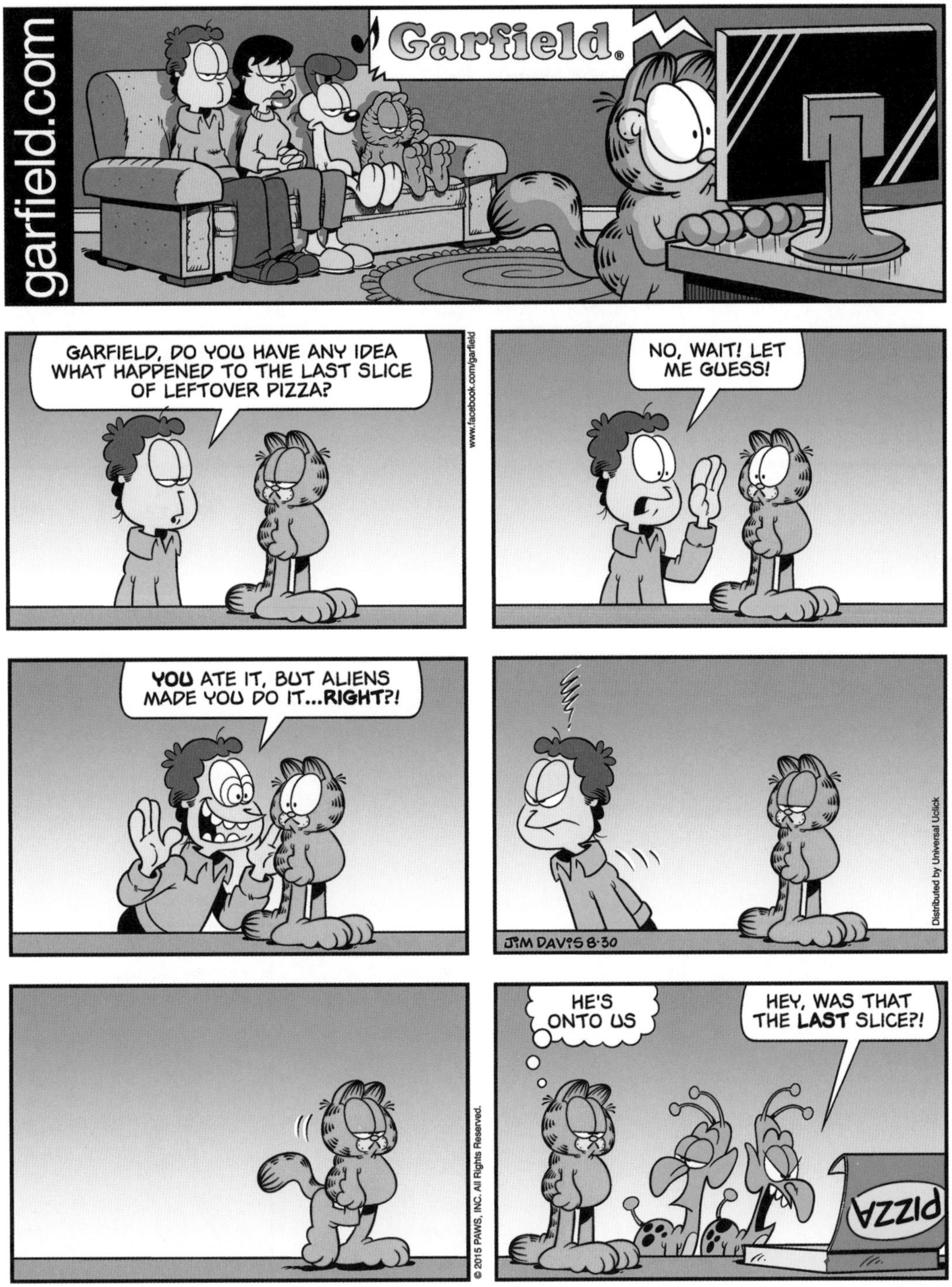
garfield.com
Garfield®
GARFIELD, DO YOU HAVE ANY IDEA WHAT HAPPENED TO THE LAST SLICE OF LEFTOVER PIZZA?
www.facebook.com/garfield
NO, WAIT! LET ME GUESS!
YOU ATE IT, BUT ALIENS MADE YOU DO IT...RIGHT?!
JIM DAVIS 8-30
Distributed by Universal Uclick
© 2015 PAWS, INC. All Rights Reserved.
HE'S ONTO US
HEY, WAS THAT THE LAST SLICE?!
PIZZA

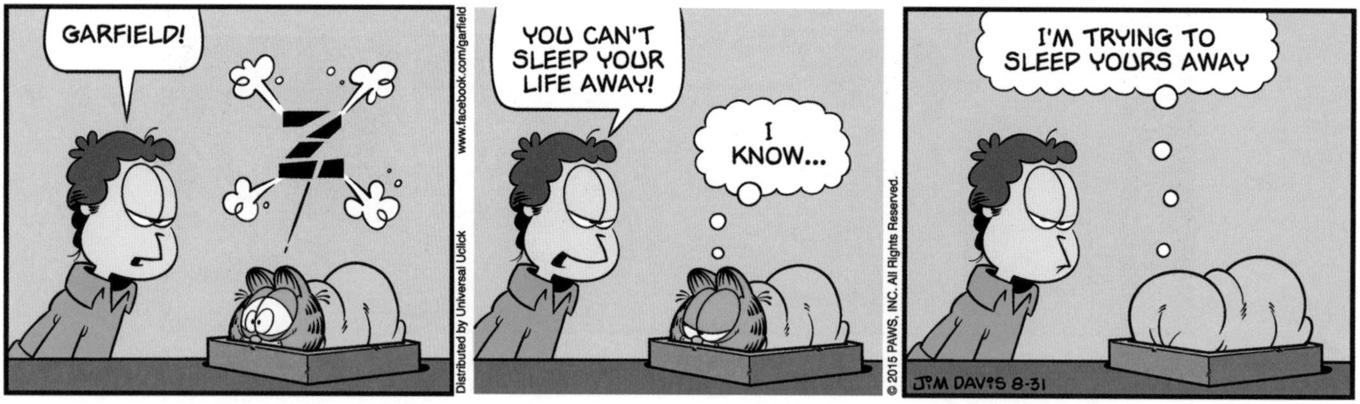
GARFIELD!
YOU CAN'T SLEEP YOUR LIFE AWAY!
I KNOW...
I'M TRYING TO SLEEP YOURS AWAY
JIM DAVIS 8-31
www.facebook.com/garfield
Distributed by Universal Uclick
© 2015 PAWS, INC. All Rights Reserved.

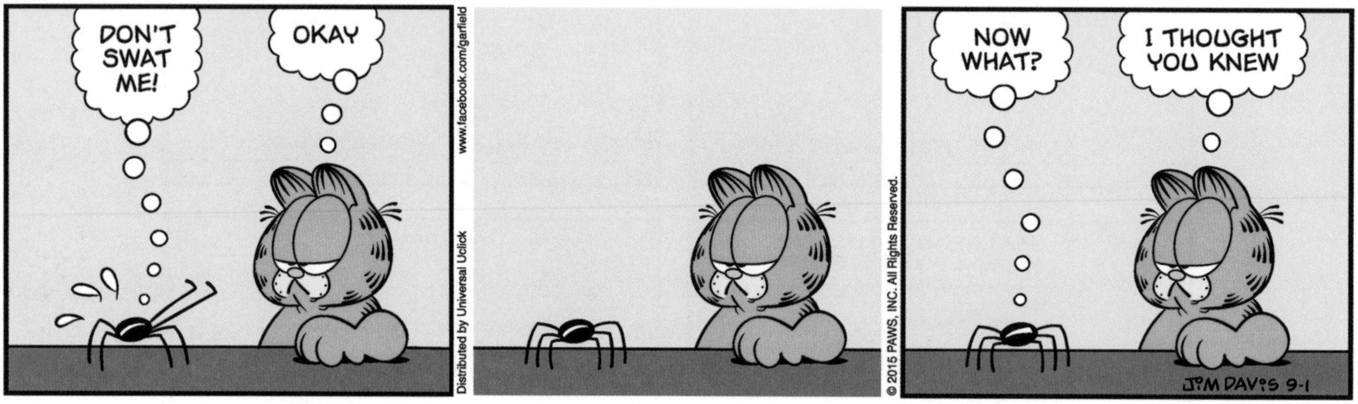
DON'T SWAT ME!
OKAY
NOW WHAT?
I THOUGHT YOU KNEW
JIM DAVIS 9-1
www.facebook.com/garfield
Distributed by Universal Uclick
© 2015 PAWS, INC. All Rights Reserved.

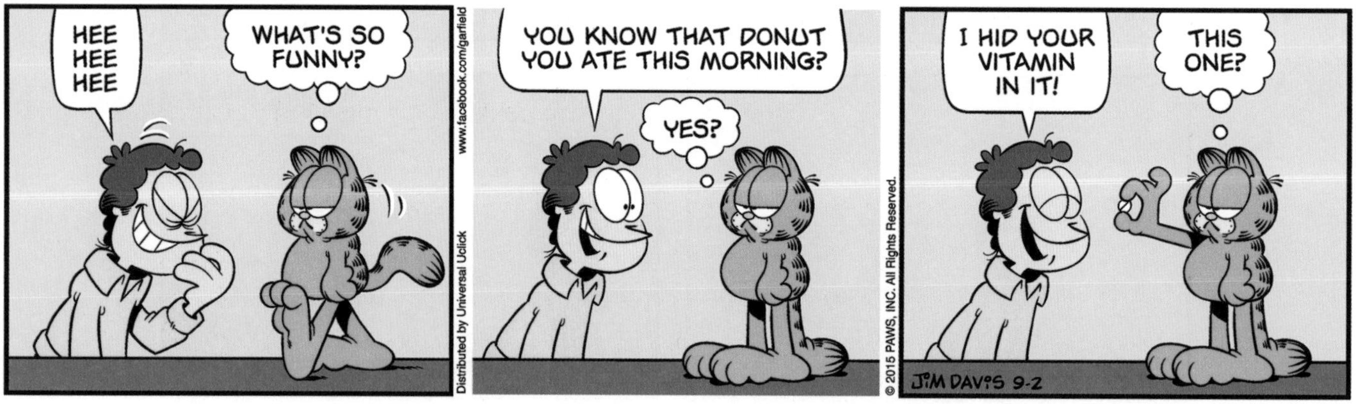
HEE HEE HEE
WHAT'S SO FUNNY?
YOU KNOW THAT DONUT YOU ATE THIS MORNING?
YES?
I HID YOUR VITAMIN IN IT!
THIS ONE?
JIM DAVIS 9-2
www.facebook.com/garfield
Distributed by Universal Uclick
© 2015 PAWS, INC. All Rights Reserved.

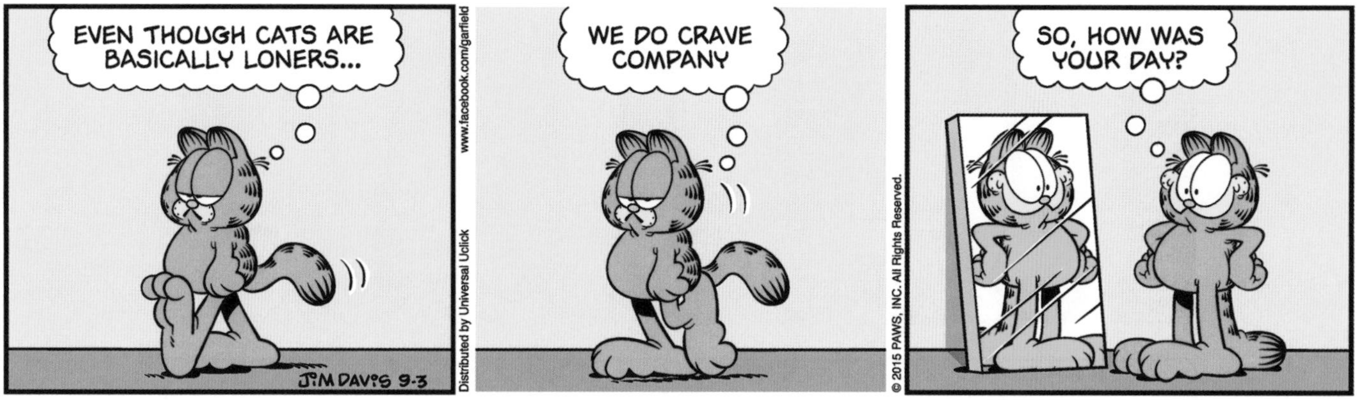
EVEN THOUGH CATS ARE BASICALLY LONERS...
JIM DAVIS 9-3
Distributed by Universal Uclick www.facebook.com/garfield
WE DO CRAVE COMPANY
© 2015 PAWS, INC. All Rights Reserved.
SO, HOW WAS YOUR DAY?

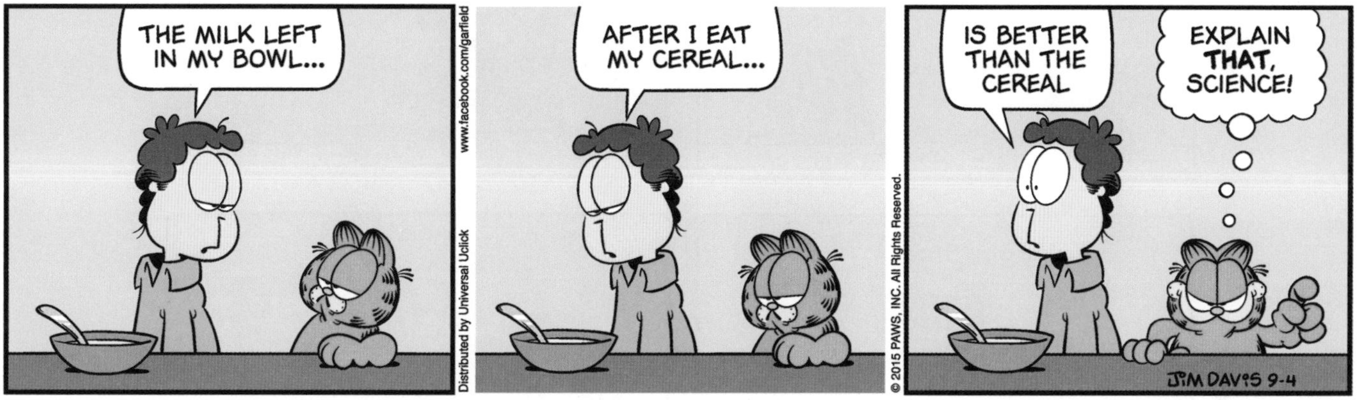
THE MILK LEFT IN MY BOWL...
Distributed by Universal Uclick www.facebook.com/garfield
AFTER I EAT MY CEREAL...
© 2015 PAWS, INC. All Rights Reserved.
IS BETTER THAN THE CEREAL
EXPLAIN **THAT**, SCIENCE!
JIM DAVIS 9-4

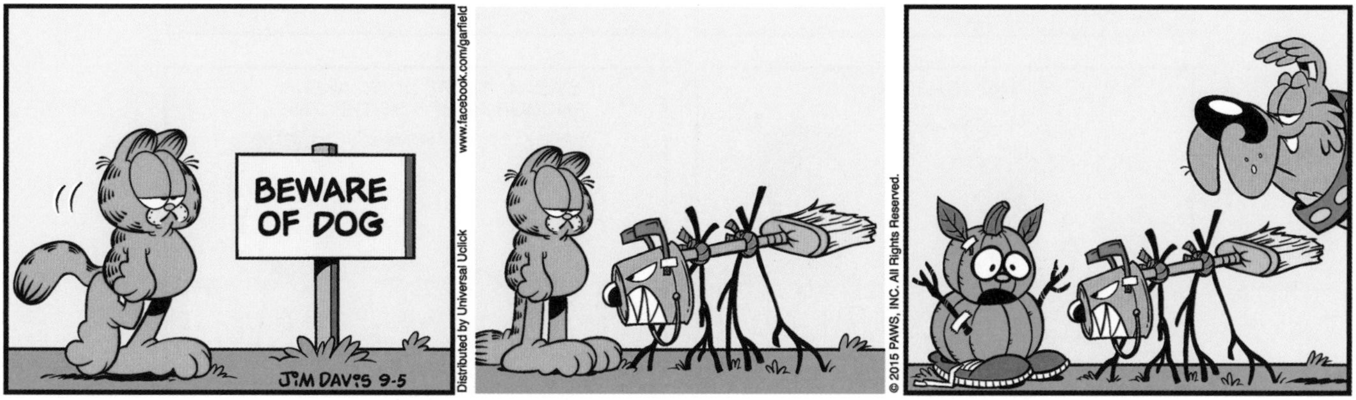
BEWARE OF DOG
JIM DAVIS 9-5
Distributed by Universal Uclick www.facebook.com/garfield
© 2015 PAWS, INC. All Rights Reserved.

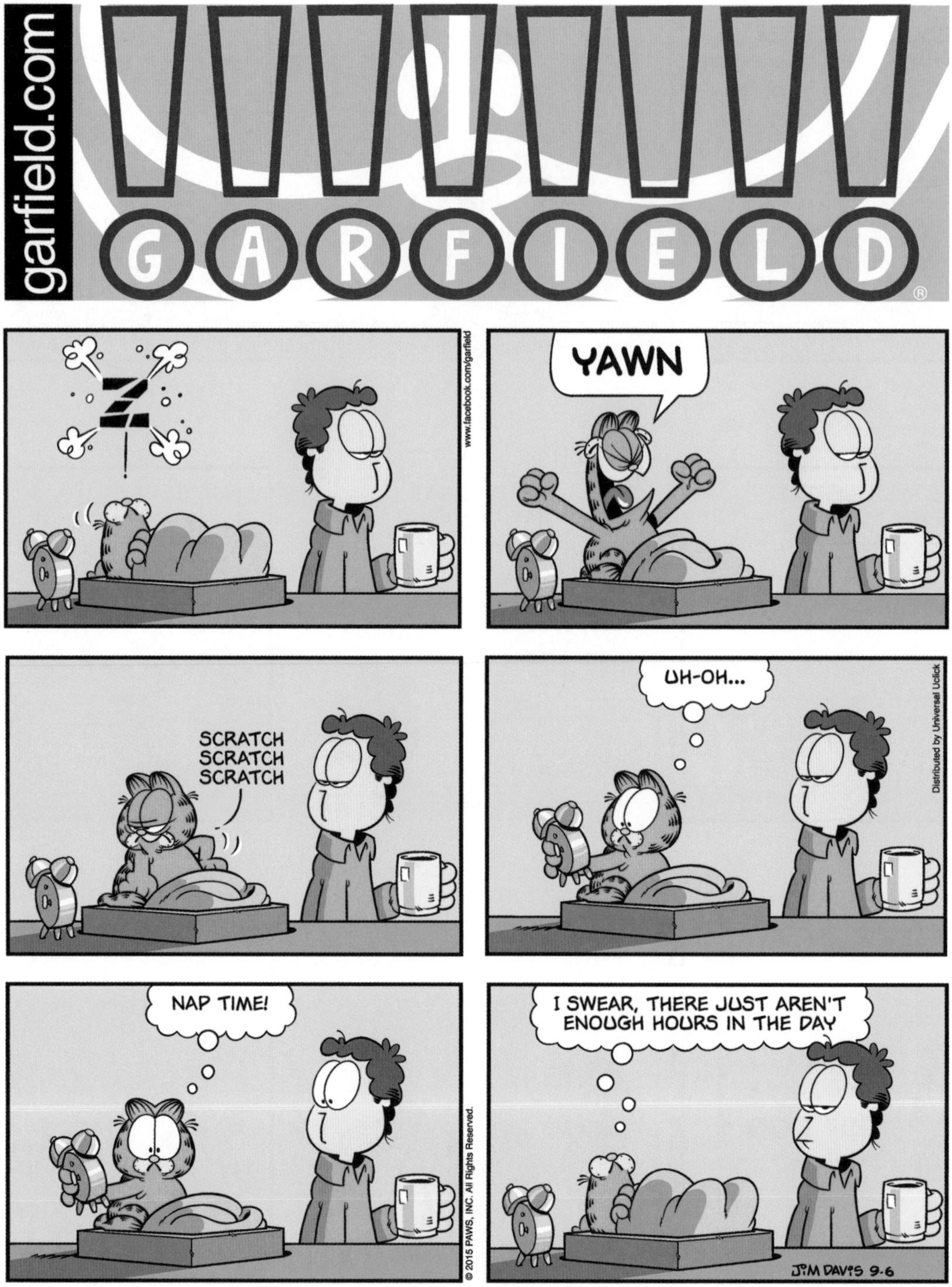
garfield.com
GARFIELD
www.facebook.com/garfield
Z
YAWN
SCRATCH
SCRATCH
SCRATCH
UH-OH...
Distributed by Universal Uclick
NAP TIME!
© 2015 PAWS, INC. All Rights Reserved.
I SWEAR, THERE JUST AREN'T ENOUGH HOURS IN THE DAY
JIM DAVIS 9-6

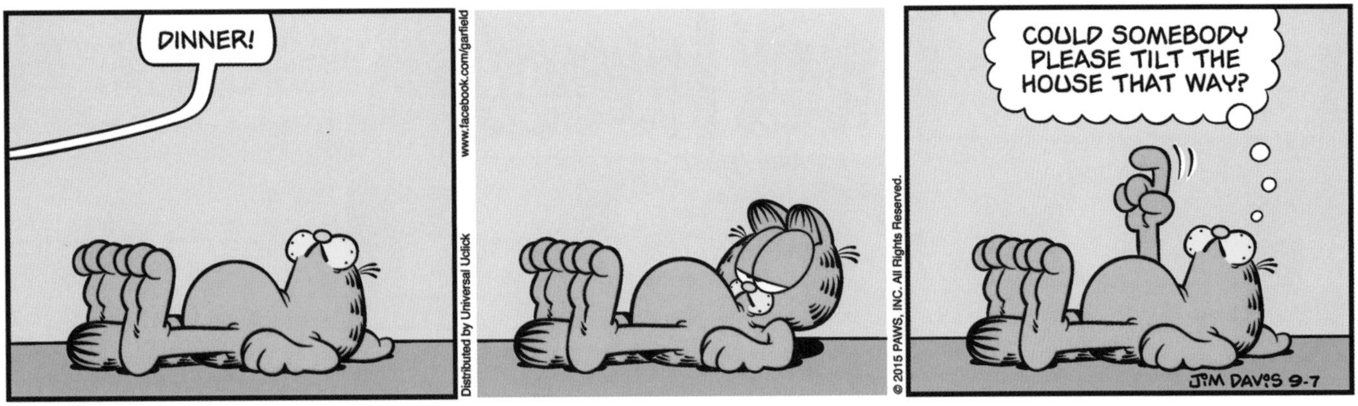
DINNER!
COULD SOMEBODY PLEASE TILT THE HOUSE THAT WAY?
JIM DAVIS 9-7
Distributed by Universal Uclick www.facebook.com/garfield
© 2015 PAWS, INC. All Rights Reserved.

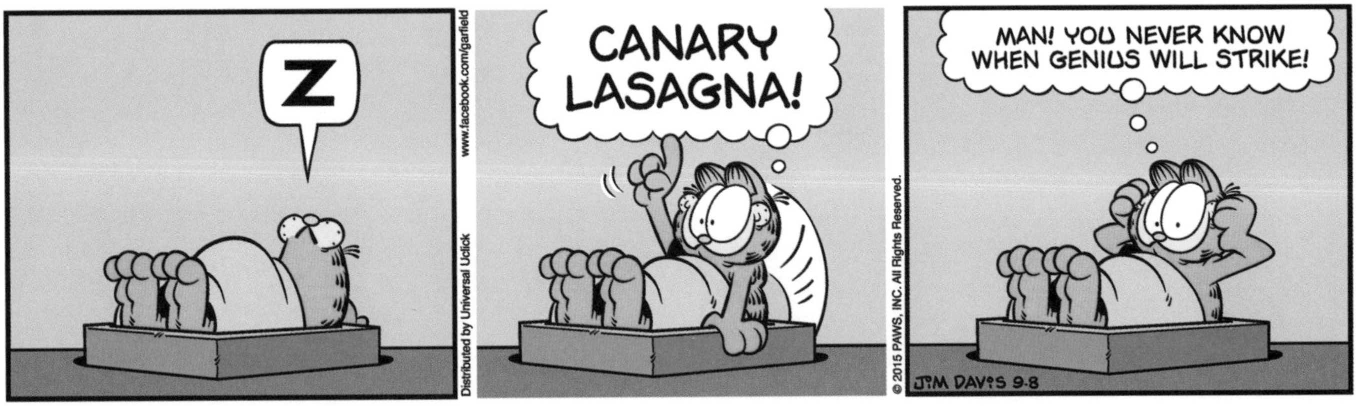
Z
CANARY LASAGNA!
MAN! YOU NEVER KNOW WHEN GENIUS WILL STRIKE!
JIM DAVIS 9-8
Distributed by Universal Uclick www.facebook.com/garfield
© 2015 PAWS, INC. All Rights Reserved.

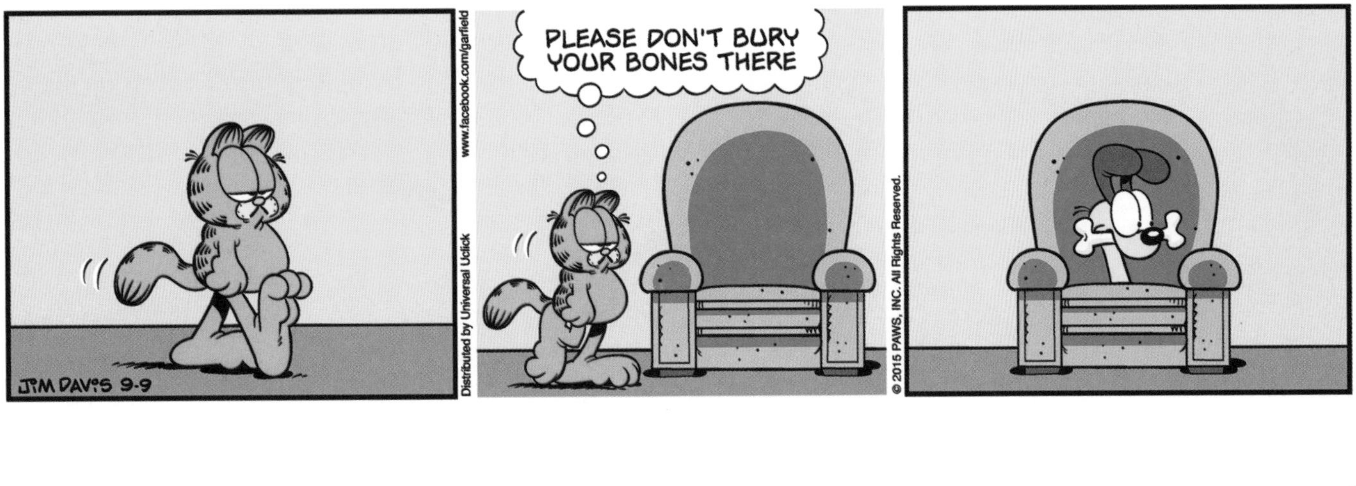
JIM DAVIS 9-9
PLEASE DON'T BURY YOUR BONES THERE
Distributed by Universal Uclick www.facebook.com/garfield
© 2015 PAWS, INC. All Rights Reserved.

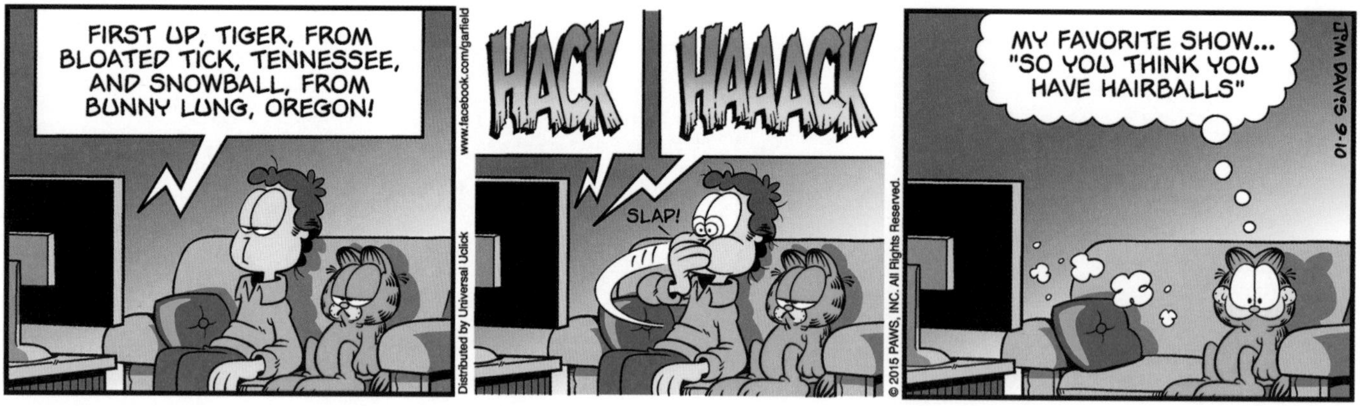
FIRST UP, TIGER, FROM BLOATED TICK, TENNESSEE, AND SNOWBALL, FROM BUNNY LUNG, OREGON!
www.facebook.com/garfield
Distributed by Universal Uclick
HACK
HAAACK
SLAP!
© 2015 PAWS, INC. All Rights Reserved.
MY FAVORITE SHOW... "SO YOU THINK YOU HAVE HAIRBALLS"
JIM DAVIS 9-10

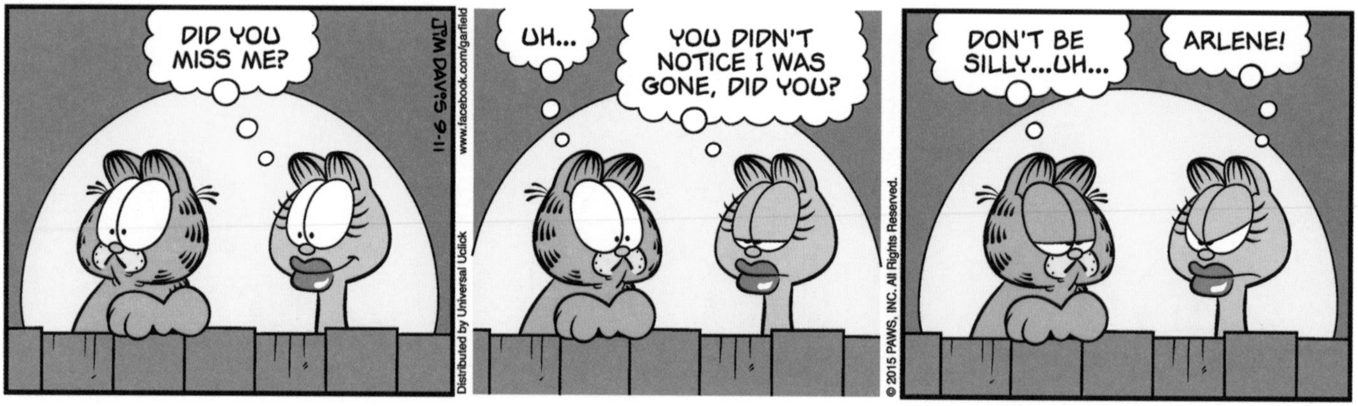
DID YOU MISS ME?
JIM DAVIS 9-11
www.facebook.com/garfield
Distributed by Universal Uclick
UH...
YOU DIDN'T NOTICE I WAS GONE, DID YOU?
© 2015 PAWS, INC. All Rights Reserved.
DON'T BE SILLY...UH...
ARLENE!

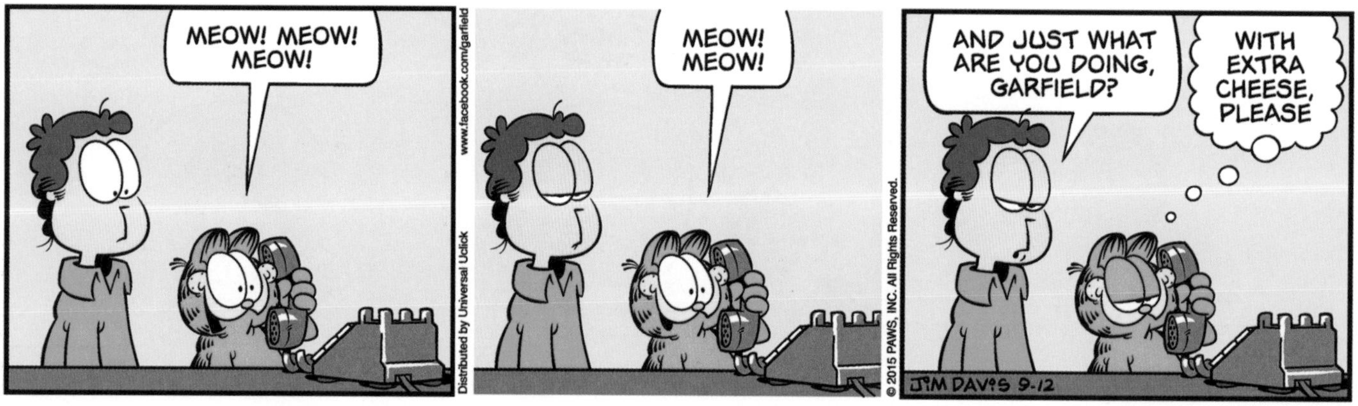
MEOW! MEOW! MEOW!
www.facebook.com/garfield
Distributed by Universal Uclick
MEOW! MEOW!
© 2015 PAWS, INC. All Rights Reserved.
AND JUST WHAT ARE YOU DOING, GARFIELD?
WITH EXTRA CHEESE, PLEASE
JIM DAVIS 9-12

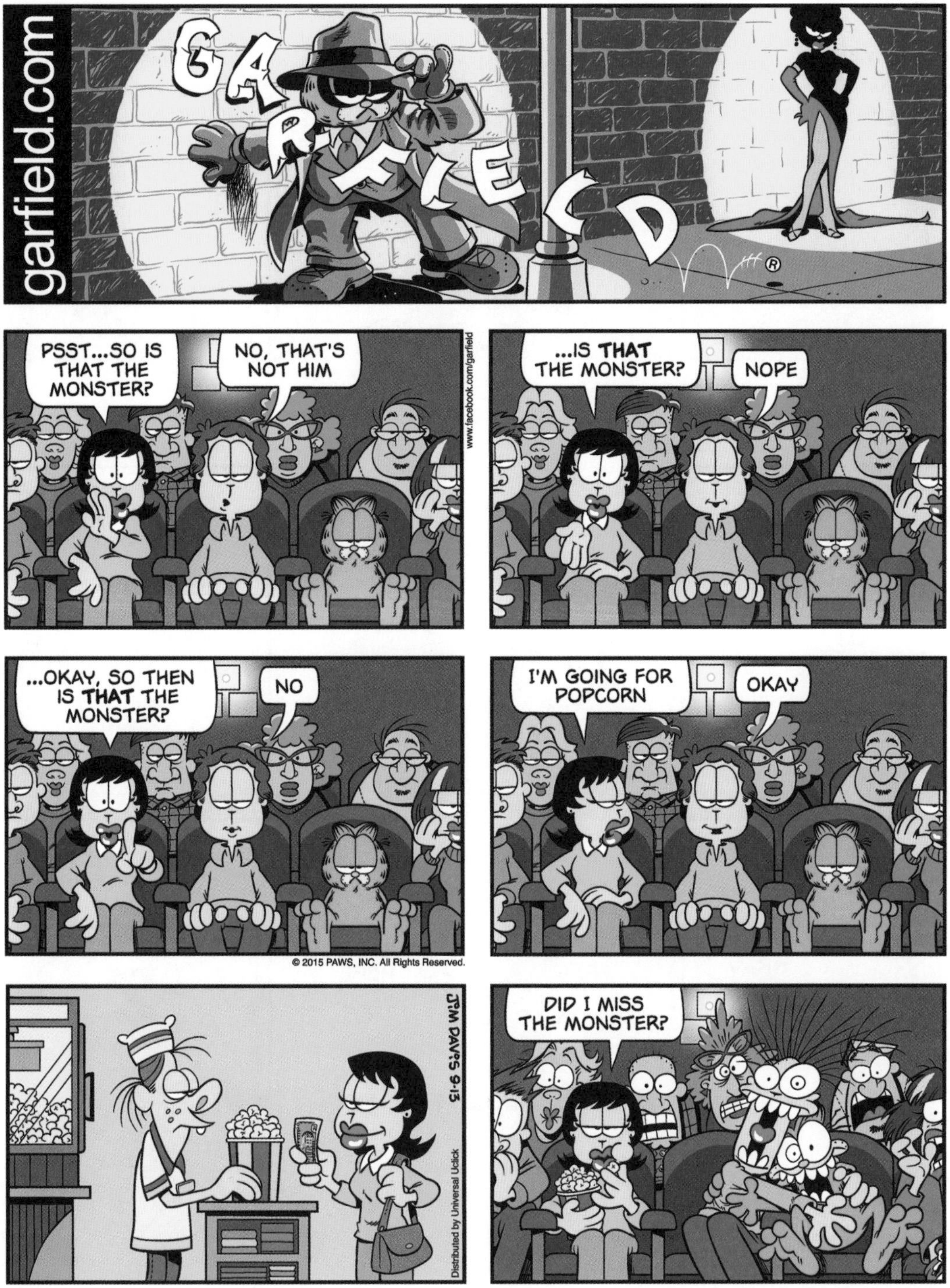
garfield.com
GARFIELD
www.facebook.com/garfield
PSST...SO IS THAT THE MONSTER?
NO, THAT'S NOT HIM
...IS THAT THE MONSTER?
NOPE
...OKAY, SO THEN IS THAT THE MONSTER?
NO
I'M GOING FOR POPCORN
OKAY
© 2015 PAWS, INC. All Rights Reserved.
JPM DAVPS 9-13
Distributed by Universal Uclick
DID I MISS THE MONSTER?

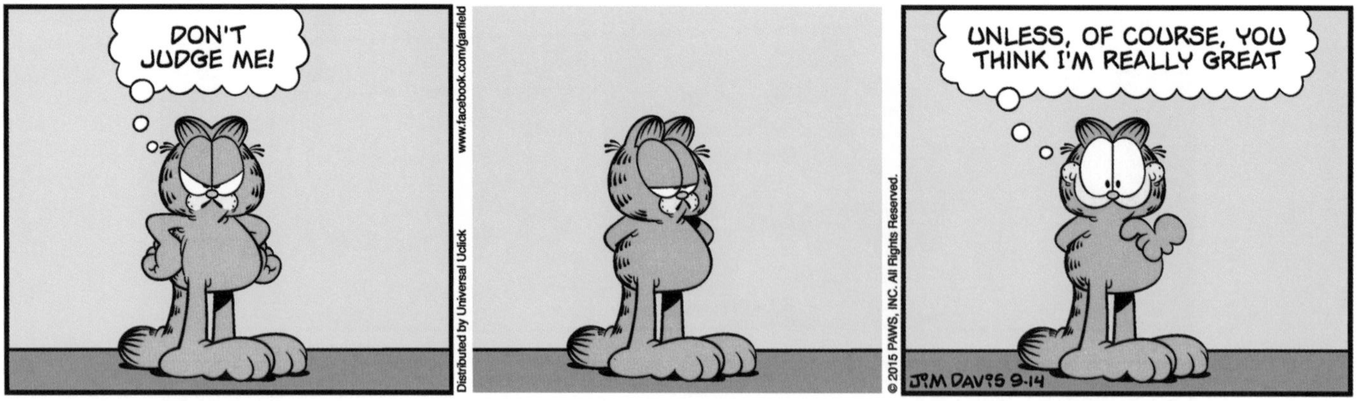
DON'T JUDGE ME!
Distributed by Universal Uclick www.facebook.com/garfield
UNLESS, OF COURSE, YOU THINK I'M REALLY GREAT
© 2015 PAWS, INC. All Rights Reserved.
JIM DAVIS 9-14

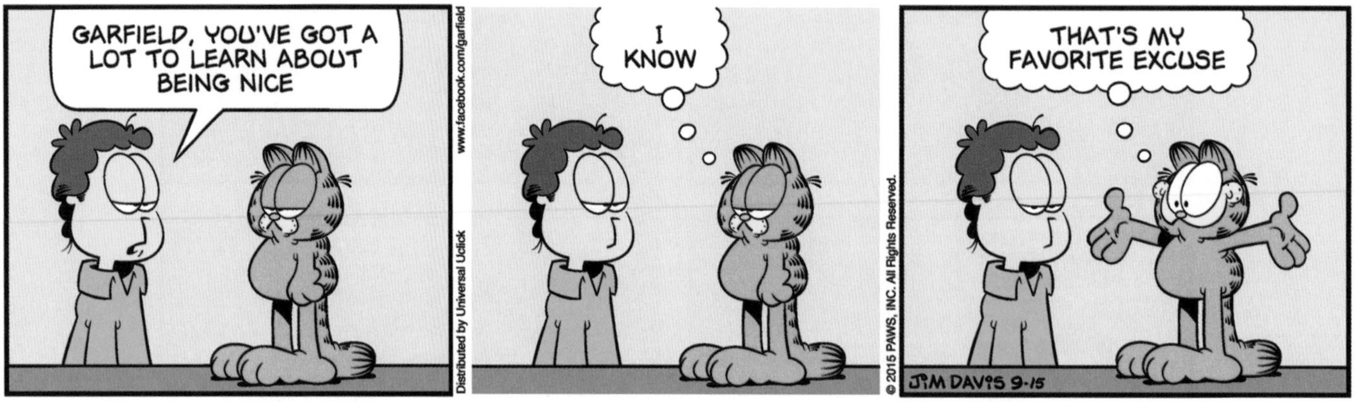
GARFIELD, YOU'VE GOT A LOT TO LEARN ABOUT BEING NICE
Distributed by Universal Uclick www.facebook.com/garfield
I KNOW
THAT'S MY FAVORITE EXCUSE
© 2015 PAWS, INC. All Rights Reserved.
JIM DAVIS 9-15

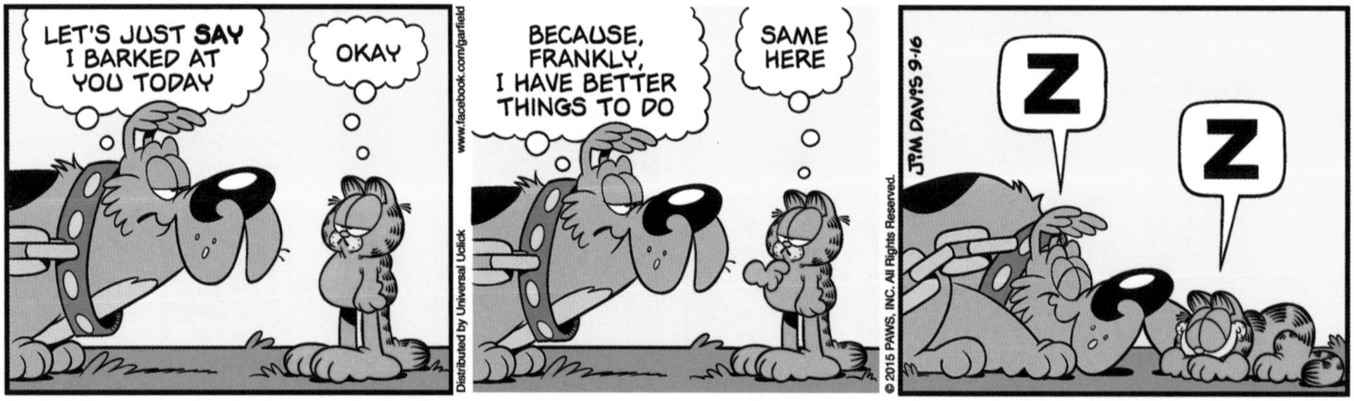
LET'S JUST SAY I BARKED AT YOU TODAY
OKAY
Distributed by Universal Uclick www.facebook.com/garfield
BECAUSE, FRANKLY, I HAVE BETTER THINGS TO DO
SAME HERE
© 2015 PAWS, INC. All Rights Reserved.
JIM DAVIS 9-16
Z
Z

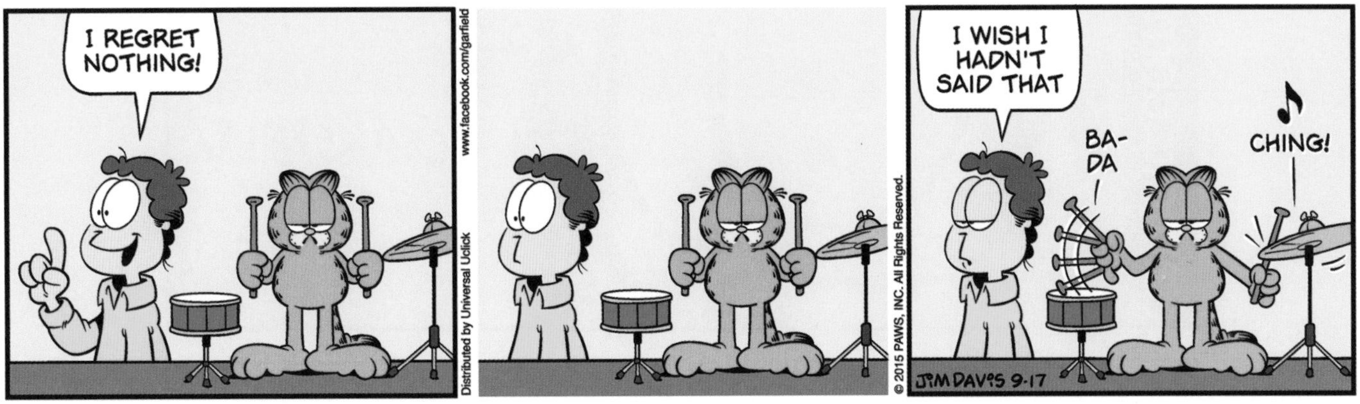
I REGRET NOTHING!
Distributed by Universal Uclick www.facebook.com/garfield
© 2015 PAWS, INC. All Rights Reserved.
I WISH I HADN'T SAID THAT
BA-DA
CHING!
JIM DAVIS 9-17

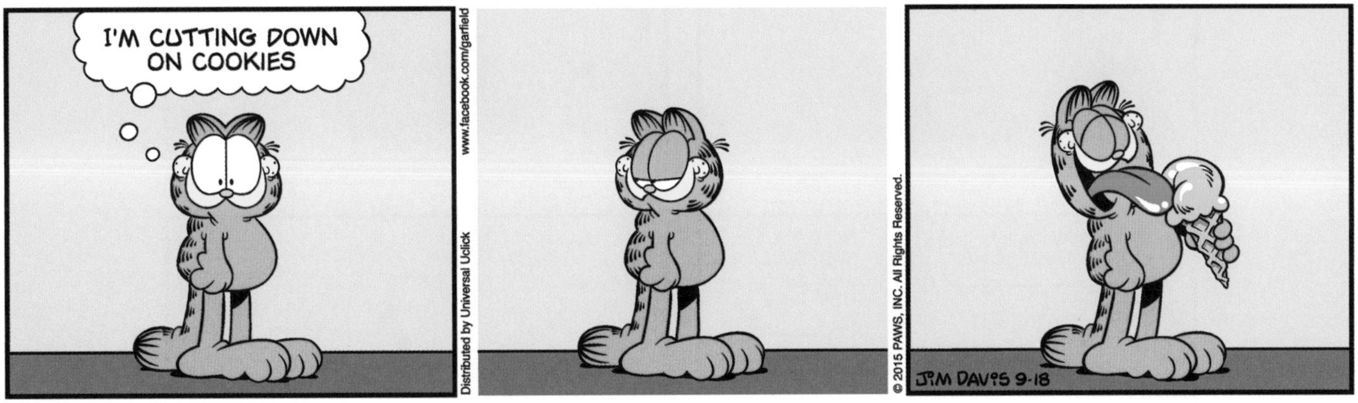
I'M CUTTING DOWN ON COOKIES
Distributed by Universal Uclick www.facebook.com/garfield
© 2015 PAWS, INC. All Rights Reserved.
JIM DAVIS 9-18

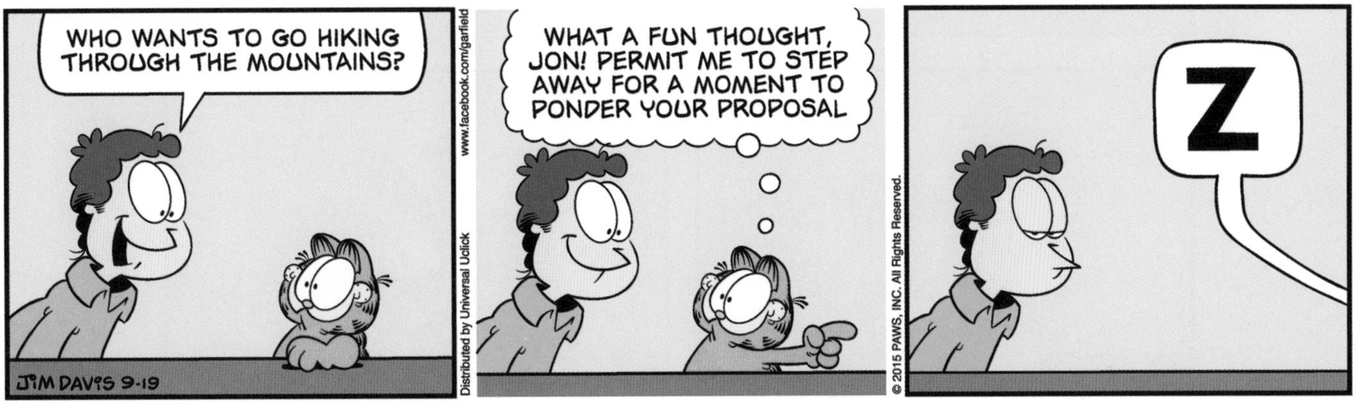
WHO WANTS TO GO HIKING THROUGH THE MOUNTAINS?
JIM DAVIS 9-19
Distributed by Universal Uclick www.facebook.com/garfield
WHAT A FUN THOUGHT, JON! PERMIT ME TO STEP AWAY FOR A MOMENT TO PONDER YOUR PROPOSAL
© 2015 PAWS, INC. All Rights Reserved.
Z

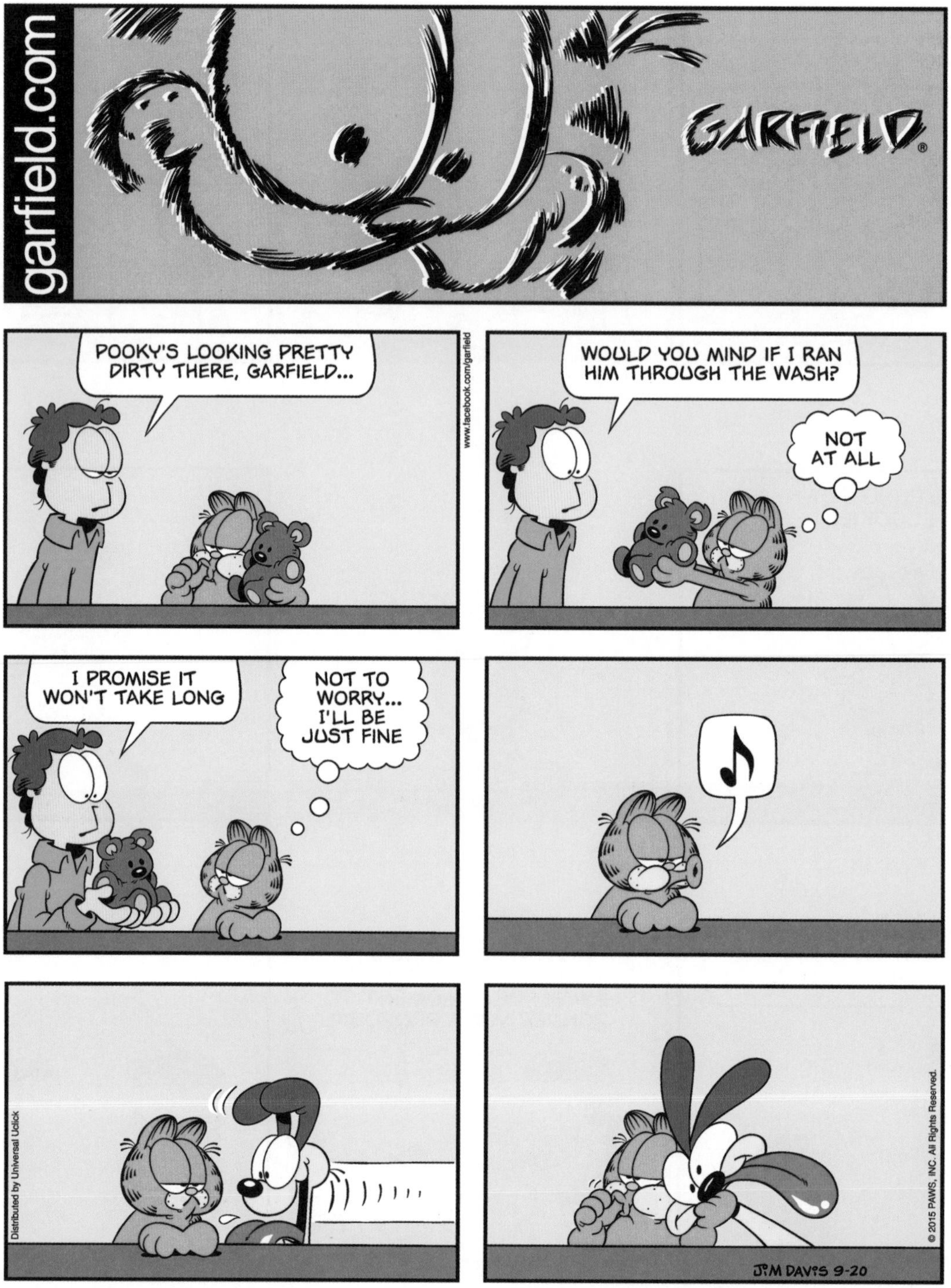

garfield.com
GARFIELD®
POOKY'S LOOKING PRETTY DIRTY THERE, GARFIELD...
www.facebook.com/garfield
WOULD YOU MIND IF I RAN HIM THROUGH THE WASH?
NOT AT ALL
I PROMISE IT WON'T TAKE LONG
NOT TO WORRY... I'LL BE JUST FINE
♪
Distributed by Universal Uclick
© 2015 PAWS, INC. All Rights Reserved.
JIM DAVIS 9-20

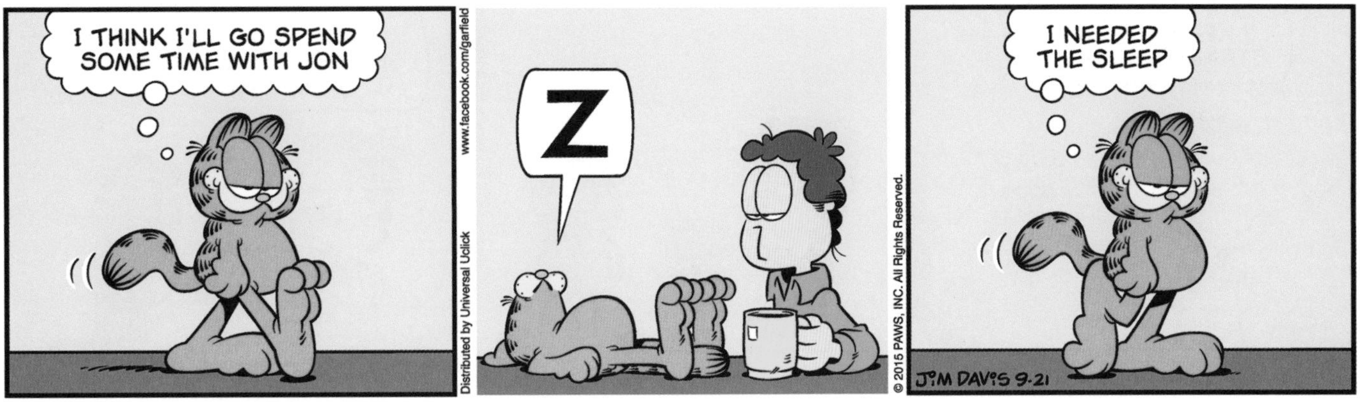
I THINK I'LL GO SPEND SOME TIME WITH JON
www.facebook.com/garfield
Distributed by Universal Uclick
Z
© 2015 PAWS, INC. All Rights Reserved.
I NEEDED THE SLEEP
JIM DAVIS 9-21

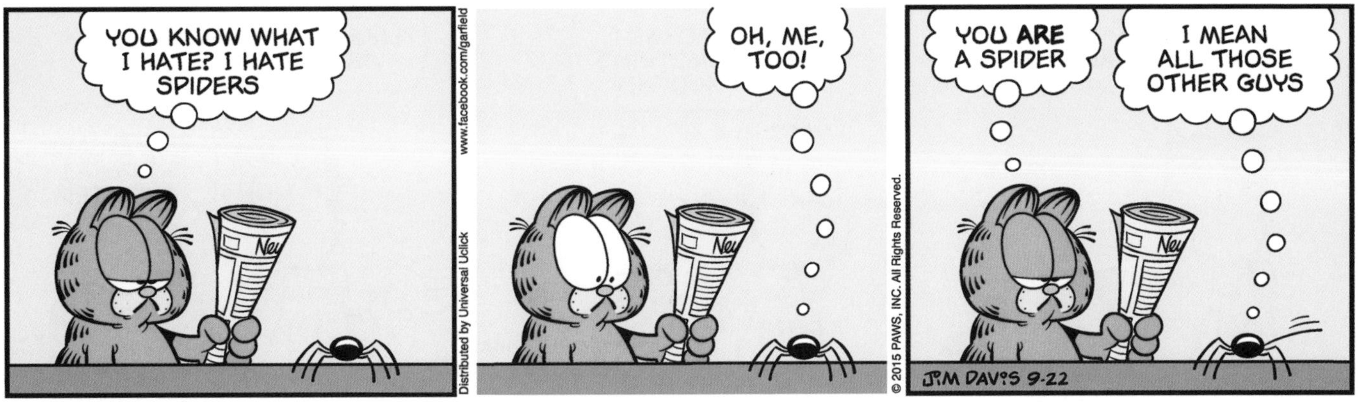
YOU KNOW WHAT I HATE? I HATE SPIDERS
www.facebook.com/garfield
Distributed by Universal Uclick
OH, ME, TOO!
© 2015 PAWS, INC. All Rights Reserved.
YOU **ARE** A SPIDER
I MEAN ALL THOSE OTHER GUYS
JIM DAVIS 9-22

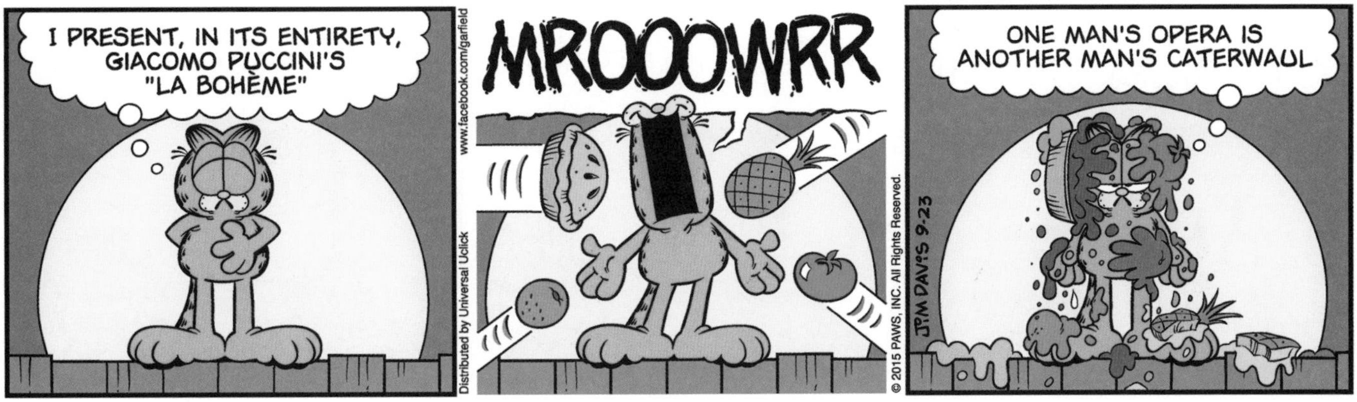
I PRESENT, IN ITS ENTIRETY, GIACOMO PUCCINI'S "LA BOHÈME"
www.facebook.com/garfield
Distributed by Universal Uclick
MROOOWRR
© 2015 PAWS, INC. All Rights Reserved.
JIM DAVIS 9-23
ONE MAN'S OPERA IS ANOTHER MAN'S CATERWAUL

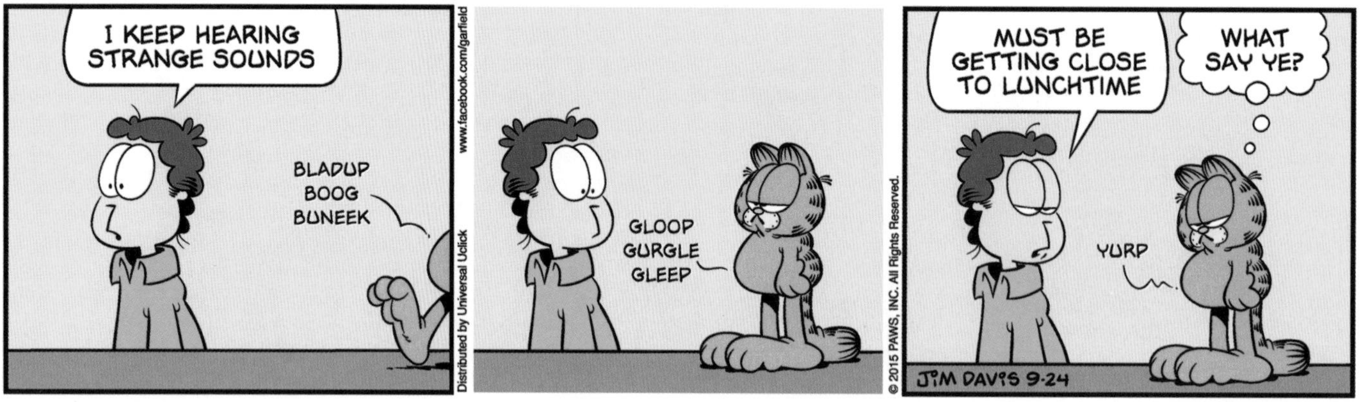
I KEEP HEARING STRANGE SOUNDS
BLADUP BOOG BUNEEK
www.facebook.com/garfield
Distributed by Universal Uclick
GLOOP GURGLE GLEEP
© 2015 PAWS, INC. All Rights Reserved.
MUST BE GETTING CLOSE TO LUNCHTIME
WHAT SAY YE?
YURP
JIM DAVIS 9-24

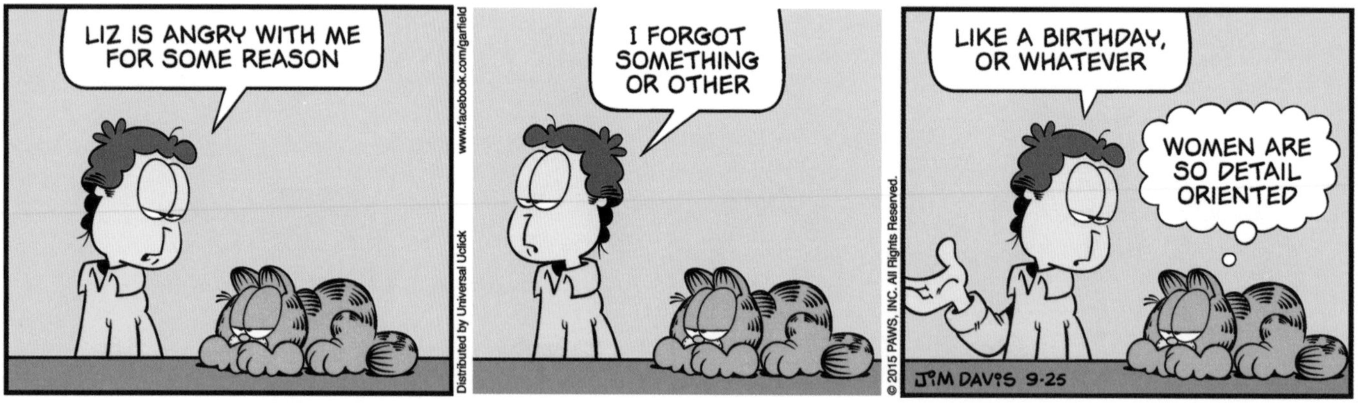
LIZ IS ANGRY WITH ME FOR SOME REASON
www.facebook.com/garfield
Distributed by Universal Uclick
I FORGOT SOMETHING OR OTHER
© 2015 PAWS, INC. All Rights Reserved.
LIKE A BIRTHDAY, OR WHATEVER
WOMEN ARE SO DETAIL ORIENTED
JIM DAVIS 9-25

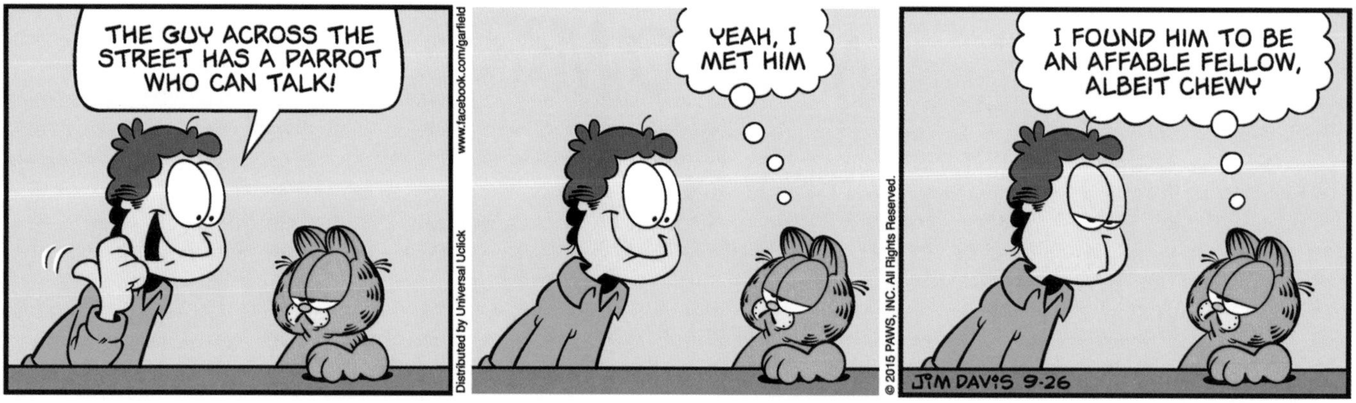
THE GUY ACROSS THE STREET HAS A PARROT WHO CAN TALK!
www.facebook.com/garfield
Distributed by Universal Uclick
YEAH, I MET HIM
© 2015 PAWS, INC. All Rights Reserved.
I FOUND HIM TO BE AN AFFABLE FELLOW, ALBEIT CHEWY
JIM DAVIS 9-26

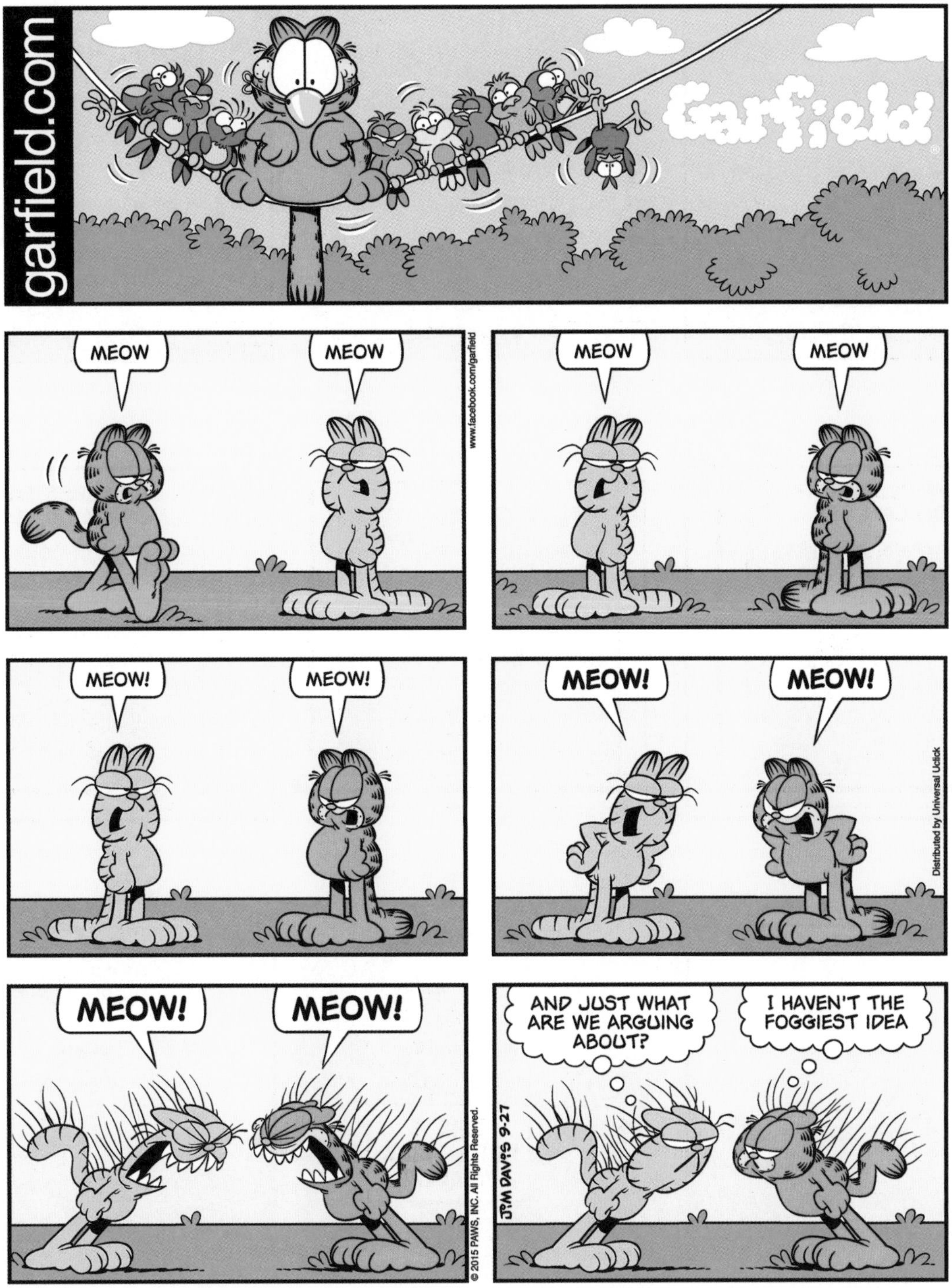
garfield.com
Garfield
www.facebook.com/garfield
MEOW
MEOW
MEOW
MEOW
MEOW!
MEOW!
MEOW!
MEOW!
Distributed by Universal Uclick
MEOW!
MEOW!
© 2015 PAWS, INC. All Rights Reserved.
JPM DAVIS 9-27
AND JUST WHAT ARE WE ARGUING ABOUT?
I HAVEN'T THE FOGGIEST IDEA

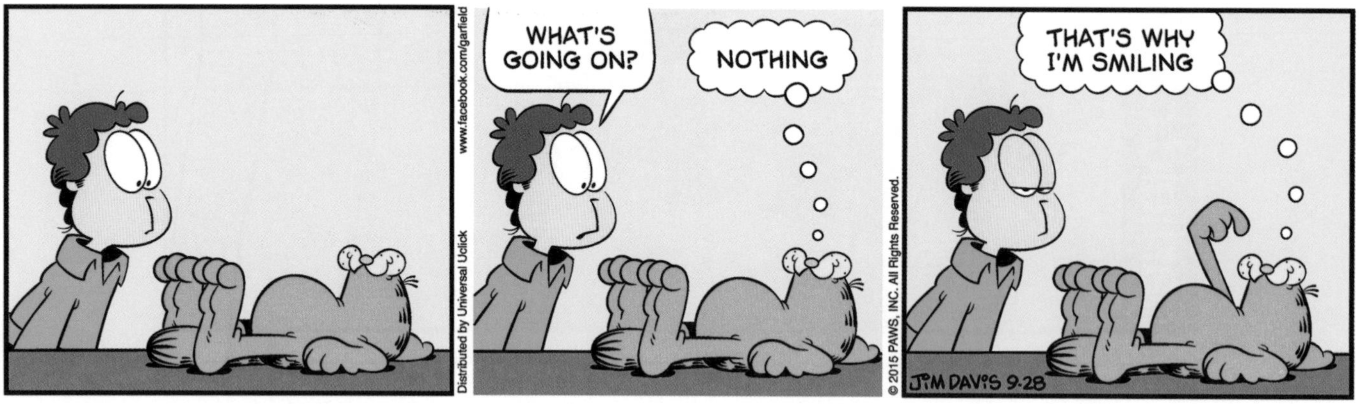
www.facebook.com/garfield
Distributed by Universal Uclick
WHAT'S GOING ON?
NOTHING
© 2015 PAWS, INC. All Rights Reserved.
THAT'S WHY I'M SMILING
JIM DAVIS 9-28

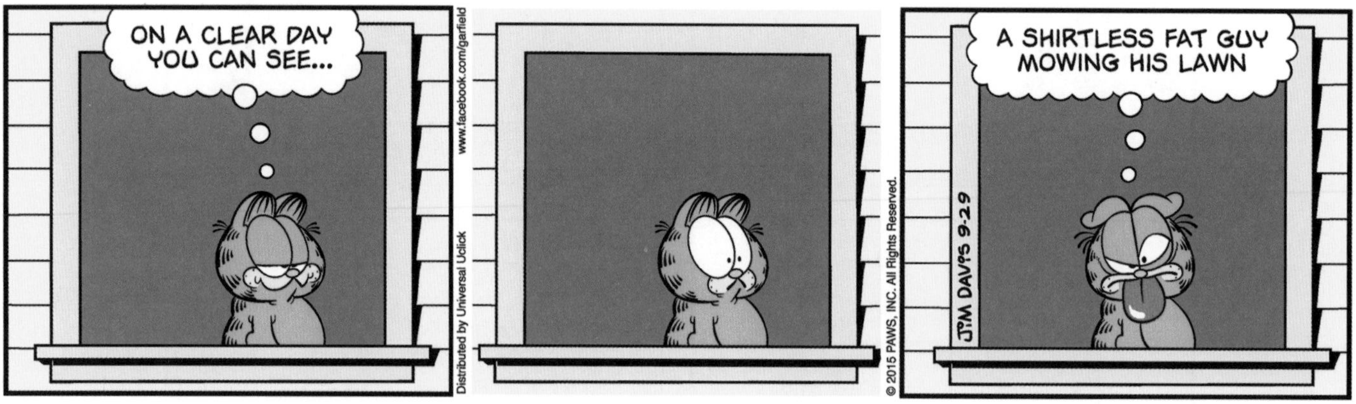
ON A CLEAR DAY YOU CAN SEE...
www.facebook.com/garfield
Distributed by Universal Uclick
© 2015 PAWS, INC. All Rights Reserved.
A SHIRTLESS FAT GUY MOWING HIS LAWN
JIM DAVIS 9-29

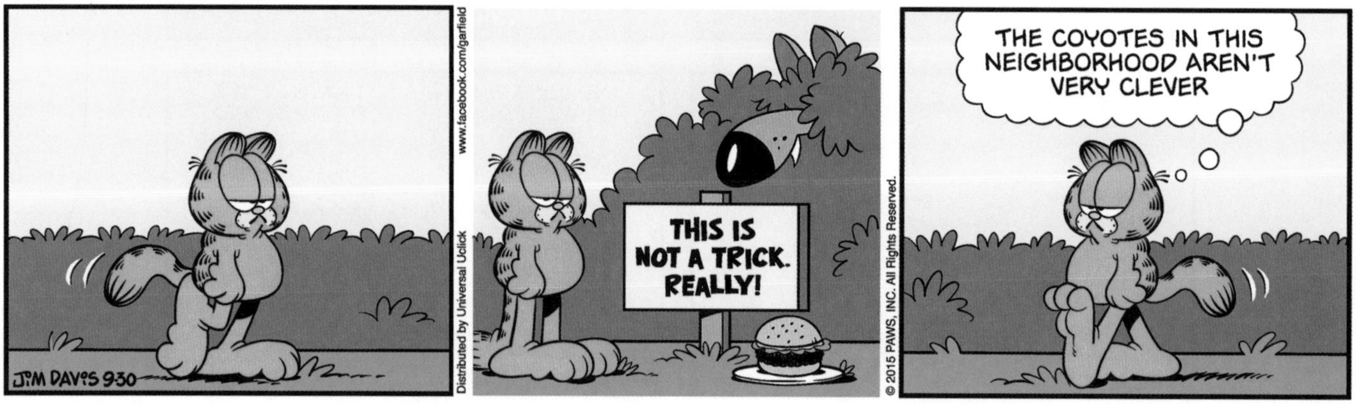
JIM DAVIS 9-30
www.facebook.com/garfield
Distributed by Universal Uclick
THIS IS NOT A TRICK. REALLY!
© 2015 PAWS, INC. All Rights Reserved.
THE COYOTES IN THIS NEIGHBORHOOD AREN'T VERY CLEVER

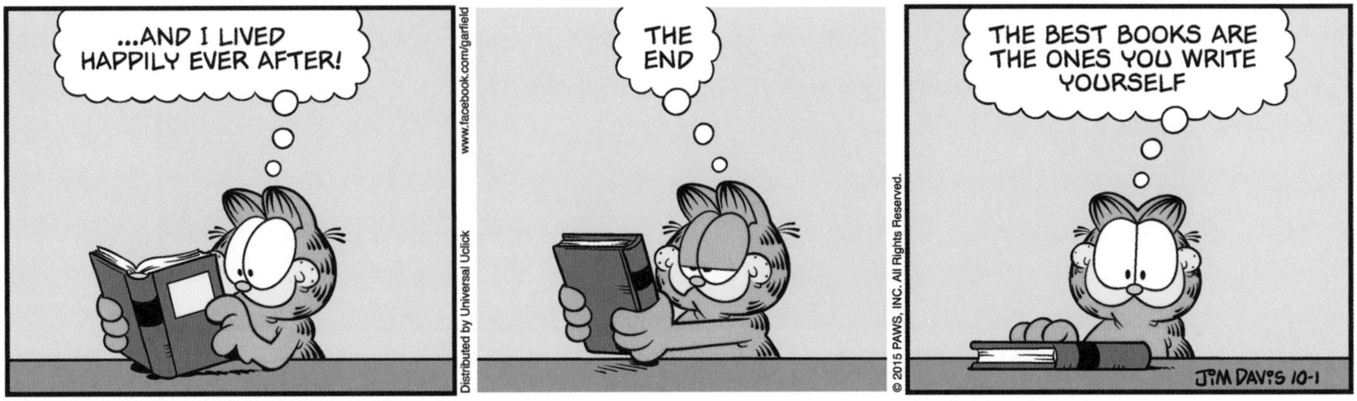
...AND I LIVED HAPPILY EVER AFTER!
THE END
THE BEST BOOKS ARE THE ONES YOU WRITE YOURSELF
JIM DAVIS 10-1
Distributed by Universal Uclick www.facebook.com/garfield
© 2015 PAWS, INC. All Rights Reserved.

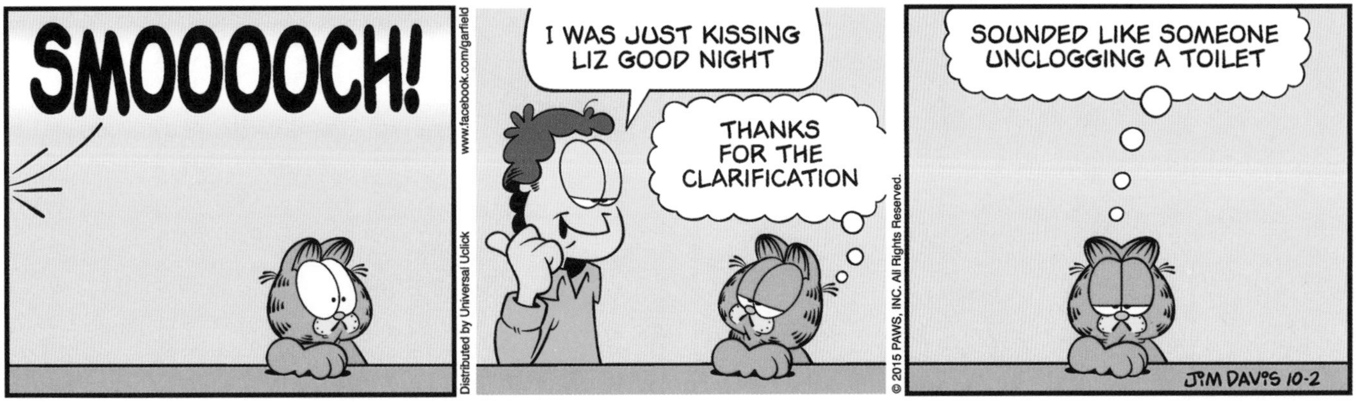
SMOOOOCH!
I WAS JUST KISSING LIZ GOOD NIGHT
THANKS FOR THE CLARIFICATION
SOUNDED LIKE SOMEONE UNCLOGGING A TOILET
JIM DAVIS 10-2
Distributed by Universal Uclick www.facebook.com/garfield
© 2015 PAWS, INC. All Rights Reserved.

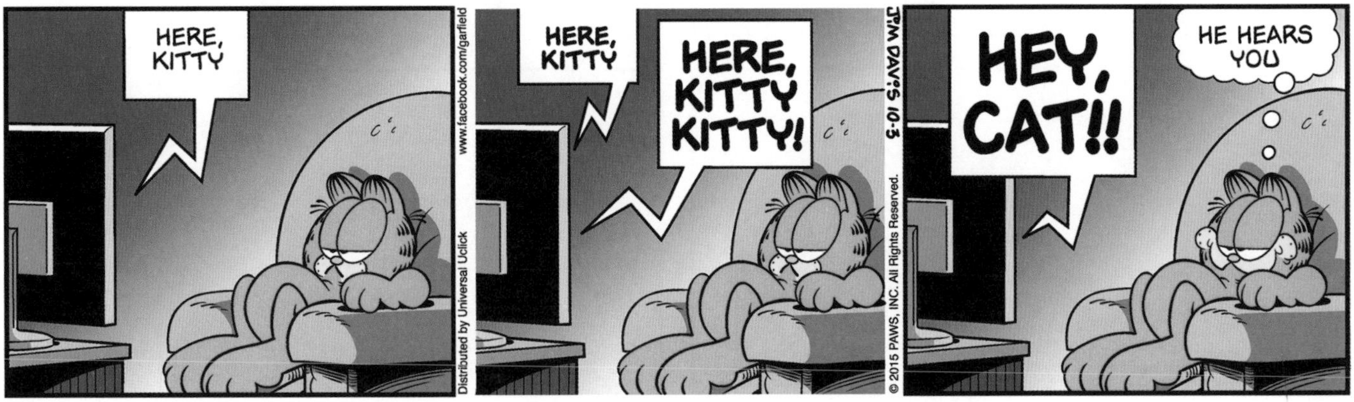
HERE, KITTY
HERE, KITTY
HERE, KITTY KITTY!
JIM DAVIS 10-3
HEY, CAT!!
HE HEARS YOU
Distributed by Universal Uclick www.facebook.com/garfield
© 2015 PAWS, INC. All Rights Reserved.

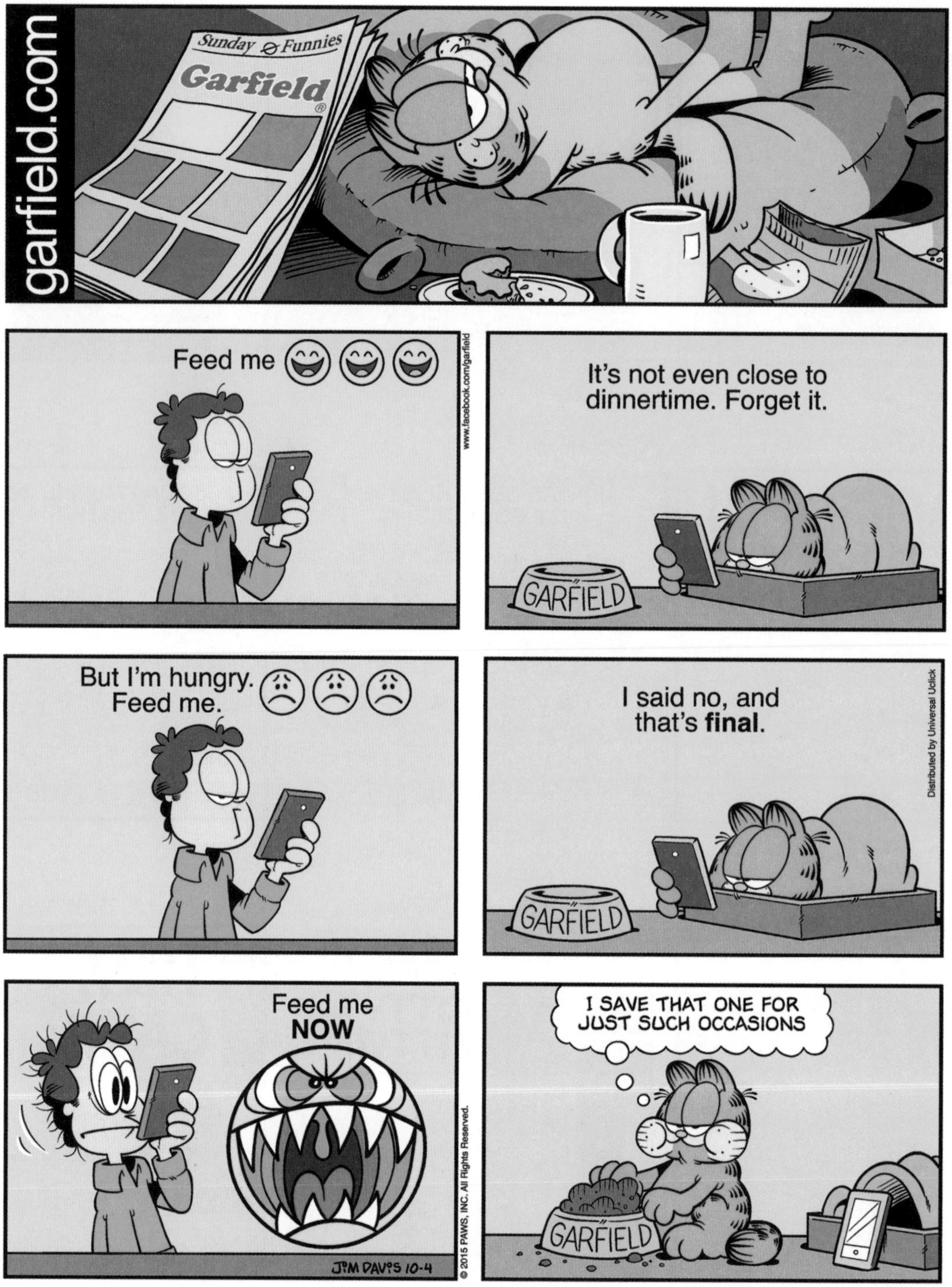
garfield.com
Sunday Funnies
Garfield
www.facebook.com/garfield
Feed me
It's not even close to dinnertime. Forget it.
GARFIELD
But I'm hungry. Feed me.
I said no, and that's **final**.
GARFIELD
Distributed by Universal Uclick
Feed me **NOW**
JIM DAVIS 10-4
© 2015 PAWS, INC. All Rights Reserved.
I SAVE THAT ONE FOR JUST SUCH OCCASIONS
GARFIELD

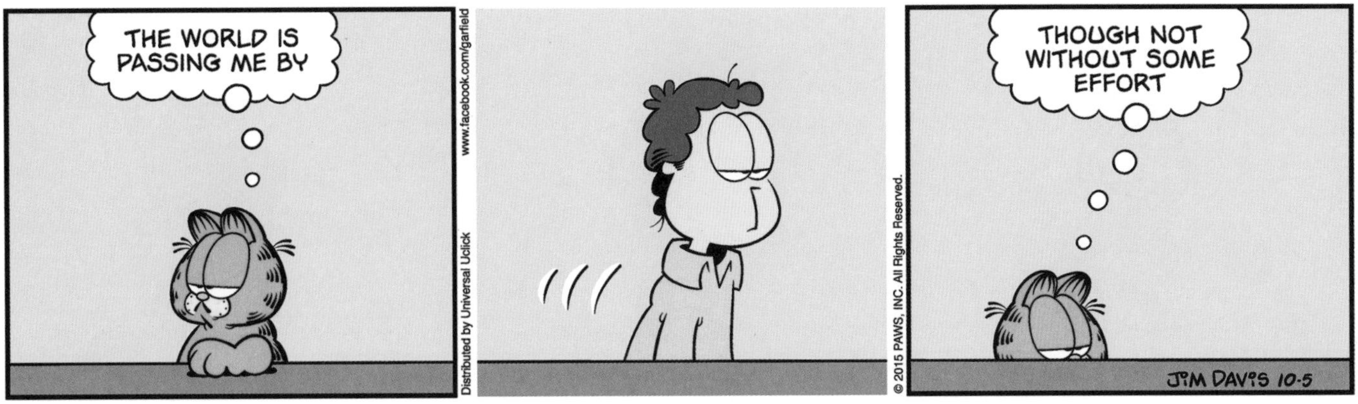
THE WORLD IS PASSING ME BY
Distributed by Universal Uclick www.facebook.com/garfield
© 2015 PAWS, INC. All Rights Reserved.
THOUGH NOT WITHOUT SOME EFFORT
JIM DAVIS 10-5

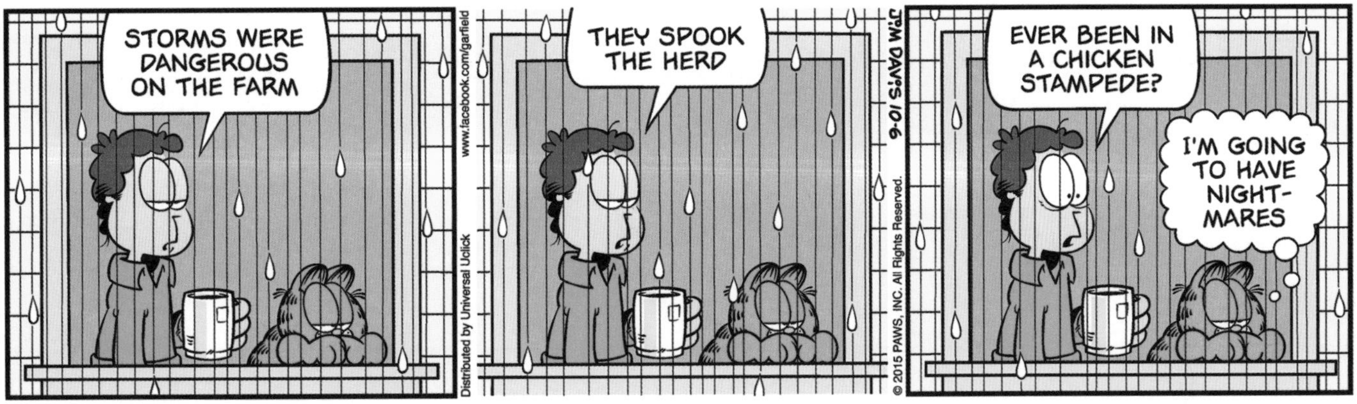
STORMS WERE DANGEROUS ON THE FARM
Distributed by Universal Uclick www.facebook.com/garfield
THEY SPOOK THE HERD
JIM DAVIS 10-6
© 2015 PAWS, INC. All Rights Reserved.
EVER BEEN IN A CHICKEN STAMPEDE?
I'M GOING TO HAVE NIGHT-MARES

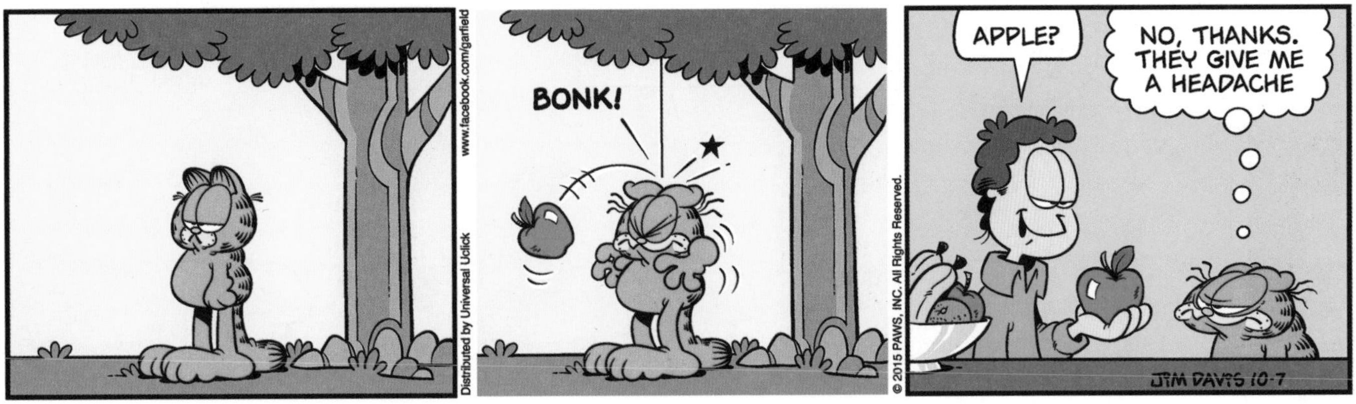
Distributed by Universal Uclick www.facebook.com/garfield
BONK!
© 2015 PAWS, INC. All Rights Reserved.
APPLE?
NO, THANKS. THEY GIVE ME A HEADACHE
JIM DAVIS 10-7

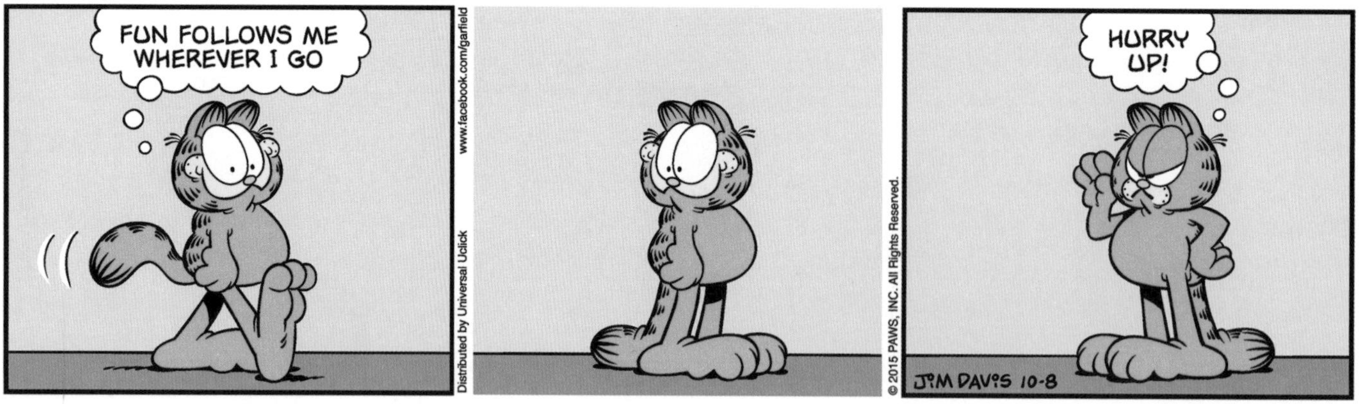
FUN FOLLOWS ME WHEREVER I GO
HURRY UP!
Distributed by Universal Uclick www.facebook.com/garfield
© 2015 PAWS, INC. All Rights Reserved.
JIM DAVIS 10-8

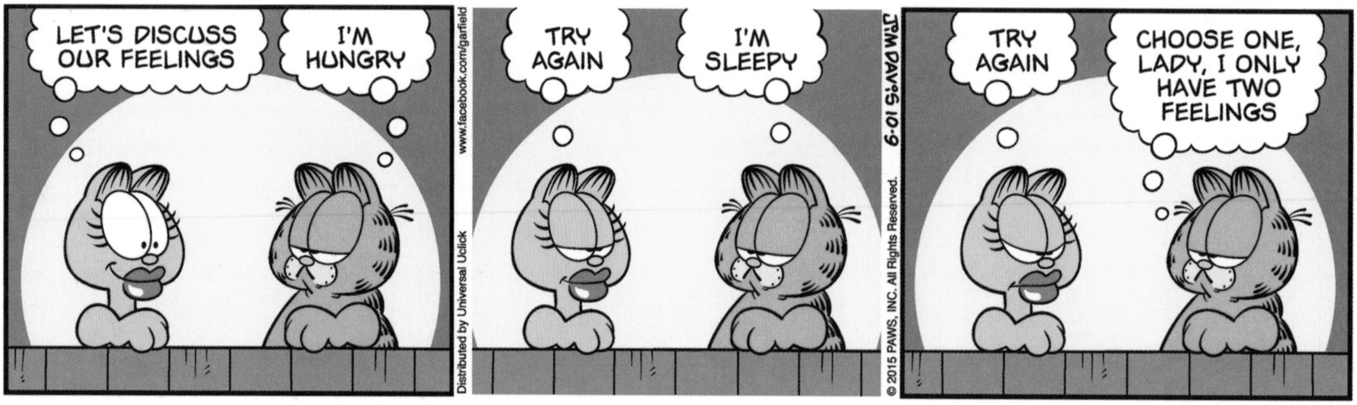
LET'S DISCUSS OUR FEELINGS
I'M HUNGRY
TRY AGAIN
I'M SLEEPY
TRY AGAIN
CHOOSE ONE, LADY, I ONLY HAVE TWO FEELINGS
Distributed by Universal Uclick www.facebook.com/garfield
JIM DAVIS 10-9
© 2015 PAWS, INC. All Rights Reserved.

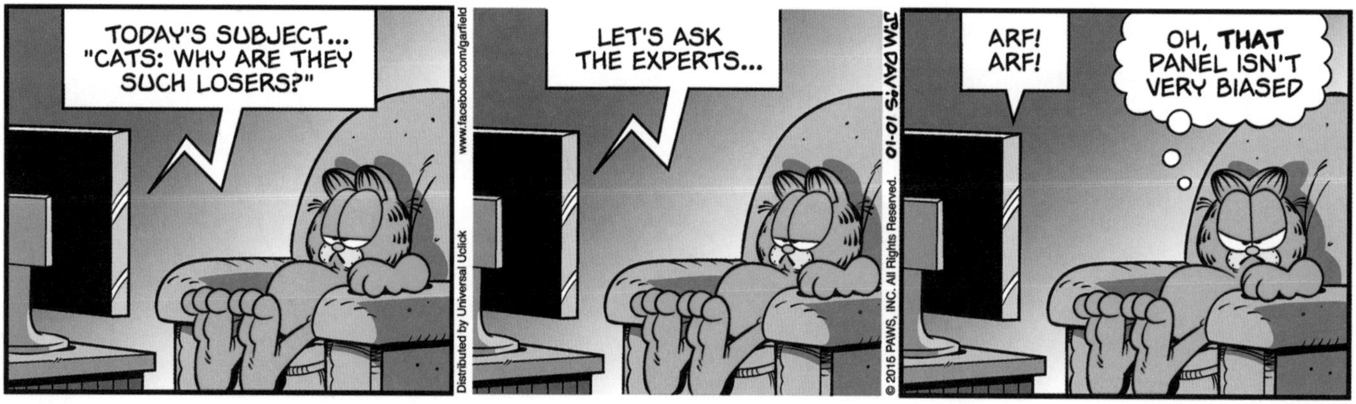
TODAY'S SUBJECT... "CATS: WHY ARE THEY SUCH LOSERS?"
LET'S ASK THE EXPERTS...
ARF! ARF!
OH, **THAT** PANEL ISN'T VERY BIASED
Distributed by Universal Uclick www.facebook.com/garfield
JIM DAVIS 10-10
© 2015 PAWS, INC. All Rights Reserved.

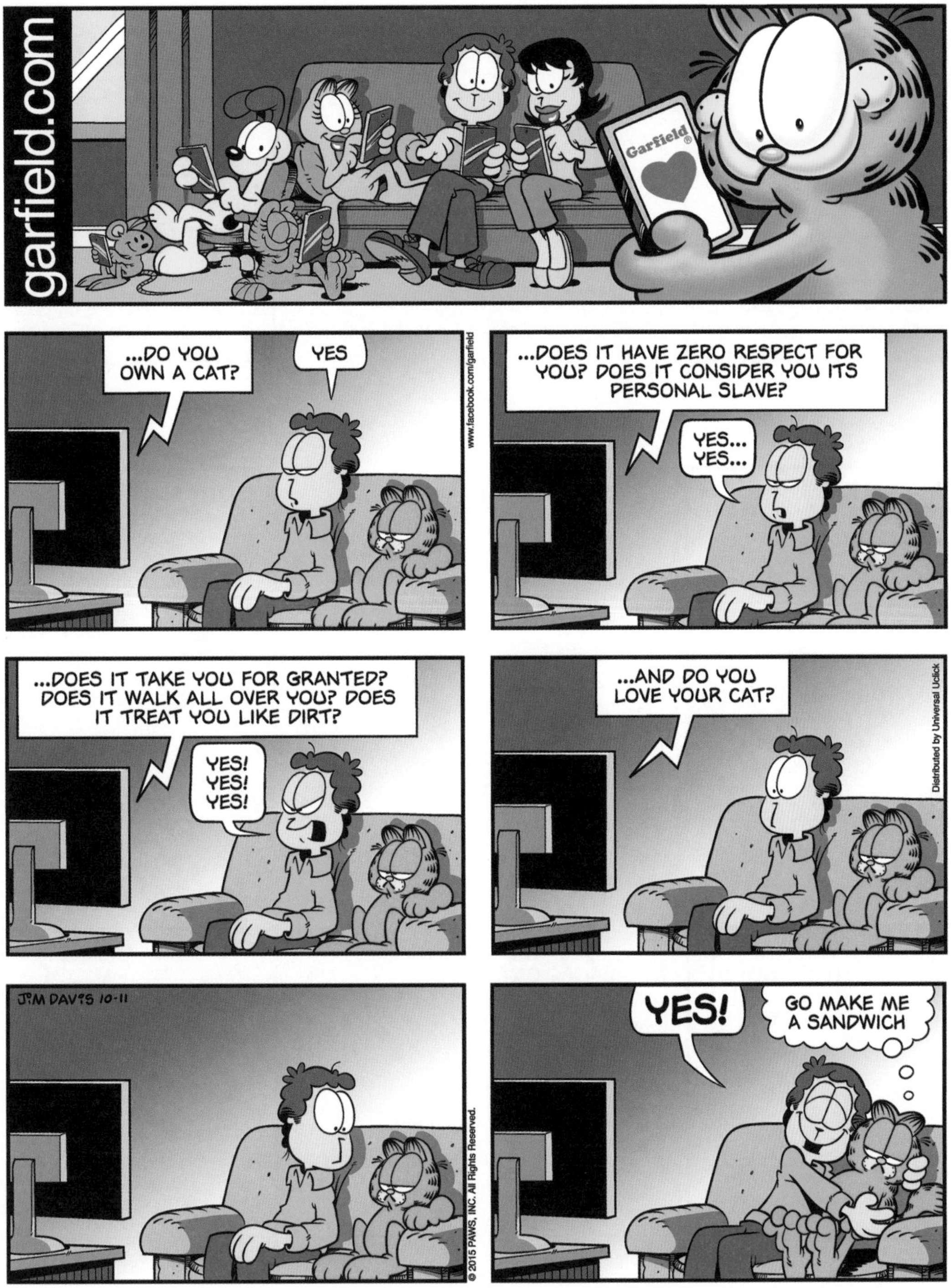
garfield.com
Garfield®
...DO YOU OWN A CAT?
YES
www.facebook.com/garfield
...DOES IT HAVE ZERO RESPECT FOR YOU? DOES IT CONSIDER YOU ITS PERSONAL SLAVE?
YES... YES...
...DOES IT TAKE YOU FOR GRANTED? DOES IT WALK ALL OVER YOU? DOES IT TREAT YOU LIKE DIRT?
YES! YES! YES!
...AND DO YOU LOVE YOUR CAT?
Distributed by Universal Uclick
JIM DAVIS 10-11
© 2015 PAWS, INC. All Rights Reserved.
YES!
GO MAKE ME A SANDWICH

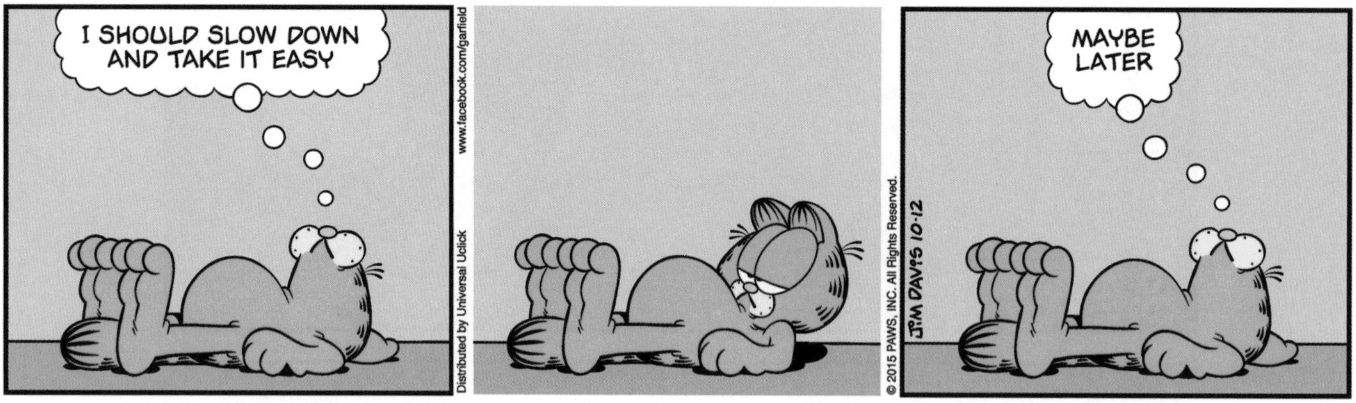
I SHOULD SLOW DOWN AND TAKE IT EASY
MAYBE LATER
JIM DAVIS 10-12
www.facebook.com/garfield
Distributed by Universal Uclick
© 2015 PAWS, INC. All Rights Reserved.

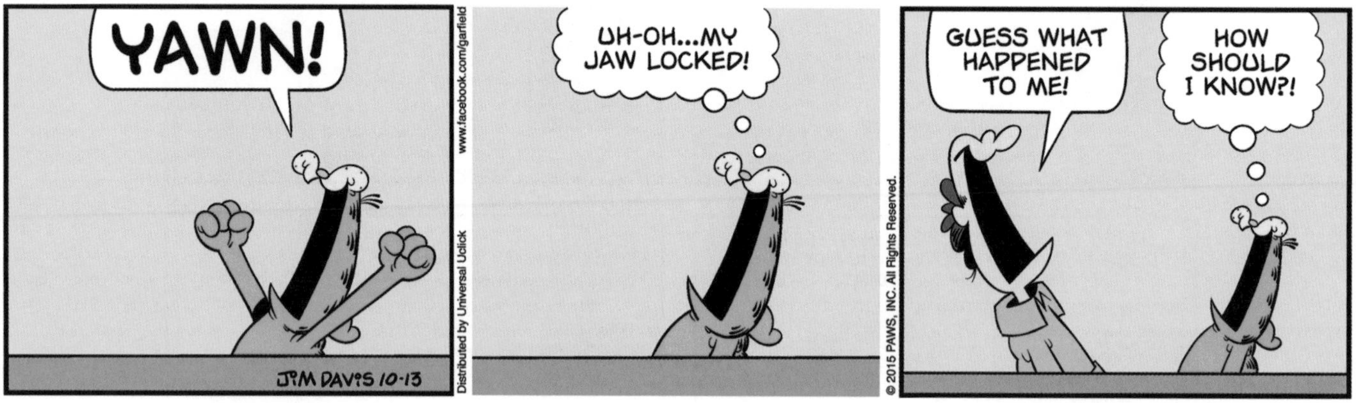
YAWN!
JIM DAVIS 10-13
UH-OH...MY JAW LOCKED!
GUESS WHAT HAPPENED TO ME!
HOW SHOULD I KNOW?!
www.facebook.com/garfield
Distributed by Universal Uclick
© 2015 PAWS, INC. All Rights Reserved.

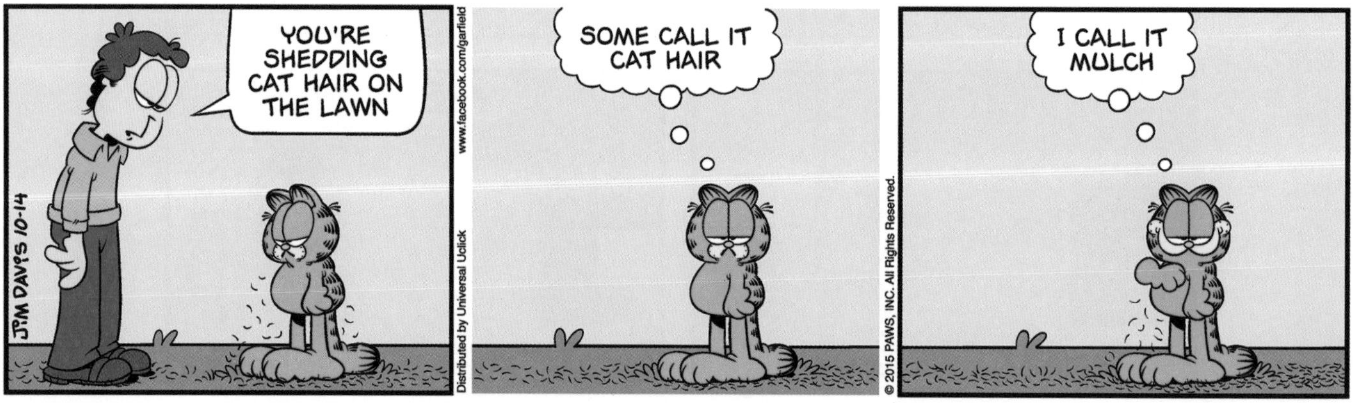
YOU'RE SHEDDING CAT HAIR ON THE LAWN
JIM DAVIS 10-14
SOME CALL IT CAT HAIR
I CALL IT MULCH
www.facebook.com/garfield
Distributed by Universal Uclick
© 2015 PAWS, INC. All Rights Reserved.

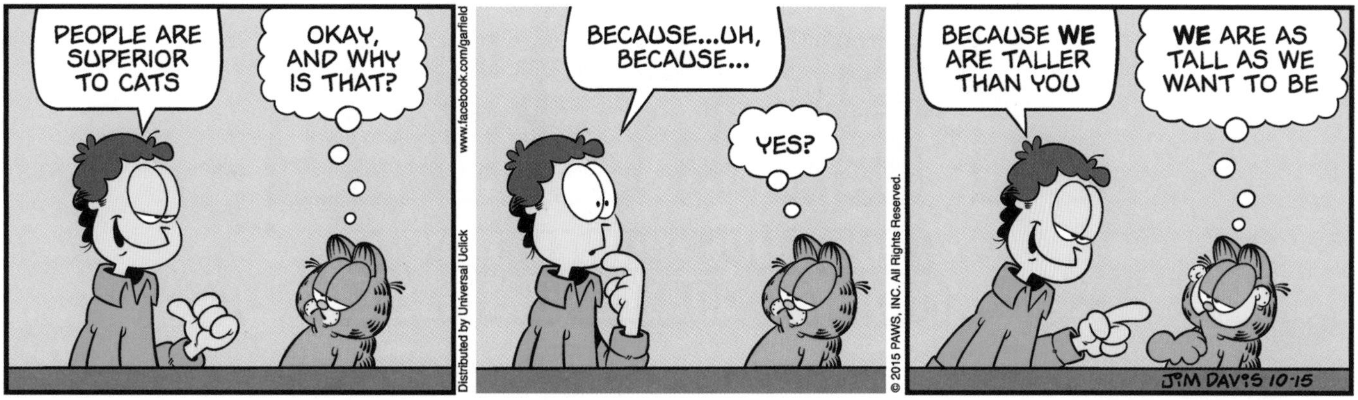
PEOPLE ARE SUPERIOR TO CATS
OKAY, AND WHY IS THAT?
www.facebook.com/garfield
Distributed by Universal Uclick
BECAUSE...UH, BECAUSE...
YES?
© 2015 PAWS, INC. All Rights Reserved.
BECAUSE **WE** ARE TALLER THAN YOU
WE ARE AS TALL AS WE WANT TO BE
JIM DAVIS 10-15

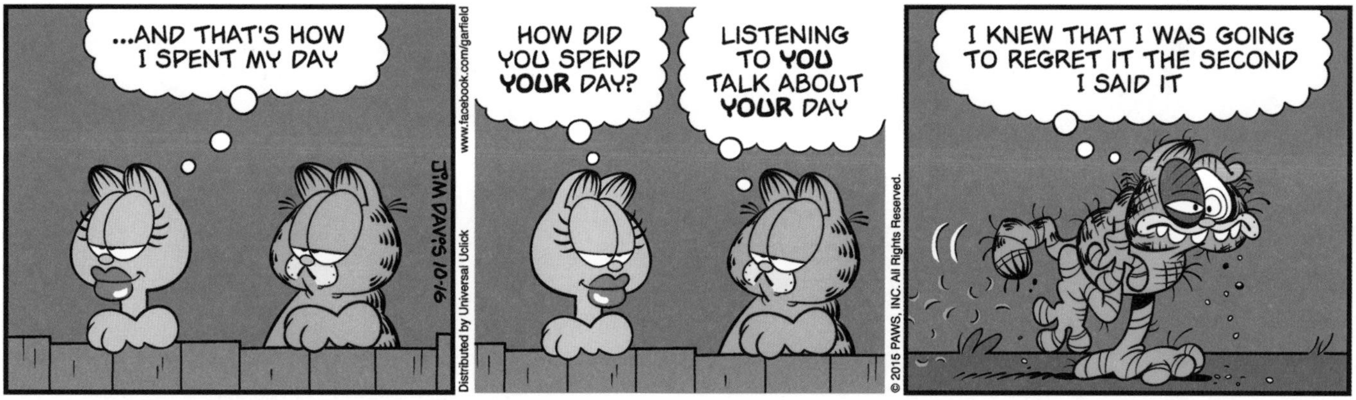
...AND THAT'S HOW I SPENT MY DAY
JIM DAVIS 10-16
www.facebook.com/garfield
Distributed by Universal Uclick
HOW DID YOU SPEND **YOUR** DAY?
LISTENING TO **YOU** TALK ABOUT **YOUR** DAY
© 2015 PAWS, INC. All Rights Reserved.
I KNEW THAT I WAS GOING TO REGRET IT THE SECOND I SAID IT

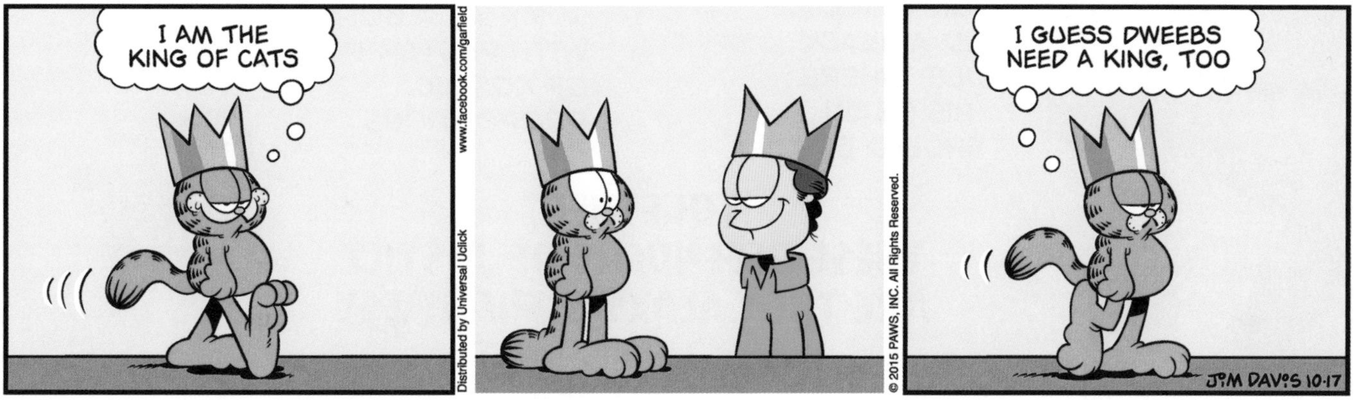
I AM THE KING OF CATS
www.facebook.com/garfield
Distributed by Universal Uclick
© 2015 PAWS, INC. All Rights Reserved.
I GUESS DWEEBS NEED A KING, TOO
JIM DAVIS 10-17

BEHOLD THE MIGHTY
PET FORCE

FOUR SUPERPOWERED PETS FROM A PARALLEL UNIVERSE!

Starlena

HER ICY STARE
FREEZES ALL
BAD GUYS
IN THEIR
TRACKS

GARZOOKA

HERO OF HEROES, WITH
THE ABILITY TO FIRE
GAMMA-RADIATED
HAIRBALLS

ODIOUS

A POTENT
STUN TONGUE,
AND A BLACK
HOLE WHERE
HIS BRAIN
SHOULD BE

ABNERMAL

QUICK AS A BLINK,
WITH PESTER-POWER
OF COSMIC
PROPORTIONS

TOGETHER,
THESE DEFENDERS OF JUSTICE
ARE THE GALAXY'S MIGHTIEST
– AND HUNGRIEST –
HEROES!

Let the fur fly!

STRIPS, SPECIALS, OR BESTSELLING BOOKS . . . GARFIELD'S ON EVERYONE'S MENU.

Don't miss even one episode in the Tubby Tabby's hilarious series!

New larger, full-color format!